JOHN HEDGECOE'S
NEW BOOK OF
PHOTOGRAPHY

JOHN HEDGECOE'S
NEW BOOK OF
PHOTOGRAPHY

DORLING KINDERSLEY
London • New York • Stuttgart

A DORLING KINDERSLEY BOOK

Project Editor
Alison Melvin

U.S. Editor
Mary Ann Bruchac Lynch

Senior Art Editor
Jane Ewart

Designer
Robyn Tomlinson

DTP Designer
Karen Mackley

Managing Editors
Rosie Pearson and Carolyn Ryden

Managing Art Editors
Carole Ash and Gaye Allen

Additional Photography
Steve Gorton

Associate Writer
Jonathan Hilton

Production
Rosalind Priestley

First American Edition 1994
2 4 6 8 10 9 7 5 3 1

Published in the United States by
Dorling Kindersley Publishing, Inc.,
95 Madison Avenue,
New York, New York 10016

Library of Congress Cataloging-in-Publication Data

Hedgecoe, John
    [New book of photography]
    John Hedgecoe's new book of photography. – – 1st Amer. ed.
        p.   cm.
    Includes index.
    ISBN 1–56458–508–5
    1. Photography. I. Title. II. Title: New book of photography.
TR146.H4228   1993
771– –dc20   93–28346
                                                                CIP

Reproduced in Singapore by Colourscan
Printed and bound in Italy by A. Mondadori Editore, Verona

CONTENTS

INTRODUCTION 6

12
THE CAMERA

*The design of the camera with an explanation
of how it works. Different types of camera, lens, and
lighting equipment are also described in detail.*

34
HOW TO SEE
BETTER PICTURES

*The secret of good photography lies in the ability to "see"
good pictures, the principal elements of which – shape,
tone, pattern, and texture – are analyzed in this section.*

66
HOW TO TAKE
BETTER PICTURES

*A comprehensive and practical behind-the-camera
guide to photographing different subjects, from formal
portraits to panoramic landscapes.*

PORTRAITS 68

INTRODUCTION

Taking exciting photographs has very little to do with buying an expensive camera or a massive array of photographic equipment. What is crucial is how the photographer sees and relates to a chosen subject and uses the various skills and compositional elements that will combine to make a good photograph.

While it may seem that some photographers have an innate ability to take superb pictures, most of that ability often comes from the photographer's passionate interest in their subject and the cumulative knowledge they have acquired through practical experience in and dedication to the medium.

A PRACTICAL APPROACH

This book adopts a practical approach to help you master photographic skills and techniques. The largest section covers a wide range of photographic genres, including portraiture, still life, landscapes, architecture, and natural history, all illustrated with behind-the-scene shots of me in a studio or out on location, actually taking the pictures. These photo set-ups reveal exactly how a shot was taken, the equipment that was used, the camera angle, and the wider settings from which the pictures were derived. The accompanying text explains how to achieve equally successful results and includes my own special guidelines.

Photographer at work
The unique photo set-ups provide a practical insight into the way I work, both in the studio and on location.

The resulting image, *above*
Subtle differences in camera angle and lighting direction can be all-important in determining the final image.

Using color, *above*
In this portrait, the contrast between colorful stripes and circles is a deliberate, amusing touch that reveals much about the subject.

Texture and light, *opposite*
This image shows how light can be used to reveal contrasting textures. The composition is simple, but the effect is striking.

A technical understanding of your camera is important, as it allows you to capture on film the pictorial qualities of a scene in the best way possible. Indeed, to take consistently imaginative and appealing photographs, you need to know what all your camera controls and lens settings do. The more familiar you are with techniques, the more attention you can pay to composition and timing.

THE SECRET OF GOOD PHOTOGRAPHS

Most good photographs capture the spirit of a subject, conveying any unique aspects or features and giving it expression and meaning. To do this you need to understand the various elements that ensure good results. The most fundamental of these is the shape or outline of a subject, which is shown most graphically when the subject is silhouetted by means of backlighting and underexposure. Another feature is the subject's color or tone; it is often the colors in a scene that initially grab

the photographer's attention. Then, form emerges – as the play of light and shade across the subject unite to produce various qualities of shape and shifting hues and intensities of color.

Form best describes the three-dimensional qualities of a subject. It gives substance to what might otherwise be a rather flat, two-dimensional representation. Allied to form is texture – the smoothness of marble, the roughness of weathered stone, the dimpled skin of an orange – which is vital because it tells us what a subject might feel like.

Deciding which of these features to emphasize in a composition is up to you, but using my photographs as examples, I show you what to look for and how to get the most out of every shot, indoors and outdoors.

Advances in technology now mean that processed slides and negatives can be scanned into computers and digitally transformed ready for electronic manipulation.

Unusual viewpoint, *left*
To maximize the potential of
any scene, photographers
should be alert to the various
opportunities it presents.

Abstract image, *above*
Simple scenes like this one
make good starting points
for creating striking, almost
abstract images.

Highlights or shadows can be added, colors
intensified or altered completely, and elements
from other images pasted in – myriad effects are
possible. Moreover, final images can be viewed
as prints or slides. Using my own photographs
again, I provide an overview of what is
possible in this exciting area of photography.

THE COMPLETE PHOTOGRAPHER

The basic equipment you need to set up a
home darkroom and studio is covered in the
last section of this book. Having a variety of
lights, reflectors, diffusers, and filters gives
you versatility in the type of images you can
produce, and having your own darkroom
gives you the freedom to experiment as much
as you want. There is no better way to learn
how various films and papers respond than
through experience and practice at home. The
fault finder section will help you see what
mistakes you might make when taking and
printing pictures, and the best way to rectify
or avoid them completely.

Use this book as a guide to developing
your own creativity and individual style:
by exploring the many possibilities of the
medium, you will discover limitless ways to
express your own particular vision.

John Hedgecoe

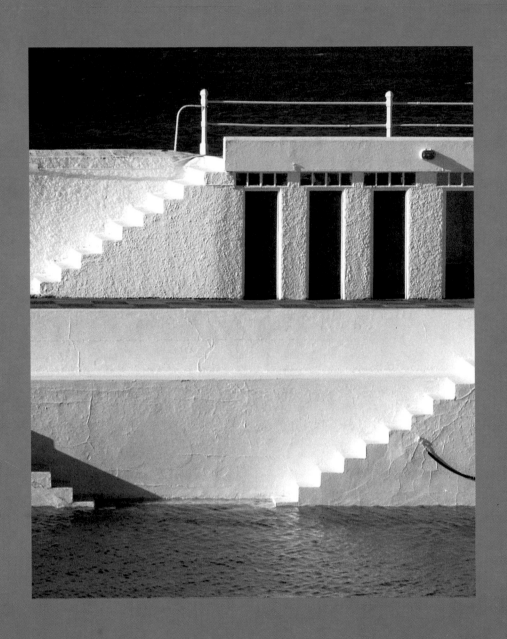

THE CAMERA

To take consistently successful photographs, it is important to understand the basic optical principles underlying how a camera works; lens types; what film speed to use in a particular situation; lighting equipment; plus the advantages and drawbacks of different camera formats. The more familiar you are with the controls on your camera, the more you can concentrate on the composition and lighting of each photograph.

THE BASIC CAMERA

If you were to strip away the electronic refinements and automatic features of any camera you would find the same basic design underneath – a lightproof container with a hole at one end over which a lens is placed and a holder opposite to accommodate a strip of light-sensitive film.

To produce a correctly exposed image in a variety of light intensities, the camera lens has an iris diaphragm that can be adjusted to leave a hole of varying diameter. This is called the aperture. On a fixed-lens compact camera, the lens also contains a shutter mechanism, known as a between-the-lens shutter, which opens to allow light to reach the film. The shutter gives you the option of choosing the precise moment of exposure, and by selecting from a range of shutter speeds you can also control the length of exposure. The shutter mechanism on an SLR camera is located inside the camera body, just in front of the focal plane, and is known as a focal-plane shutter. Without this type of arrangement, the film would be exposed to light each time a lens was removed.

Another feature common to all cameras is the viewfinder. This is basically a sighting and compositional aid that allows the photographer to aim the camera accurately and to decide what subject elements to focus on.

Camera formats

● 35mm SLR is the most popular camera format (see page 18).

● Compact cameras are light and easy to use (see page 19).

● Medium-format or roll-film cameras have a large film image size for better overall definition and quality (see page 20).

THE PATH OF LIGHT

Subject and light source
A light source to illuminate a subject is essential. Light rays reflected from the subject are transmitted through the camera to form a latent image on the film.

Subject and light source

Lens
A simple lens consists of a convex disk of ground and polished glass that refracts the widening light rays traveling away from every point of the subject, so that they converge to form coherent points. The point at which the lens focuses these rays – the focal plane – coincides with the position of the film when the lens is correctly focused.

Lens

Diaphragm

Shutter

Focal plane
This is where the rays of light refracted by the lens converge to form a sharp, upside-down image. Light traveling from different distances from the camera needs varying degrees of refraction to focus at the focal plane, so a focusing mechanism moves the lens toward or away from the back of the camera. The position of the film and focal plane coincides when the lens is correctly focused.

Viewfinder

Focal plane and film

Aperture
The diameter of the lens diaphragm can be changed by turning the aperture ring. This dictates the brightness of the image reaching the film. Moving to the next f-number either halves or doubles aperture size. Aperture size also affects depth of field (see page 17).

Full aperture   **Medium aperture**   **Stopped down**

Shutter
The shutter can be set at different speeds, which determine the length of time the film is exposed. Moving the shutter speed dial to the next stop either doubles or halves exposure time. Shutters located between the aperture and the lens or behind the aperture have overlapping blades that spring open when the release button is pressed; focal-plane shutters consist of two metal blinds that open progressively.

Blade shutter – closed   **Focal-plane shutter – closed**

Blade shutter – open   **Focal-plane shutter – open**

Viewfinder
Direct vision viewfinders on compact cameras do not show exactly the same image the lens sees. With an SLR, light is reflected by a mirror through the viewfinder window. On a TLR, the top lens is used to view the subject, while the lower lens is used to take the picture.

Direct vision   **Single lens reflex**   **Twin lens reflex**

DESIGN OF AN SLR CAMERA

The unique feature of the popular SLR (single lens reflex) camera lies in the design of its viewfinder. Light traveling from the subject enters the lens and strikes a mirror angled at 45°. It is then reflected upward, through the focusing screen, and into the pentaprism, where it exits the camera via a rear-mounted viewfinder window. This means that no matter what focal length lens is attached to the camera, the scene the photographer sees through the viewfinder corresponds exactly to that seen by the lens.

Viewfinder window

Rewind spindle

Fold-away film-rewind crank (manual cameras only)

Film take-up spool

Ring for strap attachment

Roll-film cassette chamber

Bottom spindle

Shutter

Film pressure plate

35mm SLR back view
This view shows the back of a typical SLR open to reveal the layout of the film transport mechanism as well as the position of the focal-plane shutter.

35mm SLR cutaway
This cutaway of a typical SLR shows the link between the external controls and the internal mechanisms. Although camera models may look different, the layout of the basic features – lens, diaphragm, aperture, angled mirror, shutter, focusing screen, and pentaprism – is the same.

Rear viewfinder window

Flash hot shoe contains electrical contacts that fire the flash when the shutter is triggered

Pentaprism has mirrored inside surfaces to correct the laterally reversed image transmitted by the lens and to direct the light out through the rear viewfinder window

Shutter speed dial with exposure times ranging from up to 8 seconds or longer to 1/2000 second or briefer can be set

Frame counter

Light path through the camera

Aperture control ring

Internal mirror corrects the upside-down image transmitted by the lens. It is angled at 45° to direct light up through the focusing screen and into the pentaprism

Ring for strap attachment

Film

Film take-up spool

Shutter release button – on most SLRs, half depressing this often activates the light meter and automatic exposure controls

Focal plane shutter

Internal lens elements

Lens housing

Front lens element

OPTICAL PRINCIPLES

The main lens controls are the focus control and aperture ring. Most lenses also have a distance indicator, telling you how far away the lens is focused, and a depth of field scale, indicating the extent of the zone of sharp focus. The three factors affecting depth of field are aperture, subject-to-camera distance, and the focal length of the lens. Greatest depth of field results from the smallest available aperture on the shortest lens,

focused on infinity (∞). As apertures get larger, focal lengths longer, and subject distances nearer, so depth of field diminishes.

The aperture setting is a key element in film exposure. The best setting to select depends on how much depth of field a scene requires and also the shutter speed setting. A fast shutter speed freezes subject movement and keeps camera shake from affecting the image, while a slow setting produces a blurred image.

Choosing a lens

Choose the "fastest" lens you can afford – that is, one with the widest maximum aperture. The speed of a lens affects exposure in low-light situations.

FOCUSING AND APERTURE

Depth of field

The zone of acceptably sharp focus surrounding a subject is critical to the appearance of the final image. To make full use of all apertures a lens offers, position the camera on a tripod to prevent camera shake. The two pictures shown here are identical in terms of exposure, but while the first one (*below*) was shot at 1/60 second at f2, the second one (*bottom*) was shot at 1 second at f16. All other aperture and shutter speed combinations in between would also produce a correctly exposed image.

Exposure: 1/60 second at f2

Exposure: 1 second at f16

f2 - 1/60 sec

f2.8 - 1/30 sec

f4 - 1/15 sec

f5.6 - 1/8 sec

f8 - 1/4 sec

f11 - 1/2 sec

f16 - 1 sec

The f-stop and aperture size

Any type or size of lens set at a specific f-stop transmits an image of near identical luminance, because the diameter of the aperture is directly related to focal lenth. For example, an 80 mm lens used with an aperture 5 mm in diameter must be set at f16. Thus, the focal length of the lens, divided by the diameter of the aperture, gives the corresponding f-stop number.

Fixed reference mark

Focusing distance indicator
The lens extends from the camera by means of a screw thread operated by the focusing ring. As you turn the ring, you can see the distances being focused on by reading the indicator against the fixed reference mark.

Focusing ring

Aperture settings
Moving the aperture ring up to the next f-stop (from f4 to f5.6, for example) halves the aperture size (and so halves the amount of light reaching the film), while moving the ring down (from f4 to f2.8, for example) doubles the aperture size.

Depth of field scale
With the lens focused on the subject, look for the aperture numbers on either side of the fixed reference mark that correspond to (or approximate to) the f-stop of the set aperture. Read these against the focusing distance indicator below to determine the effective depth of field.

EFFECTS ON DEPTH OF FIELD

	5ft (1.5m)	10ft (3m)	15ft (4.5m)	20ft (6m)	25ft (7.5m)	30ft (9m)

Changing aperture size

With the same focal length lens focused at the same distance, this diagram shows how depth of field can be altered by adjusting the aperture size. Depth of field usually extends in front of the subject by one-third and by two-thirds behind. The smaller the aperture the greater the depth of field. An aperture of f2 gives a much smaller depth of field than one of f16.

f2

f8

f16

Subject-to-camera distance

This diagram shows how depth of field is partly dependent on the distance of the subject from the camera, even when an identical focal length and aperture setting are used. The closer the subject is to the camera, the narrower the depth of field. Focusing the lens on 15ft (4.5m) yields a greater depth of field than focusing on 5ft (1.5m).

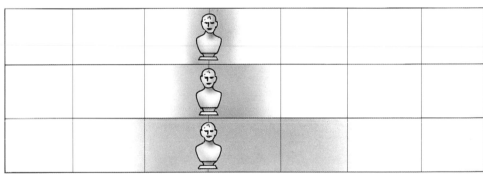

5ft (1.5m)

10ft (3m)

15ft (4.5m)

Changing lenses

With the subject at the same distance from the camera and with the same aperture size, depth of field can be altered using lenses of different focal lengths. The shortest lens results in the greatest depth of field. Focal length can be so significant a factor with extreme (8–15mm) wide-angle lenses that they do not need to be focused, since depth of field at every aperture setting is sharp.

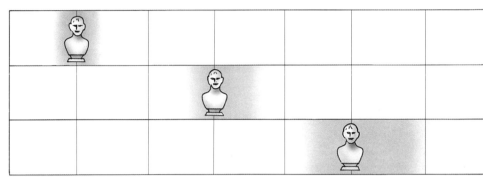

135mm lens

50mm lens

28mm lens

SELECTIVE FOCUSING

This series of photographs shows three subjects positioned 3ft (1m) apart, with the closest 5ft (1.5m) from the camera. A 35mm SLR with an 80mm lens was used throughout, and an aperture of f2.8 for the first three shots. First, the lens is focused on the near figure; depth of field is shallow.

The difference here is that the camera is focused on the middle figure. Depth of field is such that the first figure is now blurred, but because depth of field increases as the point of focus moves farther away, the rear figure is slightly sharper even though the camera setting has not changed.

With the focus shifted to the figure farthest away, depth of field has not only increased to the point where the middle figure is less blurred but also extended beyond the point of true focus to include the rear wall. The first figure, however, is now very blurred.

To bring all three subjects into sharp focus, from foreground to background, a smaller aperture size is set. For this final image, the aperture is changed from f2.8 to f22, with the middle figure as the main focusing point.

35MM-FORMAT CAMERAS

The 35mm is far and away the most popular camera size. It is small, lightweight, easy to use, and generally produces good technical results. Its popularity has led to a steady increase in technical, optical, and design innovations, and cameras are now available with every conceivable automatic feature. For 35mm single lens reflex (SLR) users, there is the bonus of a wide range of lenses with different focal lengths from which to choose.

AUTOMATIC FEATURES

Autofocus systems in general target anything positioned center-frame and assume it to be the subject of the photograph. Problems may arise, however, if the subject is off-center, is photographed through glass, or is framed by foreground features.

Autoexposure systems vary in how they are programed to control exposure. Some cameras measure exposure in the center of the frame (assuming that this is where the subject will be). Other cameras take samples from different parts of the frame, combining them to calculate a sophisticated average reading.

Additional automatic features include film-speed recognition (DX recognition), which picks up the speed of the film from a code printed on the cassette and calibrates the exposure meter accordingly. Automated film transport not only speeds up film loading and unloading, but winds on the film by one frame each time a picture is taken. When automatic wind-on is continuous, allowing you to take up to four frames per second, this function is known as motor drive.

COMPACT CAMERAS

Apart from SLRs, the other popular types of 35mm camera are compact, or point-and-shoot, models. These are less bulky than SLRs and have a fixed lens that cannot be changed. The main design problem with compact cameras is that the view seen through the viewfinder is not exactly the same as that seen through the lens. This can result in framing errors at close distances, such as chopping off the top of a subject's head. To help frame a subject correctly, most compacts have parallax correction marks visible in the viewfinder.

MANUAL SLR

After threading a film into a manual SLR, use the wind-on lever to advance the film to its starting position. The film also needs to be wound on between frames. Through-the-lens metering signals correct exposure when the aperture and/or shutter speed is adjusted. Focus manual SLRs by making adjustments while you monitor the image on the focusing screen.

Shutter release button
Shutter and film speed dial
Flash sync socket
Self-timer lever
Lens
Lens release button

AUTOMATIC SLR

Although features such as automated film transport make for easy handling, an advanced automatic SLR may have so many different controls that it becomes very complex to use. When choosing an automatic SLR, check that it has a mechanical shutter speed control option (in case of battery failure) and that automatic focusing and exposure can be overriden if necessary.

Self-timer button
Shutter release button
Command dial
Camera grip and battery
Lens

BASIC COMPACT

A basic compact camera has a fixed focal length lens – usually a 28 or 35mm slight wide-angle lens. This lens cannot be changed as with an SLR and if you want to close in on a subject, simply move nearer. Autofocus, if available on a basic compact, may not be lockable, forcing the main subject to be always positioned center-frame.

Shutter release button
Autofocus window
Viewfinder
Flash
Lens

Shutter and film speed dial

Flash hot shoe

Film rewind knob

Frame counter

Shutter release button

Aperture scale

Distance scale

Lens

Manual SLR can be used for low light levels

Manual SLR

- Ideal for technically minded photographers.

- Shutter speeds tend to be incremental and intermediate settings are not usually possible.

- Viewfinder shows the scene that will be recorded, no matter what lens is used.

- Manual focusing allows you to decide which area of the image to concentrate on.

Exposure information panel

Flash hot shoe

Command dial

Shutter release button

Lens release button

Lens

Automatic SLR can be used for close focusing

Automatic SLR

- Automatic film loading and wind-on make for quick and easy handling.

- Autoexposure is ideal for those not interested in making technical decisions about the appearance of the final image.

- Autofocus is useful for those with poor eyesight, or when the camera is being used in low-light situations.

ADVANCED COMPACT

An advanced compact camera is usually fitted with a zoom lens, within the range 35–105mm, which gives you flexibility in framing shots. This type of compact should have lockable autofocus, which allows off-center framing of your subject. There should also be a choice of exposure modes so that you can override the automatic exposure.

Shutter release button

Autofocus window

Viewfinder

Flash and red-eye reduction lamp

Camera grip and battery compartment

Zoom lens

Basic compact picture

Advanced compact picture

Compact

- Point-and-shoot features make this camera ideal for non-technical users.

- Scene in viewfinder is not the same as that recorded on the film, so use the parallax marks to frame scene.

- Most compact cameras are lighter and less intrusive to use than SLRs.

MEDIUM-FORMAT CAMERAS

Medium-format roll-film cameras fill the gap between the lightweight 35mm compacts and SLRs and the unwieldy sheet film cameras. For many professional photographers, roll-film format cameras are ideal. Although it is not too bulky, this type of camera produces a much larger negative than a 35mm, which results in better definition and tonal qualities of prints and transparencies.

ADVANTAGES OF ROLL-FILM CAMERAS

Most roll-film cameras accept interchangeable film "backs" that allow you to change from color to black and white, or from negative film to slides even halfway through a film. Medium-format cameras are not designed for casual snapping, and in most situations must be used with a tripod. The majority of these cameras have through-the-lens reflex viewing systems, so that no matter what focal length lens is attached, the subject is always accurately framed in the viewfinder.

A pentaprism viewfinder may be attached to the top of many models of medium-format camera. This allows eye-level operation and, as with the pentaprism on a 35mm SLR camera, it also corrects the laterally reversed image formed by the lens. Without a pentaprism attachment, you hold the camera at about waist-level, lift up the top flap of the camera and view and focus the subject on a ground-glass screen. However, the image you will then see will be reversed left-to-right, which makes composition slightly more difficult.

Roll-film SLRs

- Professional images of high quality result from the large film image size.

- Convenience of changing the film back to change quickly and easily from color to black and white film.

- Camera body is part of an extensive system with a wide range of interchangeable lenses, different viewfinders, and other accessories.

6 x 4.5cm CAMERA

A 6 x 4.5cm roll-film SLR camera is smaller and lighter to use than other medium-format cameras. It produces an image the full height of the 6cm (2¼in) roll film, but only 4.5cm (1¾in) across. A wide range of different camera grips, viewfinders, lenses, and interchangeable film backs can be attached to the core part of the camera body, which allows you a greater degree of flexibility than with a standard 35mm SLR. The Mamiya 645 (*right*) resembles a Hasselblad camera in shape and has a similar range of accessories.

6 x 4.5cm format picture

Shutter and film speed dial

Pentaprism viewfinder hood

Lens

Film wind-on lever

Shutter release button

6 x 4.5cm camera

- Film image size measures 6 x 4.5cm.

- Selection of different viewfinders can be used, ranging from eye-level pentaprism types to waist-level and angle finders.

- Lenses range from 24mm to 500mm, including 55–110 and 105–210mm zooms.

6 x 6cm CAMERA

This type of medium-format roll-film SLR is also known as a 2¼in square camera and produces an image 6cm (2¼in) square. Some photographers are devoted to this format while others prefer the compositional possibilities of rectangular-format images. In terms of reliability and durability, the Hasselblad shown on the right is the choice of many professional photographers. It is supported by a comprehensive range of different lenses, film backs, and auxiliary viewfinders, including a pentaprism correction viewfinder.

6 x 6cm format picture

Protective flap for waist-level finder

Removable film back

Lens

Film wind-on lever

Shutter release button

6 x 6cm camera

- Film image size measures 6 x 6cm.

- Lenses range from 30mm to 500mm.

- Selection of different viewfinders can be used, from eye-level pentaprisms to waist-level and angle finders.

- Bellows can also be attached to the camera.

DIRECT VISION CAMERA

If the bulk of a medium-format camera is daunting, then you might want to consider a 6 x 6cm direct vision camera. Rangefinder focusing considerably lessens the overall size and weight of the camera, making it resemble a larger 35mm compact, but with all the advantages of an increased film image size (approximately four times larger than the size of a 35mm negative).

Shutter release button / Accessory shoe for flash / Rangefinder window / Camera grip / Lens

6 x 6cm format picture

6 x 6cm camera

- Film image size measures 6 x 6cm.
- Direct vision coupled rangefinder.
- Interchangeable 50mm wide-angle, 75mm standard, and 150mm telephoto lenses are available.

6 x 7cm CAMERA

The 6 x 7cm camera produces a 6 x 7cm (2 ¼ x 2 ¾in) rectangular-format image, which is ideal for landscape photography. It is similar in appearance and operation to an enlarged 35mm SLR camera. However, the range of available lenses is not as extensive as you would find with a standard 35mm SLR camera, and because of their size and bulk, the lenses are much more expensive to buy. This type of medium-format camera uses 120 or 220 roll film (*see page 30*).

Shutter release button / Pentaprism / Focus control ring / Lens

6 x 7cm format picture

6 x 7cm camera

- Film image size measures 6 x 7cm.
- Larger overall size than a 35mm SLR, but similar handling characteristics.
- Interchangeable lenses are available, ranging from wide-angles to telephotos.

6 x 9cm CAMERA

This roll-film camera produces a rectangular image measuring 6 x 9cm (2 ¼ x 3 ½in). The large negative or positive film original ensures excellent enlargements. This model has a rangefinder split-image viewing system, rather than standard through-the-lens reflex viewing, making it very lightweight. The lens, however, is not interchangeable, but there is a choice of models available with two different focal lengths.

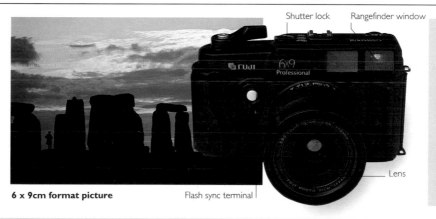

Shutter lock / Rangefinder window / Lens / Flash sync terminal

6 x 9cm format picture

6 x 9cm camera

- Film image size measures 6 x 9cm.
- Direct vision rangefinder viewing.
- Models are available with either a 90mm wide-angle or 65mm very wide-angle lens.

Twin lens reflex camera

Although a well-established design, very few twin lens reflex (TLR) cameras are still made. TLRs accept the same film as other medium-format cameras, and produce square images measuring 6 x 6cm (2¼ x 2¼in). They are designed with two lenses, one above the other, mounted on a lens panel. The upper lens is the viewing lens and the lower lens is the picture-taking lens. You view the subject with the hood up and the camera at waist level. A magnifier in the hood also allows the focusing screen to be viewed from chest level.

6 x 6cm format picture

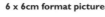

Viewing hood / Viewing lens / Picture-taking lens / Focusing knob

TLR camera

- Allows you to see the image on the focusing screen at all times, unlike an SLR camera.
- Several different viewfinders can be attached, including pentaprism types.

SPECIAL TYPES OF CAMERA

Although a 35mm or roll-film SLR will produce excellent results for most general photographic purposes, there are other cameras available that have been designed for specialized applications. Some of these cameras were designed to operate in environments too hostile for normal cameras, such as underwater, and have grown in popularity as people have become more adventurous in their leisure activities. To cater to the needs of professional landscape and architectural photographers, wide-view and panoramic cameras have been developed.

These cameras can also be used to great effect in other areas of photography.

Cameras such as the large-format camera have changed little since their introduction in the early years of the twentieth century. The modern version of this camera is the monorail or baseboard camera, which is now mostly used by professional photographers for specialist purposes. At the other end of the scale, the still video camera has incorporated the latest technological advances and applied them to the still image, and the instant-picture camera contains its own developing laboratory.

Special cameras

- Pocket cameras are useful for snapshots, but size limits image quality.

- Half-frame cameras (no longer produced) take pictures half the ordinary 35mm size.

- Disposable 35mm cameras are ideal for informal, fun shots.

INSTANT CAMERA

Instant-picture cameras produce a finished image just a few seconds after exposing the film. As well as the model shown here, which uses an integral film, cameras taking peel-apart film are also available. Color and black and white 35mm instant-picture films are available for ordinary 35mm cameras, and there are also instant-picture film backs for roll-film cameras.

Instant camera for snapshots

Lens with automatic shutter · Photocell · Built-in electronic flash · Coated Glass Lens · Polaroid · ImagePro · Film exit slot

Key features

- Focusing is fully automatic through a standard 125mm lens.

- Viewing through the lens, via a reflex mirror.

- Ten images per roll.

- Electronic flash.

WATERPROOF CAMERA

Specially adapted waterproof cameras have moisture-proof bodies and sealed controls for taking photographs in the rain and other wet conditions. Most waterproof cameras have automatic focusing and a choice of standard and wide-angle lenses. Waterproof cameras can be submerged in water, but are not designed for deep underwater photography.

Waterproof camera for wet conditions

Shutter release · Viewfinder window · MINOLTA · AF · Built-in electronic flash · Hand grip · Glass lens cover

Key features

- Twin lens with 35 and 50mm focal lengths.

- Automatic focusing above water, and fixed focus underwater.

- Waterproof to a depth of 16ft (5m).

UNDERWATER CAMERA

A 35mm camera body designed for underwater photography has special dials that are easy to read in water and large external controls for focusing and selecting the shutter speed and aperture. Underwater lenses must have slightly shorter focal lengths than ordinary lenses because of the refracting effect of the water, which increases the degree of magnification.

Underwater camera for marine life

Shutter release · Exposure compensation/ film speed dial · Nikon · 202898 · Nikon-R-UW AF FUJIKKOR · 28mm 1:2.8 · Hand grip · Lens

Key features

- Large viewfinder.

- Range of lenses.

- Choice of automatic or manual exposure.

- Enlarged controls for easy handling.

- Waterproof to a depth of 160ft (50m).

WIDE-VIEW CAMERA

A camera with a very wide-angle lens produces a rectangular image that is designed for landscape and architectural photography. Some wide-view cameras are fitted with a shift lens, useful for photographing buildings. Another way to photograph a panoramic view is to use an ordinary camera and build up a mosaic by changing the viewpoint between exposures.

Wide-view panorama

Entire facade of a building can be photographed in one frame

Spirit-level

Electronic flash unit

Lens

Cable for shutter release button

Key features

- Roll-film camera with variable film width.
- Some models are fitted with a shift lens.
- A rear-mounted, recessed hot shoe for an electronic flash.
- Built-in spirit-level.

PANORAMIC CAMERA

A special panoramic camera makes landscape photography easy by encompassing a 120°, 180°, or 360° view in one exposure. Most cameras do this by rotating the lens or the whole camera while the shutter is exposing through a vertical slit at the rear of a drum containing the lens. This type of camera must be mounted on a tripod to ensure that the horizon remains level.

360° Panoramic view

Resulting cityscape is a striking optical illusion that shows a 360° scene on one plane

Rotating lens drum can be set to turn a full circle during one exposure if desired

Lens

Support for steadying and elevating camera

Key features

- Uses a 35mm lens in a rotating drum.
- Uses 35mm film.
- Lens drum can be manually rotated to preview the scene.

LARGE-FORMAT CAMERA

Large-format cameras have either a monorail or baseboard design. Focusing is achieved by extending the flexible bellows, holding the lens panel and lens, and moving them along the rails on the monorail or fold-down baseboard. This camera uses individual sheets of 4 x 5in (10.2 x 12.7cm) film per image. Since the negative is so big, it requires little enlargement to produce prints of superb quality and definition.

Large-format camera for architecture

Viewfinder

Bellows

Handle

Lens panel

Baseboard

Key features

- Direct vision coupled viewfinder.
- Front lens panel can be removed and swapped for one of a different focal length.
- Uses 5 x 4in (10.2 x 12.7cm) sheet film.

Still video camera

Although a still video camera has a traditional lens, it records images on a floppy disk instead of photosensitive film. Inside the camera behind the lens is a CCD (charge-coupled device) etched with thousands of receptors. Each receptor produces an electrical charge that varies according to the amount of light falling on it. Prints can be produced from the disk but viewing is usually on a television.

Shutter release

Information display panel

Floppy disk

Lens

Built-in electronic flash

Key features

- Automatic infra-red focusing system.
- One disk holds about 50 images.
- Images can be stored on video tape.

STANDARD CAMERA LENSES

Camera lenses can be broken down into three broad groups: wide-angle, standard (normal), and long-focus (telephoto). It is not easy to assign focal lengths to each lens group, however, because these are dictated by the camera format. The focal length of a standard lens is approximately equal to the length of the diagonal of that format's image size. For a 35mm camera, the diagonal of the negative size measures about 50mm, so a lens with a focal length of 50–55mm is considered standard, and a lens of 80mm is a moderate long-focus lens. The diagonal of a 6 x 6cm negative measures about 80mm, so an 80mm lens is standard for a medium-format camera. The same scene taken with 35mm and medium-format cameras with standard lenses would show the same subject elements in approximately the same proportions, but the negative sizes would be different.

FOCAL LENGTH AND ANGLE OF VIEW

The illustration and sequence of photographs below, which are all taken from the same viewpoint, show that as camera lens focal length increases so the angle of view decreases.

Fisheye lens
Extreme wide-angle lenses of 6–8mm are known as fisheyes. They record a circular image of at least 180°, with some lenses even looking behind the camera with a 220° angle of view. The resulting image is very distorted, with vertical and horizontal lines bowed.

Wide-angle lens
Wide-angle lenses of 18–35mm have more general applications than fisheye lenses. Angles of view are generous and depth of field at all apertures is extensive. Poor-quality wide-angle lenses may sometimes show some distortion toward the edges of the image.

Standard lens
A standard 50mm lens is fitted on most 35mm SLRs. Useful for most types of subject, it often has a wide maximum aperture, making it good in low light. It does not show the same distortion as a wide or long lens, and its angle of view is similar to that of the human eye.

Long-focus lens
Angles of view of long-focus lenses of 80–300mm start to diminish rapidly. With so little of the scene filling the frame, the subject is shown very large, making a long lens ideal for distant subjects or detailed close-ups. Depth of field decreases as the lens gets longer.

Extreme long-focus lens
Long-focus lenses of 400–1200mm are specialized. A tripod to support the lens is essential because of its weight. A long lens has a shallow depth of field and a small maximum aperture, and requires long exposure time even in moderate light (unless you use a fast film).

STANDARD LENS

A standard, or normal, lens produces an image that is roughly equivalent to the way a scene appears when viewed with the naked eye. Most 35mm SLRs come with a standard lens, but this can be swapped for a shorter or longer lens. Standard lenses often have wide maximum apertures, making them useful in low light situations.

Depth of field scale

Aperture ring

Lens

Focusing ring

Standard 50mm lens

Standard lenses are useful for most outdoor subjects

WIDE-ANGLE LENS

A wide-angle lens takes in a larger angle of view than a standard lens, and is ideal for photographing a group of people or when you are working in confined space. If used too close to a subject, however, distortion may be a problem. Depth of field at each aperture setting is generous, which is useful when all parts of a subject must be sharply rendered.

Depth of field scale

Aperture ring

Lens

Focusing ring

28mm wide-angle lens

Wide-angle lenses are useful for interiors

ZOOM LENS

A zoom lens allows you to fine-tune subject framing by adjusting the focal length of the lens. Each zoom lens covers a range of three or four fixed focal length lenses, giving you great flexibility at a reasonable cost. Since you do not have to think about changing lenses, there is less chance you will miss an important shot.

Depth of field scale

Aperture ring

Lens

Focusing ring

28–85mm zoom lens

Zooms are useful for action shots

LONG-FOCUS LENS

Long-focus lenses are useful for large images of distant subjects or when you cannot move close enough to use a shorter lens. Long lenses tend to be heavy, which makes the use of fast shutter speeds to avoid camera shake more important than with lighter, shorter lenses. A telephoto lens is a long-focus lens with a compact design that makes it shorter.

Depth of field scale   Focusing ring   Lens

Aperture ring

135mm long-focus lens

Long-focus lenses are useful for natural history subjects

SPECIAL CAMERA LENSES

A 35mm SLR or medium-format camera body can be thought of simply as the film holder and control center for a vast array of different add-on attachments, including lenses, each with its own application. The lenses shown on these pages, all designed for the 35mm format, are just a selection of the many focal lengths and designs available.

ZOOMS AND SPECIALIZED LENSES

A zoom lens allows you to vary subject magnification without moving your camera position, which makes it popular with SLR users. Zoom lenses are also fitted as a standard feature on some advanced compact cameras.

Specialized lenses, such as extreme long-focus lenses and ultra wide-angle fisheye lenses, have more limited applications. These lenses are expensive to buy, but they can also be rented for short periods. Macro lenses are designed for taking close-ups of small subjects or isolating details of larger subjects. These lenses allow the camera to focus extremely close to a subject to record a detailed image. Used for photographing buildings, shift lenses correct perspective to overcome the problem of converging vertical lines.

MIRROR LENS

Instead of using groups of glass elements to bend light rays entering the lens and traveling down the barrel, a mirror lens uses a combination of glass elements and mirrors. These mirrors bounce the light up and down the lens barrel, manipulating the light rays to allow a long focal length to be contained within a physically short space.

Mirror lens image

600mm mirror lens with colored filters

Advantages of a mirror lens

The compact design of a mirror lens reduces the bulk and weight associated with extreme long-focus lenses. Whereas the traditional 500mm long-focus lens (*below right*) is 9.25in (235mm) long and weighs 35.25oz (1,000g), the mirror lens (*right*) of equivalent focal length weighs only 17oz (485g) and is 3.4in (87mm) long.

Distance scale
Frontal mirror
Focusing ring

Mirror lens

Focusing ring

Long-focus lens

WIDE-ANGLE ZOOM

A wide-angle zoom ranging from 21–35mm is effectively three lenses – 21mm, 28mm, and 35mm – with the added advantage of being able to select any intermediate focal length setting. However, a wide-angle zoom is likely to be slower and heavier and to show more image distortion than a wide-angle fixed focal length lens.

Lens mount
Depth of field scale
Focusing ring
Aperture ring

21–35mm zoom lens

21mm setting

35mm setting

TELEPHOTO ZOOM

A telephoto zoom lens ranging from 75–300mm encompasses about six fixed focal length lenses. This type of zoom is popular with sports and wildlife photographers. It is also useful for portraits and for moving subjects such as children. Unlike a wide-angle zoom, a telephoto zoom should not show any obvious distortion.

Aperture ring
Distance scale
Focusing ring
Depth of field scale

75–300mm zoom lens

75mm setting

300mm setting

FISHEYE LENS

Severely bowed and circular images are the hallmarks of a fisheye lens. Depth of field is so extensive that all you need do is set the focus for the approximate distance of the subject. Because of the extreme angle of view, filters cannot be mounted on the front of this type of lens. Some types of fisheye lenses have filters that are built in.

Lens mount

Focusing ring

Aperture ring

Distance scale

15mm fisheye lens

Standard lens image

Fisheye lens image

SHIFT LENS

A shift lens (also known as a perspective control lens) gets its name because it can be shifted off-center in relation to the film frame. Instead of tilting the camera back to include the top of a tall structure and so distorting the perspective, with a shift lens you can keep the camera parallel and shift the lens upward to record an undistorted image.

Aperture ring

Shift control

Lens mount

Focusing ring

28mm shift lens

Standard lens image

Shift lens image

MACRO LENS

This type of specialized lens is designed primarily to be used at very close focusing distances (*see pages 188–189*). Macro lenses are available in focal lengths ranging from 50mm to 200mm. When taking close-ups outdoors, longer macro lenses produce a large image from farther back. Moving in close with a shorter macro lens may block out the light.

Aperture ring

Distance scale

Focusing ring

Lens mount

50mm macro lens

Standard lens image

Macro lens image

TELEPHOTO LENS

A telephoto lens has specially designed optics that allow it to have a long focal length in a relatively short barrel. This name has become so widespread that it is commonly applied to all long-focus lenses irrespective of their design. Telephotos of 400mm, even lightweight ones, require some sort of camera support.

Camera body

Focusing ring

400mm telephoto lens

Focusing ring

1000mm telephoto lens

Tripod mount

Standard lens image

1000mm lens image

FLASH LIGHTING EQUIPMENT

Flash lighting units can be divided into several groups: studio equipment, built-in flash, and portable add-on or hand-held units. Although built-in flash is a convenient source of lighting, which can also be used to supplement daylight, it does have disadvantages. First, light output is limited in strength and, if it is the sole illumination, has to be used relatively close to your subject. Second, the flash is always front facing and tends to produce a harsh, unattractive light. Third, the flash and lens are very close together and this causes red eye, in which the pupils of the subject's eyes appear red. Add-on and hand-held flash units are far more versatile. In general, they have a more powerful output, the flash head can be angled to bounce light off a wall or ceiling for a softer and more natural look, and the flash head is far enough away from the lens to avoid the problem of red eye.

> ### Flash fall-off
>
> • The farther the subject is from the flash, the less light it receives.
>
> • If the flash-to-subject distance is doubled, the light is spread over four times the area.

Direct light from built-in flash

Bounced light from add-on flash

Bounced light from hand-held flash

Built-in flash
This type of built-in flash is more useful as a supplementary or fill-in light source than as the main illumination for a picture. Its low-output beam and front-facing position make its application rather limited for any creative flash effects. One useful feature of the camera shown below is an infra-red light transmitter, which bounces a beam of invisible light off the subject and helps the autofocus detector locate the subject when it is too dark to see.

Add-on flash
This flash fits into the hot shoe on top of the pentaprism. Electrical contacts connect with the camera shutter, automatically triggering the flash. This type of flashgun can be very sophisticated for its size, and a fully integrated unit (dedicated flash) allows great versatility.

Hand-held flash
This type of unit has a long handle for hand holding, but it can also be attached to the side of the camera. It may have a separate battery pack, allowing faster recharging and more flashes per charge. A synchronization chord coordinates the flash firing with the shutter.

Pentaprism

Built-in flash head

Autofocus light projector

Tilt and swivel flash head

Flash tube

Flash light sensor

Hot shoe connection

Pentaprism

Tilt and swivel flash head

Flash hot shoe attachment unit

Flash sync socket

Flash sync cord

Battery holder and handle

STUDIO LIGHTING EQUIPMENT

Tungsten or flash lighting can be used for indoor photography. Tungsten lights plug into standard outlets, are adjustable, and work independently of the camera. Flash lighting stays cool during operation and is portable, which makes it a popular choice. You must use the correct type of film with artificial lighting because the color temperature of tungsten is different from that of daylight. Do not mix daylight and tungsten. Flash lighting is used with normal film and, because it has the same color temperature as natural light, can be used to supplement daylight. Flash units cannot be battery-powered due to the intensity of their light output.

Basic flash unit
An adjustable lighting stand is required for each flash unit, and accessories can be used to modify light quality. A control switch allows you to alter the strength of the light. Larger units require a power pack, linked to the flash head and shutter by a synchronization lead.

Flood flash head
A flood produces an even spread of illumination over the whole subject.

Wide beam of light

Barn doors flash head
A set of four hinged flaps placed around the flash keeps light from reaching certain parts of the subject.

Adjustable beam of light

Flash meter

Because of the immediacy of flash, a light meter is required for accurate exposure measurement. Some meters are designed for use with flash and ambient light. Hold the meter where you want to take your reading and fire the flash manually.

Size and shape of the reflector surrounding the flash head determine the spread of light

Central column of lighting stand is telescoped up or down to alter the height of the head

Power pack is connected to mains supply; larger packs can be used for a higher output

Cable connects the flash head to the power pack

Snoot flash head
A snoot is similar to a spot and gives a narrow, concentrated beam of light with dark shadows.

Narrow beam of light

Diffused lighting

Softbox diffuser
A diffuser produces a soft, wide spread of light. Flashlight travels through the gauze material of the softbox, making the front panel the light source.

Bounced lighting

Umbrella reflector
This device bounces light back onto the subject. The inside of the umbrella can be white or silver, according to the light quality desired.

Adding a reflector

Portable reflector
A collapsible reflector is a useful accessory when working indoors or on location. Made of reflective material, it is used to soften shadows.

CHOOSING FILM TYPES

Of all the film sold worldwide, more than 90 percent is color negative intended for color prints. The remaining 10 percent comprises mainly color positive or slide film, with black and white film now only a minority interest.

NEGATIVE OR POSITIVE FILM

Color negatives show subject colors as their complementary colors, and there may also be an overall pinkish-orange color-cast. When printed, colors are reversed to show the scene correctly rendered. Black and white negatives have reversed tones – what was a dark tone appears as a light tone, and vice versa. As with color negatives, when a black and white negative is printed the tones are reversed to show the correct distribution of light and dark. Positive film images are known as slides or transparencies, and are intended to be projected and not printed. Therefore, the colors or tones on the film correspond to those of the original scene.

PRINTS OR SLIDES

The advantage of using color negative film is that color prints are easy and convenient to view. They can be stored in the envelopes supplied by the processors or mounted in albums. In addition, extra copies can be printed at little cost and enlargements made. In contrast, color slides must be mounted and loaded into a projector before they can be viewed in a darkened room. A projected slide, however, is far more impressive than a print, since the image quality is superior, and the colors tend to be richer and truer to life.

Black and white negative (*above*)
Black and white print (*right*)

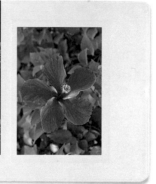

Color negative (*above*)
Color print (*right*)

Slide (*above*)
Mounted slide (*right*)

BLACK AND WHITE

The image tones on a black and white negative appear reversed, with light areas corresponding to dark areas of the subject, and dark areas of the negative corresponding to light areas of the subject. Black and white prints can be made from a color original, but a black and white negative will usually give the best-quality results.

COLOR PRINT

The colors on a color negative appear as the complementary colors of the subject, which makes judging image quality from the film difficult. After printing, colors should appear normal. If necessary, color can be corrected with filters during printing. You should ask for replacement prints if colors are inaccurate or there are color differences within a set.

COLOR SLIDE

Since there is no intervening printing stage with slides, the colors should be extremely accurate. Before it is ready for projection, each image has to be cut from the film strip and mounted (*see page 242*). This is done for you automatically with process-paid slide film. Color and black and white prints can also be made from slides.

Film formats

Each format of camera must be used with its corresponding film format. Film for 35mm cameras comes in metal or plastic cassettes, while roll film used in medium-format cameras has a paper backing for protection. Large-format film comes as individual sheets.

110mm film
The once popular 110mm film format is so small that the resulting prints are usually of poor quality. The film is conveniently packaged and comes in a drop-in plastic cartridge.

35mm film
This is the most popular film format, with a large range of brands. It is available for prints or slides, and in varying lengths and film speeds.

Roll film
Also called 120 or 220mm film, roll film is used in all medium-format cameras, which all have a 2¼in (6cm) image dimension.

Sheet film
Sheet film comes in individual sheets that are loaded into holders.

DAYLIGHT AND TUNGSTEN FILM

Film is manufactured to produce best results, in terms of color, when used under specific types of lighting. Most film is balanced for use in bright daylight or for use indoors with electronic flash, both of which have the same color temperature. If daylight-balanced film is exposed using domestic lighting, or when using tungsten studio lights, then it will show a pronounced orange color-cast. With color prints, this cast can largely be corrected during the printing stage. Color slide film, however, does not go through a printing stage, so it is vital to make sure that you buy the correct type of film for the light source under which it will be used. Black and white print and slide film can be used under any type of lighting without risk of distorting its tonal response.

Incorrect use of daylight-balanced film

Correct use of daylight-balanced film

DAYLIGHT FILM

Color film designed for use in daylight or flash will show a distinct orange cast if used under tungsten lights. These two pictures were shot on daylight-balanced film. In the first shot (*far left*), the tungsten of the domestic lights gives the room a distinct orange cast. In the second picture (*left*), the scene is lit by natural daylight alone and is correct in color.

Correct use of tungsten-balanced film

Incorrect use of tungsten-balanced film

TUNGSTEN FILM

Color film intended for use in tungsten light will show a strong blue cast if used in daylight (or with daylight-balanced flash). These two pictures were both taken on tungsten-balanced film. In the first picture (*far left*), the scene is lit by domestic tungsten lights and has correct color rendition. In the second picture (*left*), daylight gives the scene a distinct blue cast.

Brand color bias

Different brands of color film use different dyes, which result in subtle color variations. Color may also vary between different speeds of film from the same manufacturer. These differences are most obvious when using color slide film, since there is no intermediary printing stage.

Film with blue bias

Film with yellow bias

Film with red bias

FILM SPEED AND CAMERA EQUIPMENT

Films are referred to as being fast, medium, or slow – a reference to their sensitivity to light. Fast films have high ISO (International Standards Organization) numbers and slow films, low ones. Fast films are useful in low-light situations, since they increase the chances of achieving a correctly exposed image when a less-sensitive, slower film may result in underexposure. The drawback of this increase in speed, however, is a reduction in image sharpness and an increase in contrast. Slow films are ideal when light levels are good and you need the highest-quality prints.

SLOW FILM

This marble bust was shot using a very slow-speed film (ISO 32). Note the delicate, almost creamy texture of the statue's surface and the soft gradation of tones between the lit right-hand side and the shadowy left-hand side. Even in the enlargement (*see inset*), the appearance of any grain is negligible.

Choosing slow film
A slow film is ideal for brightly lit subjects, or where a degree of subject movement or blur is required. It is often used for still life subjects that need to be enlarged while still retaining a lot of detail and a fine-grained image. Even if light is poor, the camera can be set up on a tripod and a long exposure given.

MEDIUM FILM

Using the same lighting as above, the bust was shot using a medium-speed film (ISO 200). Note that grain becomes coarser the faster the film. Here the film is much faster than the ISO 32 film (each doubling of the ISO number is a doubling of the sensitivity), but the quality is still good, and the grain can only just be detected.

Choosing medium film
A film in the medium-speed category is suitable for a wide range of different subjects and lighting conditions. Although ambient light levels are high in this bright Mediterranean scene, medium-speed film can also be used in less light earlier or later in the day when the sun is much lower in the sky.

MODERATE-FAST FILM

With the film speed doubled to ISO 400, the appearance of the bust on the full-frame image is slightly different. The surface of the bust looks less fine and the contrast between light and shade is beginning to increase slightly. As you would expect with a faster film, the grain is now fairly noticeable in the enlargement.

Choosing moderate-fast film
This shot of a seagull in flight requires a fast shutter speed to capture the movement of the subject and avoid camera shake, as well as a small aperture to cover any slight error in focus. The speed of a moderate-fast film enables you to photograph subjects in even extremely dim lighting conditions.

ULTRA-FAST SPEED FILM

The ISO 1000 film used for this photograph of the bust is 1.5 times more sensitive than the ISO 400 film, and now the grainy nature of the film emulsion is apparent. Note, too, that the soft gradation of tone apparent in the version using the slow film is now more abrupt and that there is a slight color shift.

Choosing ultra-fast film
Choose an ultra-fast film when light levels are really low, for example, in a dimly lit interior or outdoors at dusk. This type of film is so sensitive that it will give you acceptable results even by the light of a match. The graininess of the resulting image can add to the dramatic impact and atmosphere of the shot.

BASIC CAMERA EQUIPMENT

For the 35mm SLR user there is a wide range of equipment and accessories available to cover every area of photographic interest. In terms of lenses, your camera may come with a standard 50mm lens already fitted. Additionally, you should consider a wide-angle lens between 28 and 35mm for shooting a broad panorama or when working in a confined area. A long-focus lens between 90 and 135mm is useful for portraits as well as more distant subjects. However, a zoom lens gives you flexibility without changing lens. A tripod guarantees sharp images of stationary subjects and may be essential to avoid camera shake during a long exposure.

If there is room in your camera bag, then you should also include a few filters, a basic lens- and camera-cleaning kit, a notepad and pen, a portable flashgun, and some spare film of different speed ratings.

Front and rear lens caps
When a lens is not in use, always keep the front lens cap on. The rear lens cap should be fitted when the lens is removed from the camera.

Camera strap
Use a camera strap and keep it around your neck in case you let the camera slip. Wider straps spread the weight of the camera and lens.

Electronic flashgun
An electronic flashgun is useful when light levels are low, when working indoors, or when you want to lessen contrast by adding some light to areas of shadow.

35mm camera
The body of the camera forms the heart of a system for which there are numerous accessories and lenses. Always use a body cap to protect the interior of the camera when a lens is not attached.

Tripod
A lightweight tripod is essential when you need steady images.

Cable release
Releases the shutter on a tripod-mounted camera and avoids the risk of camera movement.

Filters
A clear ultra-violet filter can be left on the lens as protection. Strongly colored filters are used with black and white film or for special effects with color film.

Lenses
Choose lenses according to the type of shots you want to take. Wide and long lenses increase flexibility. Extension rings allow you to get in closer to a subject.

Notepad and pen
These are invaluable for noting the location of a particular shot or for details of a particular subject.

Film
Always carry several rolls of spare film. If you have fast film you will be able to take photographs in dimly lit places.

Camera care kit
All you need for cleaning your camera and lenses are (from left to right) a soft lint-free cloth, special dust-free tissues, lens-cleaning fluid, and a blower brush. Use the cleaning fluid very sparingly. If a hair or piece of film debris gets lodged in an awkward area, then a pair of tweezers might be needed. A small screwdriver is also useful.

Camera bag
A camera bag should be well padded inside and have adjustable compartments for holding equipment.

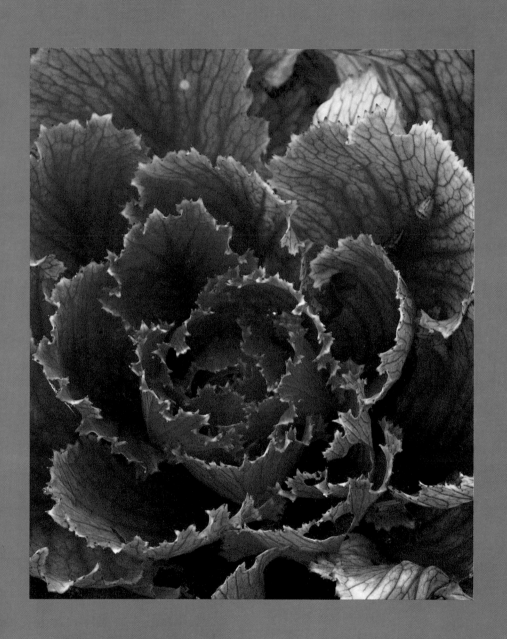

How to See Better Pictures

Taking photographs that have appeal and impact
depends in part on your ability to see
the potential in a subject and then interpret it
in your own way. This section reveals how light
affects form, color, texture, shape, and pattern, and
how to compose excellent photographs
by considering the different qualities of light.
It also illustrates the importance of selecting
the viewpoint that will show your
subject in the most effective and telling fashion.

THE ESSENTIAL PICTURE ELEMENTS

It is difficult to define precisely what it is that makes a "good" photograph. With pictures taken on vacation or of members of your family, what constitutes a good photograph may be a personal judgment. However, some photographs do communicate to a broader audience because of the revealing way the subject has been treated or the way in which the elements are composed to convey mood.

The photographs on these pages are all different in terms of subject matter, but each has a quality that invites closer inspection. Some images work because the photograph has captured the subject's intriguing shape or some aspect of its form that makes it appear three-dimensional. In other photographs, the main element may be color – subtle and moody or vibrant and contrasting – or a humorous juxtaposition of subject elements.

Adding humor, *above*
Looking like companionable old friends, and showing almost the same amount of teeth, this Peruvian woman and her llama makes for a very humorous picture.

Color harmony, *left*
Natural brown and green hues come together in this photograph of a decorative piece of fungus to create an image that has strong shape and color harmony.

Main subject
A well-composed picture needs to have a main focal point. In this image, a central cloud directs the gaze to the distance and gives a feeling of depth.

Vibrant color
The color of this cabbage has been intensified by moving in close to exclude extraneous details and fill the whole frame with a deep, vibrant pink.

Lens effect
Extra punch is given to this photograph of Indonesian paddy fields by shooting the scene using a long lens. This has the effect of squashing the different subject planes, so that the background is enlarged relative to the foreground. A clue to the scale of the landscape is provided by the figure, whose shirt provides a splash of contrasting color.

Simple detail
Even a simple still life photograph of seemingly mundane objects such as these thermometers can be an image of considerable dramatic impact.

UNDERSTANDING COLOR HARMONY

Ideally, a photograph should have one main subject and one main color – with any other colors being supplementary to give added emphasis to the most important element. In terms of mood, a composition made up of harmonious colors of similar tones tends to be restful and calm, unlike the discordant feeling of compositions based on contrasting colors.

Even contrasting colors can be blended and subdued to create a harmonious picture if photographed in the appropriate type of lighting. The choice of lighting can affect color, but you can also affect color through exposure: slightly underexposing to give a low-key result, and slightly overexposing or using colored filters to lessen color contrast.

Restricted palette
The stark simplicity of this bathroom is reinforced by restricting the color palette to cream and beige, with a panel of delicate, gray-blue tiles used to link the flat bands of color.

Strong hues
Although blue and green are harmonious colors, the strength of the hues in this landscape would appear strongly contrasting if it were not for the intervening band of light gold acting as a buffer between the two.

Sunset colors, *above*
As the sun dips below the horizon, red wavelengths of light dominate, turning all colors in the scene into harmonious shades of the same single hue.

Low-key image, *left*
The green, blue, and red colors of these wooden boats are blended into a harmonious scheme by underexposing the image to give a low-key result.

Faded hues
A gentle, autumnal blend of color characterizes this photograph of dried rose blooms and hips.

Morning light
Red and blue – opposites in the color spectrum – feature in this portrait, but in the morning light the colors complement each other rather than compete.

Natural colors
An abandoned wagon, slowly being absorbed back into the natural world, is the focal point of this image composed of harmonious shades of green and brown.

USING COLOR CONTRAST

Color has an emotional content, conveying atmosphere and affecting how we interpret an image. Strong, bold colors can create a feeling of vitality and, if used with restraint, small areas of color contrast can draw attention to a section of an image without overwhelming it as a whole.

Color contrast is caused by the juxtaposition of primary colors – red, blue, and yellow – or results from placing a primary color next to its complementary color – green, orange, and purple, respectively. Large areas of contrasting color can have a detrimental effect on subject form, destroying depth and masking detail. Although the use of color is dependent on personal preference, as a general rule bold colors should be balanced with weaker ones.

Unusual view, *above*
An abstract composition consisting of strong color contrast is created here by showing part of the boat's red keel and its reflection in the inky blue water.

Flower contrasts
The petals of the yellow sunflower (*top*) and the pink daisy (*above*) contrast strongly with the dark, shadowy backgrounds.

Light and color
The light by which an object is viewed has an effect on its coloration. Here, strong, directional evening light produces intense hues of red.

Muted contrast, *top*
Color contrast can give
even a simple picture, such
as this still life detail,
greater pictorial interest.
The yellow string is most
pronounced when seen
against the area of shadow
to the right of the pipe.

Spatial abstraction, *above*
Two large blocks of strong,
contrasting color destroy
the sense of depth in this
picture. Although the
yellow field is more distant,
it is the green grass closer
to the viewer that appears
to recede, creating a spatial
abstraction with both
elements interpreted as
sitting on the same plane.

Touch of color
Although only very small
in the frame, the red of
the Senegalese tribesman's
headdress contrasts with
the blue both of his gown
and of the sky, drawing
immediate attention to a
particular area of the image.

WORKING WITH SHAPE

One of the most powerful ways to emphasize shape in a photograph is to ensure that, at least in outline, it contrasts strongly with its surroundings in either tone or color. The shape of a subject with a lot of pattern or detail can be emphasized by photographing it against a plain, neutral background that will not compete for attention. Another technique is to use an extreme form of lighting contrast, as you would for a silhouette, to suppress all details and allow the subject to become a strong graphic outline of equal-density tone.

The shape of an object is not fixed and you can alter its appearance by changing your camera position. Shooting down on a subject can reduce its bulk overall, as well as the apparent size of its different parts, making some seem larger in relation to others. You can also manipulate shape by shooting from below the subject, or by using different lenses, from very wide-angle to long-focus.

Viewpoint and shape
It is necessary to look for an unusual viewpoint to convey something of the Amazon River's huge size. This aerial shot reinforces the twisting nature of the river, making shape of paramount importance.

Competing shapes
The presence of two powerful shapes such as the Great Pyramid and the Sphinx in the same image needs careful handling to ensure a well-balanced, harmonious composition.

Using shadows, *above*
Two ways of emphasizing shape in a photograph can be seen in this image. First, the dark outline of the man contrasts with the pastel color of the wall behind. Second, a low afternoon sun has cast a well-defined shadow onto the wall, strengthening the element of shape in the composition as a whole.

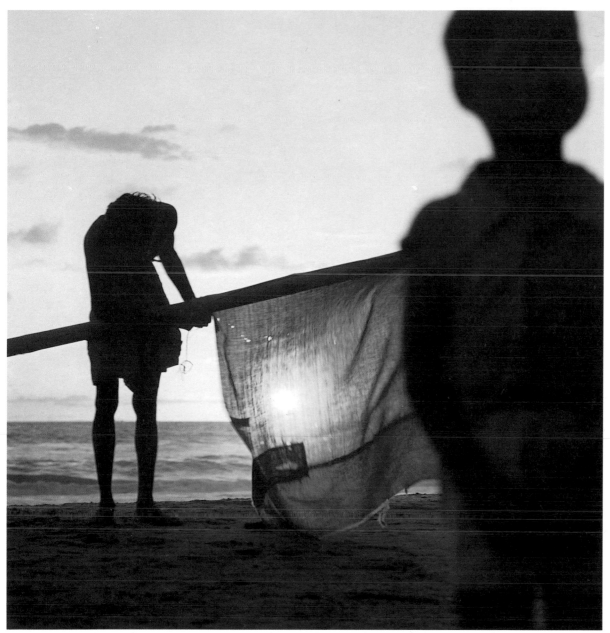

Concentrating attention
The close-up figure on the right of this photograph acts as an effective frame and counterbalance to the more distant one, helping to direct and then hold attention within the picture boundaries. Both figures are reduced to silhouettes by the strong backlighting, and the diagonally held pole helps unify the composition by bridging the gap between them.

Silhouette, *below left*
A low camera angle is used here to show off the striking Gothic silhouette of a ruined abbey against a neutral backdrop of sky. A high camera position would have shown more of the dark hills behind the building and lessened the impact of its shape.

Rim lighting, *below*
A dramatic silhouette is achieved by positioning the model directly between the sun and the camera. The sunlight is so intense that a halo of rim lighting has spilled past the subject, perfectly outlining her face, neck, and upper body.

USING LIGHT AND DARK TONES

The term tone refers to any area of uniform density on a print, negative, or transparency that can be distinguished from lighter or darker parts. In its most extreme form, a photograph may consist of just two tones – black and white – with no shades of gray in between. More often, however, images are composed of a wide range of intermediary tones between these two extremes.

Tone is also used to refer to the visual weight – the perceived darkness or lightness – of an image. A photograph consisting of predominantly heavy dark tones and black is known as a "low-key" image; while one that is made up mostly of light bright tones and white is referred to as "high-key."

These terms are not restricted just to black and white photography. A color photograph can also be described as high- or low-key. We talk about shades and tints of a color to describe its different intensities, and the grays making up a tonal range also form part of our color perception. The latter is mainly governed by the intensity and angle of light striking an object and you can manipulate this for effect.

High-key color, *below*
Directional window light bathes one side of this pitcher and bowl in bright illumination that dispels any hint of deep shadow. This high-key result is helped by the white wall behind, which acts as a reflector, increasing light levels and lightening dark shadows.

Low-key results
Low-key pictures do not have to exclude all bright tones. In the portrait (*right*), daylight illuminates one side of the man's face, but most of the image is in shadow. In the still life (*below right*), the pots show a whole range of tones in what is a low-key picture.

Dark imagery, *left*
This low-key image of a windmill has a brooding atmosphere. The sky seems full of foreboding and the dark landscape has a hint of menace. A red filter is used to darken the sky and other light tones, except for the path in the foreground.

Bright imagery, *above*
A combination of smoke and mist has given a light-toned, high-key result. Although practically no detail has survived, the imagery has an old-world tranquillity and there is an overwhelming feeling of space and emptiness.

High contrast, *far left*
Contrast in a photograph refers to the difference in tone between the brightest highlight and deepest shadow. This image is high contrast because of the presence of both bright white and deep black tones.

Low contrast, *left*
The tones in this misty woodland scene all come from the middle of the tonal range. There are no strong black or stark white tones, and so this image is a low-contrast picture.

EMPHASIZING FORM

Whereas shape describes the two-dimensional outline of a subject and is recognizable even if an object is backlit with no surface details showing, form or modeling describes not only the surface characteristics of an object but also its three-dimensional qualities, such as its roundness and substance. In a photograph, form is shown by the gradation of light and shade, and the color strength, which is also related to the amount of light reflected or absorbed by the subject's surface.

Lighting that produces a flat color or tone, with little or no variation across the surface of the subject, tends to suppress the appearance of form. To accentuate form, it is therefore best to avoid harsh, frontal lighting and to use angled lighting or sidelighting, which tends to produce a gradation in color or tone. This in turn emphasizes the surface texture and tactile nature of the subject. The still life on these pages was shot in daylight and also with flash to show how the angle of light striking an object affects the sense of form.

Natural daylight
Positioned by a window, these lemons are directly lit by natural daylight as well as by reflected light from the white window ledge. Note that adjacent to the window, where the lemons are most strongly lit, form is least obvious.

Low sidelighting

Light source at 90°

This still life is part of a sequence showing different lighting effects. Here a light is positioned low down at about the same height as the lemons, so that only one side is lit. Contrast between the lit and unlit sides is very strong.

Overhead lighting

Light source above

The light is shining down from directly above the still life group, and, apart from the area near the dividing line between light and shade on each lemon, there is little sense of roundness. As a general rule, overhead lighting destroys form.

Angled lighting

Light source at 45°

An angle of about 45° is ideal to give an impression of the form of the lemons. There is a now a gradual transition between light and shade, noticeable on the right of the group, which was in shade before.

REVEALING TEXTURE

The appearance of texture in a photograph gives the viewer additional information about the tactile qualities of an object. It is only by seeing the pitted quality of the skin of an orange, the coarseness of a length of woven cloth, or the smooth perfection of a piece of fine porcelain that we can imagine what it would be like to touch the object.

The most revealing type of illumination for texture comes from directional lighting, since it is the contrast between the lit, raised surface areas and the shadows in the hollows that creates a three-dimensional illusion (*see page 46*). This is the reason why the soft, directional light of early morning or evening sunshine has been the basis for so many successful landscape photographs.

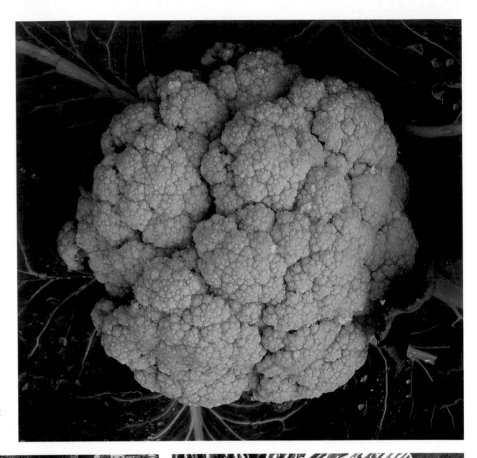

Diffused lighting
Working in diffused light ensures that the shadows do not hide too much of the surface of this giant tree trunk. Note that the top ridges have all caught the sunlight, while the hollows are filled with deep shadows.

Depth and texture
Shot from overhead with weak sunlight striking the front of the cauliflower, it is easy to imagine the feel of the vegetable's surface. Tonal contrasts define the tactile qualities of the object and also give the picture an impression of depth.

Magnified texture, *above*
By photographically enlarging a small object you can record its texture. The individual hairs on the body of this hornet and the hollows of the fungus are emphasized by the use of strong, directional lighting.

Wood surface, *above left*
Soft, oblique light reveals the texture of otherwise uninteresting pieces of old and weathered wood. Remember that individual surfaces absorb and reflect different quantities of light and must be lit accordingly.

Light and shade, *above*
The rusted and peeling surface of this sheet of metal is partly in sunshine and partly in shade. The directional lighting reveals the texture and adds to the overall composition.

Surface sheen
An old tarpaulin exposed to the weathering effects of the elements has taken on a character of its own. The lighting is subdued, since the sheen would be lost and the appearance of texture and form would be diminished if harshly lit.

DISCOVERING PATTERN

Representing order and harmony, pattern is something pleasing to the eye. To record the patterns abounding all around us, you need to choose the right viewpoint. By carefully selecting your camera position, you can record patterns even when looking at a seemingly random array of subject elements.

PATTERNS IN NATURE

As a photographer, you can draw attention to abstract patterns and repeating forms in the natural world, such as fallen autumn leaves or the frost-covered branches of a tree. Sometimes pattern is only transitory and is gone in an instant. A flock of birds, for example, can be seen as a collection of repeating colors and shapes, or sunlight on a row of houses may create a pattern of dark triangles in an otherwise bright scene.

Importance of viewpoint
To concentrate attention on the repeating shapes, colors, and forms of this flock of geese, a high camera viewpoint is vital. A lower camera angle would show more of the background and so dilute the pattern's impact.

Seeing pattern
A vortex of repeating shapes seems to draw the eye upward, following the relentless spiral of this staircase toward a distant highlight. Without the curiosity to explore different camera angles, unusual shots are easily missed.

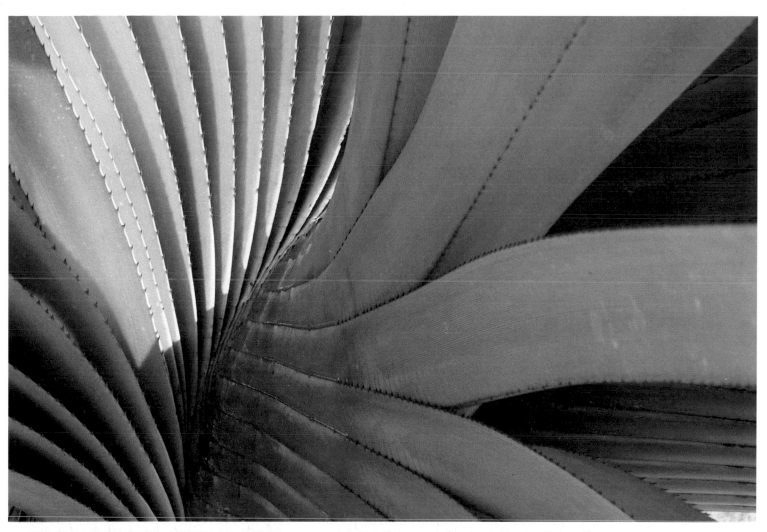

Layers of pattern, *above*
In this close-up of an aloe, many different layers of pattern can be seen in the overlapping fronds.

Isolating design, *below*
A jumble of rope can be framed in the viewfinder to create an interesting design. The twisted strands making up the rope itself represent a pattern within a pattern.

Random pattern, *left*
Although the pots are not arranged, their repeated curved shapes and the dark circles of their shadowy openings create a sense of pattern. The uniform color of the composition is another vital element.

Effective detail, *above*
The pleasing effect pattern has on the eye is illustrated in this detail of two cogs. Not only do the teeth of the cogs themselves form an obvious motif, but the interplay of light and shade also reinforces the effect.

THE BENEFITS OF BLACK AND WHITE

Black and white photography, although now a minority interest, continues to have a band of dedicated adherents. The enduring appeal of working in this medium stems from its powerful graphic potential and its ability to evoke mood and atmosphere.

Black and white film allows you a lot of flexibility in how the image will look when printed. You can use a wide range of colored lens filters to change the relative strength of tones within an image. It is also far easier than with color to manipulate the image in the darkroom, by giving a weak part of the negative extra exposure through the enlarger to increase local density, or by printing on a type of paper that gives an overall cold-blue image or a warm-brown one. Inevitably, once color is extracted from some scenes they lose much of their impact, and thus subjects such as gardens or natural history, in general, may not be ideal for black and white treatment.

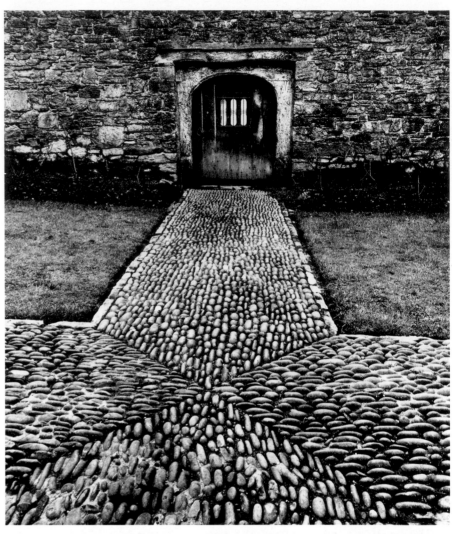

Dominant color
A wide range of tones is the main feature of the black and white picture (*right*). Although linear perspective draws attention to the door itself, the patchwork effect of the tones leads the eye in different directions. By contrast, the colors of the door (*below*), serve to emphasize the textures.

Distracting color
The color content is so overwhelming in the detail of a wall (*above*) that it does not allow the image to be seen as anything other than a color composition. Seen in black and white, a similar detail of a brick wall (*left*) has visual attributes such as texture, pattern, form, and shape.

Darkroom manipulation
An atmosphere of isolation pervades this image of a solitary figure walking along a winding road. To heighten this effect, the countryside surrounding the road was given extra exposure during printing.

The human form
Black and white is ideal for showing the form and modeling of the human body by bringing out subtle gradations of tone. Sidelighting accentuates the skin texture so that every line is palpable.

Infra-red film
Infra-red film is sensitive to wavelengths in ordinary light that are invisible to the naked eye, and gives some subjects an unusual appearance. The sky in this image is unnaturally dark while the roadside foliage is unnaturally light. An infra-red or a deep red filter over the lens will exaggerate the tonal shifts when using infra-red film.

FRAMING THE IMAGE

To create a unified effect you need to decide how best to arrange the elements making up the image – what to include or omit, the angle at which to shoot, and how to show one subject element in relation to others. Just as a painter must work within the dimensions of his canvas, a photographer uses the camera viewfinder as the creative space within which to build a pleasing composition. One way of composing a picture is to use a frame within a frame. In order to emphasize the main subject of a picture you can show it surrounded and balanced by another element.

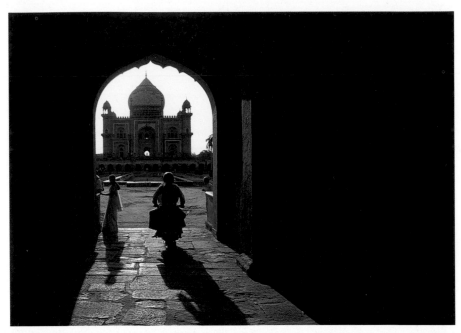

Stonework surround
The foreground stonework through which the distant landscape is viewed gives the scene an added feeling of space and distance.

Framing a building
By using an arch as a framing device, the image is simplified. Unwanted details are cut out to focus attention on the building.

Balancing shapes, *left*
Careful composition within the viewfinder creates an evocative composition, with well-positioned silhouetted figures and the diagonal shape of the platform.

Frame effect, *above*
The viewer's gaze is drawn to the group of figures at the window by showing them within a natural frame created by a gap in the wall covered with ivy.

Framing choices
If using a 35mm camera, you can frame a picture vertically or horizontally. In the horizontally framed shot (*above*), there is a feeling of being enclosed by the hills rising on either side. By turning the camera around for a vertical shot (*left*), the inclusion of a greater amount of sky helps to dispel the sense of confined space.

Color contrast, *far left*
The figure is effectively framed by the red curtain as well as by the dark background against which he is highlighted.

SELECTING THE VIEWPOINT

The viewpoint from which you photograph a subject determines the apparent relationship between all the objects included in the frame and of those objects to their surroundings.

The only accurate way to determine the effectiveness of a particular viewpoint is by checking its appearance through the viewfinder. Looking at a scene with the naked eye, you are aware of a mass of peripheral information surrounding the area of interest. The viewfinder, however, shows the scene with clear-cut edges as it will appear in the finished photograph.

Look for ways to simplify the picture by positioning yourself to exclude extraneous detail, or for unusual ways to present the subject. While looking through the camera, try crouching down so that you are lower than the subject; or try standing on a small stepladder so that you can look down on it. Even by simply moving to one side you can show subject elements in a different way.

Selective viewpoint
In this unusual portrait of the sculptor Henry Moore, it is the artist's hands that are the focal point. The viewpoint forces our attention on to the strong fingers that are reminiscent of the sculptural shapes they once produced.

High viewpoint
In an overhead view, taken from standing height, these colorful toadstools growing on the forest floor seem to glow with an autumnal warmth. If taken from a lower camera viewpoint, their impact would be lessened by the inclusion of less of the background.

Varying the viewpoint
This sequence illustrates
that there is more than one
viewpoint for any subject.
The first image (*top*) is shot
from slightly above and the
next (*center*) at about level
with the snake charmer.
The final shot (*bottom*) is
taken from standing height.

Low viewpoint
Shooting directly upward
produces an extreme
viewpoint, which conveys
the immense size of these
ancient Egyptian columns.

DEPTH AND PERSPECTIVE

Perspective is a way of using spatial elements to indicate depth and distance in a photograph, giving the impression that you are looking at a three-dimensional scene. There are several different methods of using perspective to create this illusion of depth.

By placing one object behind another you can indicate that it is farther away from the camera. This is called diminishing scale and stems from our knowledge that objects of the same size appear to look smaller the more distant they are from the camera. Linear perspective describes the apparent convergence of parallel lines as they recede from the camera, and aerial perspective is the tendency of colors to become lighter in tone in distant shots. Finally, by using a large aperture and focusing on a near subject, you can make the background appear out of focus.

Using the horizon
The setting sun and the gradation of tones where the sea and sky meet creates an illusion of depth and distance in this scene.

Wide-angle perspective
A wide-angle lens produces an exaggerated perspective effect. The man's feet near the camera seem large in proportion to his head.

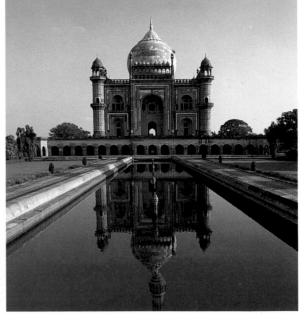

Linear perspective, *above*
The camera angle chosen for this view of a mosque in India shows strong linear perspective in the apparently converging sides of the lake.

Vanishing point
The tapering sides of these skyscrapers are an example of linear perspective. By picturing the converging parallel lines extended, you can imagine that at some distant point they will meet – this is called the vanishing point.

Aerial perspective, *far left*
A mountain lake makes an evocative foreground for the overlapping forms of a range of mountains in the Swiss Alps. Note how the peaks become lighter and bluer in tone as they fade away into the distance.

Diminishing scale, *left*
An avenue of trees leads the eye to a fountain, an effect reinforced by linear perspective. Another clue to perspective is present in the diminishing scale and apparent size of the trees.

DEFINING IMAGE PLANES

Unless you fill the camera frame with a flat, two-dimensional object, or just one face or side of a three-dimensional object, then every photograph should contain a foreground, middleground, and background, which are known as the image planes.

By ensuring that important subject elements are visible in all three image planes, you can manipulate the viewer's interpretation of the composition by leading the eye to explore the picture. However, you should try to choose a viewpoint that clearly defines one of the image planes as having a dominant compositional role, so that the idea you want to convey is not confused or lost.

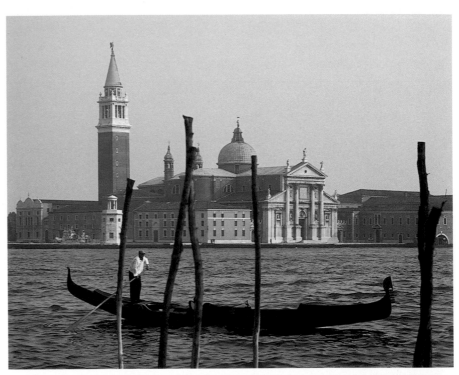

Tonal separation
In this view of ornate steps leading to a church in Portugal, it is the subtle difference in tone that helps separate the fore-, middle-, and background.

Well-defined planes
Mooring poles define the foreground, the gondola the middleground, and the church the background. Each element adds to the view of Venice as a whole.

Merging planes
A long lens is used for this shot of the temple at Luxor in Egypt. By compressing the perspective, it merges the distinction between the image planes, and makes the judgment of depth and distance more difficult.

Foreground detail
Although a full and detailed picture, with well-defined image planes, the camera viewpoint emphasizes the foreground statue by showing it against a plain green middleground with the background building reduced in scale.

Middleground, *far left*
The castle in the middle distance dominates this landscape. Although the fore- and background are important, they are only assigned supporting roles.

Focusing distance, *left*
By using a wide aperture to render the background out of focus, attention is fixed on the railings at the front of the frame.

BALANCE AND PROPORTION

Practically every photograph, whether it is a visually rich interior or an abstract composition of shapes and colors, consists of a number of different subject elements. The photographer must aim to compose the shot so that there is a balance between all of them.

The concept of balance and proportion does not mean that a good photograph must be perfectly symmetrical or that the main focal point must be positioned in the center of the frame, since this leads to static, formal images. A much-used pictorial device is to divide the photograph into thirds, both horizontally and vertically, and to place the subject one-third across and one-third up or down the picture. Balance also applies to color and shape. Two strong colors or dominant shapes will compete for the viewer's attention, but if they are positioned in a sympathetic way they can provide an effective pictorial balance.

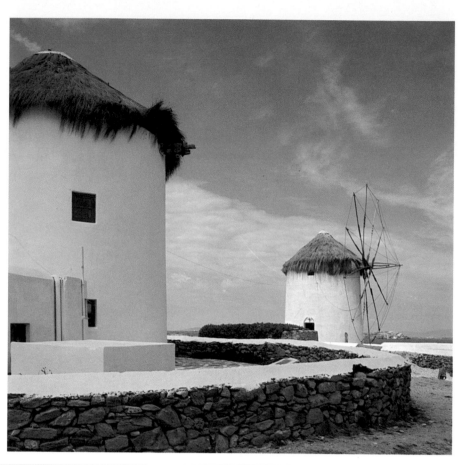

Balanced shapes
In this photograph of artist Graham Sutherland, the camera angle is chosen to balance the shapes of the seated figure and the semi-silhouetted tree stump.

Partial view
By avoiding the temptation to position the windmills in a symmetrical way, the partial view of the nearest building is balanced by the more distant structure.

Foreground interest, *above*
The Taj Mahal is one of the most photographed sites in the world. In this picture, however, a duality of focal points makes for a more unusual representation. The boatman balances the temple in the background, and also adds interest to the foreground.

Human scale
The imposing columns of the Egyptian temple of Karnak at Luxor rivet the attention of the viewer, but without the presence of the diminutive, white-clad figure, the enormous size of the building could not be appreciated.

Dynamic imbalance
Although this picture is not at all symmetrical, the silhouetted figure seems to balance the bulk of the surrounding buildings. In its simplicity, starkness of tone, and geometric forms, the composition verges on the abstract.

SELECTION FOR EFFECT

Before taking a photograph of any subject you should spend some time studying and composing the image in the viewfinder. This involves arranging the subject elements to achieve the desired effect. Sometimes you may want to emphasize balance, harmony, and symmetry, while at other times you may prefer to highlight contrast by juxtaposing different elements or colors.

First decide which are the most important elements and then choose the viewpoint, focal length of lens, and film accordingly. Scenes with landscapes or buildings have many viewpoints; the interpretation of the image depends on the photographer's skill in framing the subject to exclude details that detract from the main area of interest.

Positioning the horizon, *above*
Where you position the horizon can have a marked effect on the image. Whereas a high horizon accentuates the foreground, a low horizon emphasizes the sky.

Vertical abstraction, *below*
By framing a vertical subject such as these trees horizontally, a tension is established in the photograph. Vertical framing would weaken the overall effect.

CROPPING AN IMAGE

Although it is always preferable to make major compositional decisions through the camera's viewfinder before taking a picture, you are not restricted to using the full-frame image once the film is processed. Sometimes it may be impossible to obtain the camera position you ideally want, so cropping out the foreground or background of the final image may be necessary. Alternatively, you may want to change the composition from horizontal to vertical framing by having only part of the original image enlarged. You could crop off one side of the picture to move a subject into an off-center position in the frame. Cropping can be used to concentrate attention on particular areas of interest in the picture to create balance and harmony. All the pictures on this page show how cropping can alter the appearance of an image to convey several different messages.

Horizontal cropping shows the subject and surroundings

Vertical cropping is used to isolate a detail of the image

Close cropping isolates the figure in the photograph

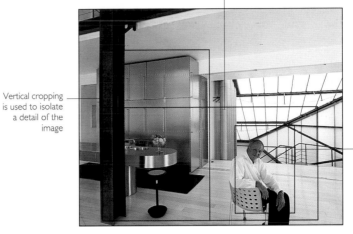

Alternative ways of cropping
The full-frame image shows architect Richard Rogers in his home. The outlined areas illustrate different ways the image can be cropped.

Horizontal image, *above*
Cropping in on both sides of the figure and down from the top of the full frame has simplified the visual content of the image and produced a distinctly enclosed feeling.

Vertical image, *above*
Strong vertical cropping of the picture is used to isolate the subject and to eliminate all background detail. However, this portrait lacks some of the atmosphere of the scene shown in the uncropped shot.

Isolating details, *left*
A side detail of the original image has been sectionally enlarged to become the subject of this cropped version. Enlarging a detail should only be attempted when the image is sharp overall and when the detail has sufficient visual content.

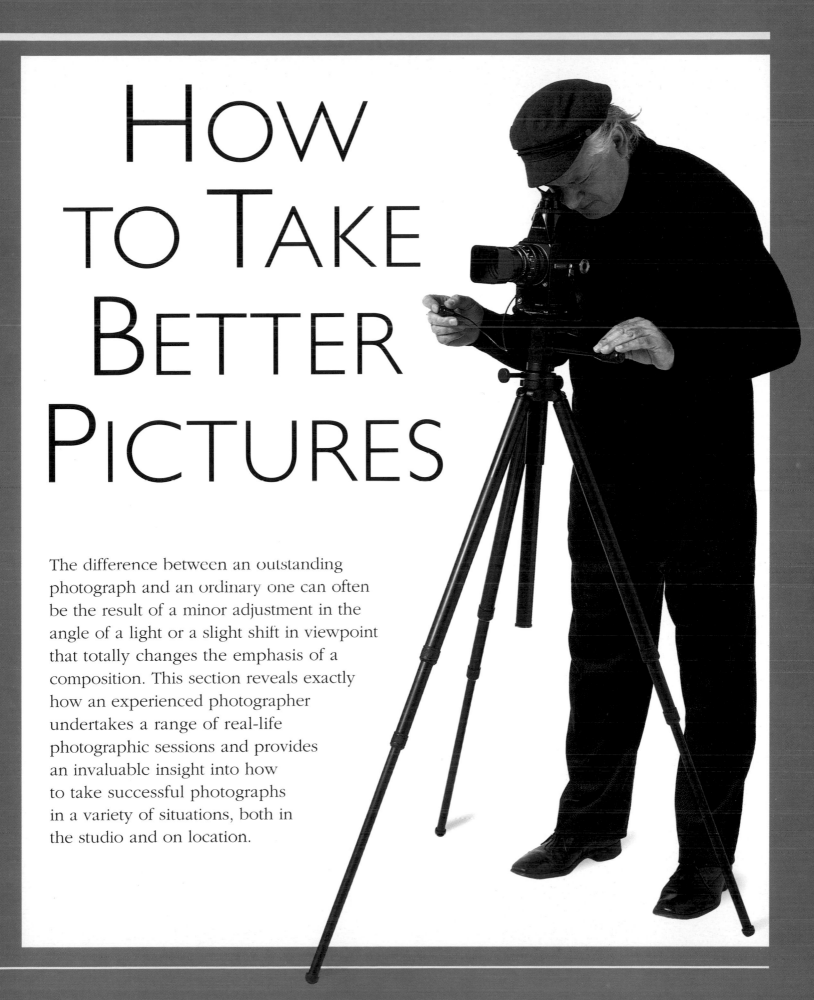

HOW TO TAKE BETTER PICTURES

The difference between an outstanding photograph and an ordinary one can often be the result of a minor adjustment in the angle of a light or a slight shift in viewpoint that totally changes the emphasis of a composition. This section reveals exactly how an experienced photographer undertakes a range of real-life photographic sessions and provides an invaluable insight into how to take successful photographs in a variety of situations, both in the studio and on location.

PORTRAITS

Photographs of people often elicit a greater response from the viewer than any other kind of subject. A good portrait photograph does not just show you the appearance of the subject. It should also be a visual biography, capturing a sitter's character and revealing their unique personality.

Fashion portraits
See pages 72–73

Character portraits
See pages 80–81

Dramatic portraits
See pages 84–85

Children's portraits
See pages 106–107

Photographing people

A portrait can be a photograph taken without the subject's knowledge, or it may be a more formal affair where the photographer has been commissioned to follow a specific assignment. As with all areas of photography, there are technical decisions to be made. Different types of camera and lens are needed for different conditions; lights must be arranged to achieve specific effects; and the camera viewpoint has to be positioned to suit the subject's face, or to enhance some aspect of the setting.

What makes a good portrait?

Portraits are not limited to posed shots of immobile subjects. Capturing moving subjects on film with flash can make lively, expressive portraits, and giving subjects an activity can have unexpected results. The latter approach works well with children, who become bored quickly. Do not underestimate the importance of background and setting in your portraits. Photographing people outdoors or in their own environment can add a dimension otherwise missing from a portrait in a studio setting.

Drawing out a subject

Another important aspect of portrait work is overcoming a subject's natural apprehension of the camera and lights. Try to put your model at ease by having all the camera equipment and lights set up well in advance of the photo session. This will leave you free to get to know and reassure the model before you start to take any photographs. Talking may help the sitter relax and allow you to achieve the desired result – a revealing, natural-looking portrait. The best photographs move beyond this to capture expressions that give an insight into a person's character and mood, resulting in wonderful and exciting portraits.

PORTRAIT SET-UP

The equipment illustrated here comprises a flexible set-up for a formal portrait photograph. It allows you complete control of the lighting and is highly adaptable. For full-length portraits you will need a room about 20ft (6m) long, although it is possible to shoot half-length portraits in a shorter space. Start by positioning the lights as shown below, and then adjust them to achieve different effects.

Umbrella reflector
This has a reflective inner surface that bounces back light directed at it, softening the lighting quality.

Fill-in light
A secondary flash unit, positioned slightly farther away than the main flash, fills in the shadowy areas.

Background light
This additonal flash unit allows you to light the backdrop independently of the main subject.

Fill-in light power pack
This provides the power for the secondary flash. It is automatically triggered when the main flash fires.

Formal portrait
This portrait is the result of the set-up below. The lighting is soft and gives good tonal separation between the model and background, with no harsh shadows across her face.

Overhead plan

Backdrop light

Backdrop

2½ft (75cm)

5ft (150cm)

2½ft (75cm)

3ft (90cm)

6ft (180cm)

Fill-in light

Camera

Main light

Main light
Build up your lighting scheme one light at a time, starting with a main light. This flash unit is positioned so that light shines at about 45° to the model's face.

Light stand
Adjustable light stand makes positioning the flash units extremely quick and easy.

Cable release
This frees you from behind the camera, which allows you to interact with the subject.

Equipment

- 35mm SLR camera and spare film
- Range of lenses
- Adjustable tripod
- Cable release
- Flash lighting units
- Umbrella reflectors
- Power packs
- Synchronization lead
- Diffuser panels

Camera and film
A 35mm SLR camera with a 100mm long-focus lens, loaded with ISO 100 film. The camera is set so that the lens is level with the model's face.

Tripod
Fixing the camera on a tripod leaves you free to adjust lights and check the results in the viewfinder.

Main light power pack
A 3,000-joule power pack provides the power source for the main flash unit. Output can be varied in one-stop increments.

Synchronization lead
The cable runs from the camera to the main power pack, enabling the flash units to fire in sync with the shutter release.

CREATING FORMAL PORTRAITS

A studio can be a challenging place to work. It is up to you to transform a stark space into an environment where your subject can be drawn out. However, if you have access to a studio, you have greater control and the opportunity to experiment with lighting quality and intensity, as well as with various shooting angles, and you will learn how to manipulate these variables for specific results.

LIGHTING EMPHASIS AND QUALITY

There is no single "correct" lighting set-up for all portraits. The three-point arrangement (*see pages 68–69*) is a good starting point. However, placing diffuser panels directly in front of the flash heads and umbrella reflectors (*below*), allows lighting to be manipulated to produce subtle variations. More obvious changes occur when whole lighting units are removed from the set-up.

Lighting variations
If directional light is used with very little fill-in light, shadows increase (*left*). No fill-in light at all results in heavy contrast (*above*).

Soft lighting, *below*
This softly lit portrait is the result of the photo set-up using the diffuser panels.

Patterned rug acts as interesting backdrop

Diffuser panel of heavyweight tracing paper on a wooden frame is positioned between the model and the lights

Flash lighting unit with umbrella reflector is positioned at 90° to the diffuser panel

Each light is powered by an individual power pack

35mm camera with an 80mm long-focus lens positioned on a tripod

Cable release

Synchronization lead

PHOTO SET-UP: Diffused lighting
Large diffuser panels made of heavyweight tracing paper are placed in front of the flash units and umbrella reflectors to increase the area of light falling on the model. This gives a low-contrast result if both lighting heads are used.

VARYING CAMERA ANGLES

A studio is the ideal type of location in which to experiment with different camera angles. By altering the viewpoint of the camera, you can bring about a variety of interesting and subtle effects. A high camera position, for example, shooting down on the model's face, tends to emphasize the forehead and the tops of the cheek bones. Moving to the opposite extreme, and taking the shot from below up toward the face, draws attention to the chin and lower jawline. This approach often results in the face taking on a slightly square appearance. The camera angle may also imply something about personality: shooting from above suggests vulnerability; while a model shot from below may appear aloof.

PHOTO SET-UP: High viewpoint
A little extra height considerably steepens the camera angle. Lighting is unchanged from the set-up shown on the opposite page. A long synchronization lead connecting the camera to the flash units allows freedom of movement.

Professional tips

- A three-quarter view of the face often makes it appear finer and less full than a frontal angle.

- For a 35mm SLR use an 80–90mm long-focus lens.

- Distortions occur when using a short lens close up.

- Using an extreme shooting angle may produce unwanted results, such as tapering features.

High camera angle
Shooting from a small stepladder gives strong emphasis to the model's forehead, eyes, and cheek bones, while the line of her jaw and chin is understated.

Low camera angle
Kneeling down and shooting up at the model from a low viewpoint changes the portrait's emphasis. Different facial features now catch the viewer's eye, with the chin and jaw looking stronger and squarer.

Subject in profile
A close-up profile is one of the most critical in portrait photography. Before starting to take pictures, study all aspects of your model's face and decide which angles to shoot from for the best effect.

TAKING FASHION PORTRAITS

Obtaining the services of a professional model for a day's session is not difficult, but it can be expensive. Model agencies usually charge for their models by the hour, so make sure you have a clear idea of the type of pictures you want before the shoot starts.

USING A PROFESSIONAL MODEL

Modeling is a form of acting that requires experience as well as an attractive face. A professional model will know how to react to the camera and how to change her pose to give the clothes an added elegance. She will be able to vary her facial expression and will be confident in the way she holds herself. In comparison, most amateur models will lack confidence and may appear wooden. Finally, if you do not want to use a make-up artist, a professional model will know how to apply make-up to suit the clothes she is wearing.

PHOTO SET-UP: Fashion portrait
Two lights pick the dark-clothed model out from the mottled gray background. The flash unit to the model's right is angled at the ceiling so that its light reflects back down to give a broad spread of illumination. The flash unit to her left gives three-quarter illumination and is fitted with a softbox diffuser. A 6 x 6cm camera ensures the type of superior quality results demanded by magazines.

Symmetrical shape
The model's almost symmetrical pose highlights the simplicity of her dress.

Wide-angle flash lighting head is angled upward at the ceiling

Canvas backdrop painted to give a neutral, mottled-gray effect

Reflector board ensures lighting is even

6 x 6cm camera on a tripod with a 120mm long-focus lens

Telescopic lighting stand, fitted with castors to make positioning easier

Cable release

Power pack

Posed portraits
Aim to direct the model into poses that emphasize the shape of her body and the clothes she is wearing. Note the way in which the model constantly changes her pose in this sequence of pictures.

Wide-angle flash lighting head enclosed within a softbox diffuser

Each light is powered by an individual power pack

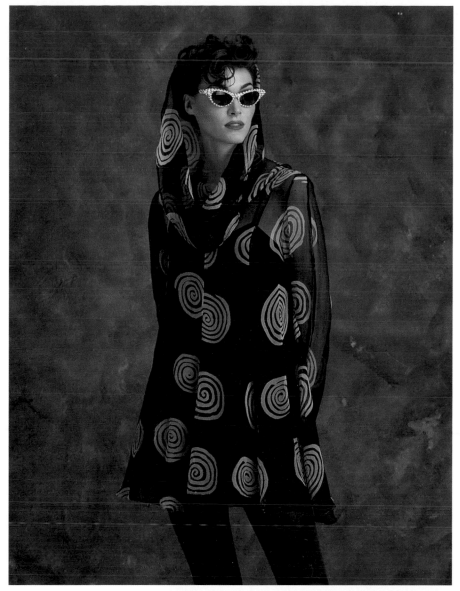

USING ACCESSORIES

Attention to detail can transform an otherwise ordinary photograph. For a fashion portrait, any accessories or props you use should be appropriate to the type of image you want to create and should complement the model's clothes. Careful selection of accessories is vital: neutral tones can be set off by simple props, and bright, saturated colors can be complemented by unusual and exciting accessories. A portrait should communicate a message to the viewer, and each and every detail should facilitate that communication.

Framing a model
The story a photograph tells is partly dictated by how the model is framed. With a nearly full-length shot, the emphasis is on the model's general appearance. The viewer can appreciate the clothes, their monochromatic coloring, and how they work together.

Close-up eyes
Viewed in close-up, the emphasis of the image is fixed on the model's face. The pearl-studded sunglasses perched on her nose demand the viewer's special attention.

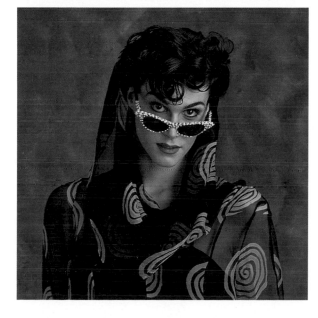

Splash of color
The use of props, such as this green hat, can complement a model's clothes and provide a bright finishing touch.

Change of mood
Confidence and poise are the hallmarks of a good model, quickly changing from one outfit to the next.

Professional tips

- Keep a variety of interesting accessories on hand so that you can experiment with different props.
- Talk to your model, directing her every movement.
- Ask someone to assist with hair and make-up.

STYLING PORTRAITS

Brief models beforehand on the look and style you want to create at the photo session. If you can afford the expense, a costume supplier will be able to provide you with everything from period costumes to evening wear, and a stylist can help furnish the set. When taking fashion portraits, be sure that the models look perfect, since the final images should appear glossier and more attractive than real life. If you are working with two models featured in the same shots, coordinating the appearance of both of them is also essential.

PLANNING THE SHOOT

Once you have identified the style of the model's clothing, you can turn your attention to choosing a suitable setting. If you do not have access to a photographic studio or suitable space indoors, you could use an outdoor environment such as a deserted beach. Whatever setting you choose, be prepared to shoot a lot of film to get the most out of the session.

Wide-angle flash lighting head is angled upward at the ceiling so that its light reflects back down to give a broad spread of soft illumination

Canvas backdrop is painted to give a realistic blue-sky-and-clouds effect

Flash units are positioned at different heights

Blue background paper is taped down to the floor

Softbox diffusers produce soft, directional light

6 x 6cm camera on a tripod with a 120mm long-focus lens

Cable release

Single power pack runs both diffused flash units

PHOTO SET-UP: Lighting for a styled portrait
The set is lit by reflected light from a wide-angled flash directed at the ceiling on the photographer's left. The models' faces are illuminated by the two softbox diffusers.

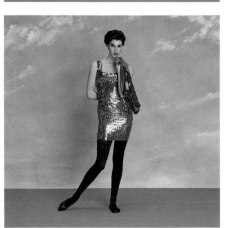

Coordinated image
The two models have a coordinated look with their matching sequined dresses. This image is emphasized by their linked-arm pose.

Making use of a prop
A silk scarf adds color as well as compositional balance. Expect to shoot a lot of film to achieve a natural-looking picture.

FILLING THE FRAME

You can achieve a close-up simply by moving the camera position closer to your subject to concentrate attention on facial features and expression. By excluding other details from the picture, the impact of the image can be dramatic if the model is well chosen. With a normal lens you may have to move very close to your subject to fill the frame with the model's head and shoulders. Alternatively, you can use a longer lens or have the central portion of the picture enlarged during printing.

The correct lighting is essential for close-up portraits. Gentle, soft lighting, such as from a window or a diffused flash, is more flattering than harsh, directional light, which tends to emphasize every fine line or misplaced hair.

Double profile
If using two models, position them so that each one is seen with her best profile toward the camera.

Critical close-up
Always check the models' appearance by looking through the viewfinder before pressing the shutter.

Unusual headwear
Hats can cause lighting problems by casting shadows over the models' faces or obscuring their eyes. To counter this, make sure the faces are lit independently, as shown in the set-up on the right.

PHOTO SET-UP: Lighting for a close-up
A wide-angle flash head reflects light bounced off the ceiling, as on the opposite page. The flash units with softbox diffusers to the photographer's right are positioned low and angled slightly upward, to throw extra light onto the models' faces.

Wide-angle flash unit angled upward to reflect light off the ceiling

Painted backdrop

Stylist makes adjustments to make-up and hair during the shoot

Flash lighting units are positioned at different heights and angled low to light models' faces evenly

Floor covering

Softbox diffuser produces soft, directional light

6 x 6cm camera on a tripod with a 120mm long-focus lens

Power pack

TAKING PORTRAITS ON LOCATION

You may have to overcome certain difficulties when you want to take a portrait of a subject in his home or workplace. You will have less control over lighting intensity and direction, and space may be cramped with furniture inconveniently arranged. However, a subject will be more relaxed in his own environment, and you gain the chance to record aspects of his life that could not be witnessed elsewhere.

LIGHTING POTENTIAL

In terms of lighting, you should be prepared for almost any situation – from direct sunlight streaming through a large window, to levels so dim that even fast film will require a wide aperture and still result in a very slow shutter speed. It is advisable to visit the location beforehand to see if you will need flash or additional equipment. You can then decide what type of camera to use and at what time of day the light will be most suitable.

Diffusing umbrella made of sheer material creates soft directional lighting effect

6 x 6cm camera on a tripod with an 80mm lens

Flash head positioned high to reflect light from ceiling and walls

Light-colored walls and ceiling are ideal for bouncing flash

Synchronization lead

Power pack

Subject and setting, *top*
The setting is as much the subject of the picture as the sculptor. Carefully placed stone figures mark the fore-, middle-, and background.

Framing a subject, *above*
Look for the best way to frame your subject in the available space. In this shot, the sculptures make strong shapes flanking their creator.

PHOTO SET-UP: Supplementary flash

To photograph sculptor Glyn Williams in his studio calls for soft, directional lighting to capture the subtle texture of the sculpted figures. The low level of natural daylight requires the use of flash lighting. The light-colored ceilings and walls make ideal surfaces from which to bounce light.

Walls are too far away from the light source to affect the overall exposure

Subject is leaning on sculpture to reinforce link with work

6 x 6cm camera on a tripod with a 150mm long-focus lens

Single flash head with a diffusing umbrella is angled to spotlight the subject's face

Power pack

SIMULATING DAYLIGHT

When taking a portrait in a working environment, it is preferable to use natural light to convey the atmosphere of the setting. If it is not possible to illuminate an interior using natural light, you can arrange the flash lighting to simulate some of the characteristics of daylight. Light entering a room through a window produces a directional effect, lighting near parts of the subject and casting distant corners into shadow. When taking a portrait, you may need to reduce this contrast by the use of fill-in lights and reflectors. However, high-contrast lighting does give a scene a naturalness that implies a lack of interference.

PHOTO SET-UP: Poor natural light

Low levels of natural light present lighting problems similar to those on the opposite page. Diffused flash is needed to light the sculptor evenly in the dark interior. A single flash unit with reflector is positioned to light the subject's face, but the background walls remain in shadow.

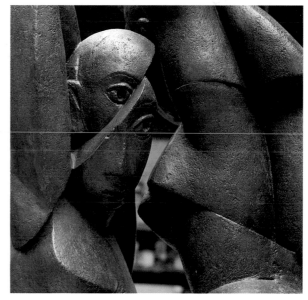

Natural daylight
Positioning the sculpture directly below a skylight produces this high-contrast lighting effect.

Simulated daylight
Diffused flash is used to supplement the weak light from an overhead skylight. The lighting direction and quality resemble natural light but ensure that the shadow areas are not too dark on the subject's face.

Professional tips

• Visit the location before the shoot.

• Exclude unwanted clutter from the shot.

• Take additional lights if daylight is very poor.

• Make sure there are sufficient power points to run your equipment.

Indirect daylight, *top*
For this portrait of artist Ivan Hitchens, indirect light bouncing off a wall produces a soft effect. *6 x 6cm camera, 150mm lens, Ektachrome 200, f11, 1/125 sec.*

Flash and daylight, *above*
Flash supplements the poor light in a gallery interior for this portrait of sculptress Barbara Hepworth. *6 x 6cm camera, 80mm lens, Ektachrome 100, f11, 1/125 sec.*

Filling the frame, *above*
With a strong personality such as artist David Hockney, stay alert and react to any chance expression. *6 x 6cm camera, 120mm lens (plus extension tube), Ektachrome 100, f16, 1/60 sec.*

Location lighting, *right*
Bounced flash was used for this location portrait of Agatha Christie. *6 x 6cm camera, 150mm lens, Ektachrome 64, f11, 1/125 sec.*

Appropriate lighting, *far right*
Artist Richard Hamilton's expressive face benefits from the punchy quality of strong natural daylight. *6 x 6cm camera, 80mm lens, Ektachrome 100, f11, 1/30 sec.*

Color statement
The color and abstract, flowing shapes of his paintings make an ideal background for this portrait of Terry Frost. The colors of the canvas are emphasized by the artist's beret and the contrasting vertical stripes of his waistcoat.
6 x 7cm camera, 80mm lens, Fujichrome 100, f8, 1/250 sec.

Integrating the background
Good photographs work at all levels, from the foreground right through to the background. And in this portrait of John Bellamy, the background of one of his canvases is as much the subject of the photograph as the artist himself. Lighting is provided by a mixture of bounced flash and daylight.
6 x 6cm camera, 50mm lens, Ektachrome 200, f5.6, 1/15 sec.

CAPTURING CHARACTER

Perhaps the most challenging aspect of taking a portrait photograph is to try to capture something more than just a likeness of the subject. In fashion portraiture (*see page 72*), for example, the models are not just vehicles for the clothes they wear; they also need to project a certain image. Similarly, an informal portrait of a person should tell the viewer something about the sitter's character.

LIGHTING FOR AN OLDER SUBJECT

Choosing appropriate lighting is critical when photographing an elderly subject. A face lined with age speaks volumes about the sitter's personal history. If you want to emphasize the wrinkles and lines that reveal character, use strong directional lighting to highlight the surface texture. However, if you want to disguise the signs of aging, you can use a soft-focus filter to blur skin texture. Diffused or reflected light as used in the images on these pages gives a flattering, subtle effect.

To lighten this dark corner, bounced flash is used to reflect light off the side walls

Softbox diffuser helps both to soften and direct the light output

6 x 6cm camera on a tripod with a 50mm wide-angle lens

PHOTO SET-UP: Diffused flash lighting

The location is a long-established reading room for retired sailors and fishermen. The walls are covered with glass-covered photographs recording long careers spent at sea. If not treated with care, the flash could cause each picture to reflect light in the form of intense highlights known as hot spots. To prevent these reflections, check the image in the viewfinder, and adjust the picture frames accordingly.

Professional tips

- A wide-angle lens allows you to include more of the setting in the frame for added atmosphere.

- A 35mm SLR is less noticeable than a medium-format camera and may seem less intimidating.

- Remove unwanted furniture from the picture area.

- Use a dulling spray to prevent reflections.

- If you are working with a flash unit, make sure the synchronization lead allows you free movement.

Creating atmosphere
Lit mainly by reflected light bounced off the side wall, the intimate atmosphere of the setting is preserved. Lighting must be adjusted constantly and the image checked in the viewfinder.

Candid moment
Capturing an unguarded moment is possible here since the subject is totally engrossed in the card game and not self-conscious.

Using the setting, *left*
Setting the subject off-center establishes a tension in the composition, and the pictures visible behind him suggest something about his history.

PHOTO SET-UP: Character in close-up

By moving in closer with a hand-held 35mm camera and an 80mm long-focus lens, you can isolate one person in the group. Try to frame the image to exclude unwanted detail so that everything in the final shot provides valuable clues to the sitter's character. Concentrate on the feature that you most want to emphasize and then wait for the right moment to release the shutter.

Subject quickly forgets about the photographer and continues playing the game of cards

Compactness of a 35mm SLR camera makes it ideal for hand-holding

80mm long-focus lens is used to isolate a single subject

Character and mood
Try to be unobtrusive and avoid drawing attention to the camera. Do not let your subject pose for too long (*top*), but follow the mood and atmosphere of the occasion (*above*).

TAKING BLACK AND WHITE PORTRAITS

Black and white film is a medium that attracts those photographers who want an added dimension in the process of image selection and interpretation. Color, even when used in a very abstract way, leaves little room for the viewer's imagination. Color also has certain associations with mood, some of which are cultural and some personal – fiery red, sunny pastel shades, cold blue tones, and so on. Because we react so strongly to the color content of a photograph, it can sometimes distract us from looking at other important aspects of the image.

TONAL VALUES

In black and white pictures, images become much simpler in content. The clutter of color falls away and is replaced by a range of tones – shades of black, ranging from gray to white (see page 44). If you think of a photograph as already being an abstraction of the real scene it records, then a black and white picture is another step away from that reality.

Black and white or color
Positioning the subject so that he appears to be part of the collection of sculpted heads works better in black and white than color.

White reflector is set at about 45° to the subject

Single flash lighting unit is pointing directly at a large circular reflector

6 x 6cm camera on a tripod with a 50mm wide-angle lens

Walls and ceiling help reflect the light

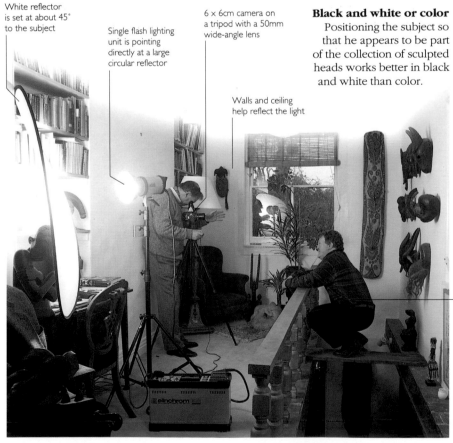

Subject is positioned against a background of sculpted heads

PHOTO SET-UP: Confined spaces

In the narrow upstairs hallway of sculptor Glyn Williams' home, there is little space for the flash lighting unit used to supplement the daylight coming through the window. In order to maneuver himself into the correct position in relation to the background of sculpted heads, Glyn improvised by standing on a plank bridging the stairwell.

Highlighting elements

The way we interpret a picture varies according to whether the image is in color or black and white. In this comical pose the viewer's eye is drawn to the sculpted hands in the immediate foreground, the sizes of which have been exaggerated by using a wide-angle lens. Although the subject's pose in the color portrait is identical to the black and white version, it is the colored checks of the subject's shirt that initially attract the viewer's eye. With the middleground demanding attention in this way, the overall image lacks the depth of the black and white portrait.

PHOTO SET-UP: Subject and background

Two aspects of Glyn Williams' work, drawing and sculpting, provide ideal background and foreground elements for this portrait, and a strange perspective is achieved by utilizing the distorting effect a wide-angle lens exerts on the apparent sizes of foreground and background objects. As with the set-up shown on the opposite page, the lighting is kept simple with a single flash lighting unit and reflector supplementing the poor natural daylight.

Winter daylight from window supplements flash lighting

Sketches taped to the wall behind are lit by a mixture of flash and daylight

Single flash lighting unit with an umbrella reflector is positioned opposite the subject

6 x 6cm camera on a tripod with a 50mm wide-angle lens

Professional tips

● Simple, strong shapes often have more impact in black and white than in color.

● Mixed lighting such as strong daylight and domestic tungsten light sources can be used in the same shot without fear of creating color-casts.

● Take into account that some colors, such as certain shades of green and red, appear as virtually the same gray when the film is developed.

CREATING DRAMATIC PORTRAITS

Injecting drama into a photograph often means using lighting creatively to produce a powerful or unusual interpretation of your subject. You can use strong, directional light to create a high-contrast portrait with bright highlights and dark shadows that accentuate a subject's bone structure and facial features.

LIGHTING COLOR AND EFFECT

You can also alter the color of the lighting for dramatic effect. It is best to make a radical change to the normal color since a minor deviation may look accidental. In the images on these pages, the flash heads are filtered in different colors and the lights lowered to cast long shadows. In additon, smoke is released during the shoot for added theatrical impact.

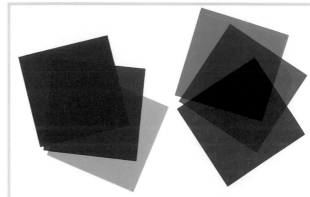

Colored gels

Colored light filters are usually made of gelatin or plastic, and come in a variety of sizes. If filters are too large, trim them to a manageable size and clip or tape them over the lighting heads or the inside surface of a diffuser.

Colored filter effects
The dancers and the lights illuminating the set are well defined before the addition of the smoke.

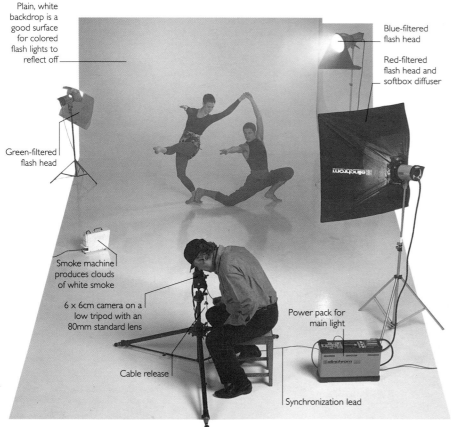

Plain, white backdrop is a good surface for colored flash lights to reflect off

Green-filtered flash head

Smoke machine produces clouds of white smoke

6 x 6cm camera on a low tripod with an 80mm standard lens

Cable release

Blue-filtered flash head

Red-filtered flash head and softbox diffuser

Power pack for main light

Synchronization lead

PHOTO SET-UP: Lighting with colored filters
Two flash units covered with blue and green gelatin filters respectively are positioned at the back of the set behind the dancers. A red-filtered flash unit with a large softbox diffuser to the right of the photographer provides general, warm illumination all over the set.

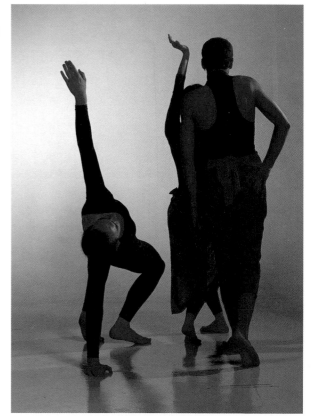

Smoke effects on lighting
When the smoke is added, the light becomes more scattered and diffused, the figures less distinct, and areas of color start to merge.

Matching effect and subject
The exaggerated movements of the modern dancers are given greater dramatic impact by the addition of special-effects smoke.

Exposure compensation
Scattered light, as shown in this sequence, can cause the meter to register more light than is present. Open the aperture an extra half to one f-stop to compensate.

Tonal contrast, *above*
The carefully positioned sculpted
heads make an ideal frame within
which to place their creator, the
sculptress Elisabeth Frink.
*35mm camera, 80mm lens, HP5,
f16, 1/30 sec.*

Rural record, *below*
A single picture can tell a life story.
The simple setting, the clothes on
the line, and the farmer's expression
tell of a way of life now extinct.
*6 x 7cm camera, 80mm lens,
Tri-X Pan, f11, 1/60 sec.*

Making a connection
An old woman holding her prized
pet pigeon makes for a revealing
character portrait. Diffused flash
is used to supplement the weak
sunlight and highlight the fine lines
on the subject's face.
*35mm camera, 105mm lens,
HP5, f16, 1/250 sec.*

Window light
Weak sunlight from a window on
the subject's right provides the
only illumination for this picture of
a Salvation Army stalwart. This
type of gentle and sympathetic
lighting masks some signs of aging
and is in keeping with the subject.
*35mm camera, 80mm lens,
Tri-X Pan, f5.6, 1/60 sec.*

Framing an idea

In any photograph of an artist you might expect the tools of the trade to feature prominently. In this portrait of sculptor Henry Moore, it is his hands that are held up to the camera, positioned as if sizing a block of stone, yet acting as a frame for his face.
6 x 6cm camera, 50mm lens, Tri-X Pan, f11, 1/250 sec.

Focusing attention

Although a face as powerful as this would command attention no matter how it was photographed, a wide lens aperture keeps the depth of field sufficiently narrow to keep details in the background from competing.
35mm camera, 135mm lens, HP5, f4, 1/30 sec.

Natural spotlight, *top*

With sidelight revealing fine details, typographer David Kindersley is thrust forward in the frame.
35mm camera, 135mm lens, HP5, f16, 1/250 sec.

Directional flash, *above*

A flash is directed at the subject to throw a band of light over the face.
6 x 4 5cm camera, 120mm lens, Tri-X Pan, f22, 1/60 sec.

TAKING A SELF PORTRAIT

Self portraiture is a photographic exercise that may require the use of one or two technical aids and a great deal of patience, but it can also be a lot of fun. The simplest way to take your own portrait is to pose in front of a mirror and to photograph your reflection by holding the camera at waist level. Alternatively, you can use a long cable release or self-timer and pose in front of the lens.

DELAYED-ACTION TIMER

Practically all cameras have a delayed-action timer designed for self portraiture. Activating this before pressing the shutter release gives you between 10 and 20 seconds (depending on the camera) to get to your predetermined position. Alternatively, if you pose close to the camera, you can trigger the shutter at the precise moment you want by using a long cable release. An adjustable tripod is essential for positioning the camera at the right height.

PHOTO SET-UP: Indoor self portrait
For this self portrait, the camera's integral delayed-action timer is used. The camera is prefocused on the exact spot the subject will occupy, and a chalk mark on the canvas sheet acts as a position guide.

Single flash unit is set high and positioned at about 45° to the subject

Umbrella diffuser gives direct but softened lighting

Synchronization lead

Hardboard reflector is positioned on the subject's shadow side to return some of the light and reduce contrast

6 x 6cm camera with a 120mm long-focus lens and with shutter set on a delayed timer

Adjustable tripod is positioned so that the camera frames the subject's head and shoulders

Self-timer sequence
Experiment with different poses to record a comic, dramatic, or serious self portrait. The exposure for these self portraits (*above*) was calculated using a flash meter, and the settings then transferred to the camera. Remember to wind the film on between shots and to reset the timer.

PHOTO SET-UP: Outdoor self portrait

The camera is focused and set manually for the distance of the subject from the camera, and an extra-long cable release allows the shutter to be released at precisely the right moment.

Silver reflector is used to lighten the subject's shadow side and even out the lighting contrast across the face

35mm camera on a tripod with an 85mm long-focus lens

Long cable release is held by the subject, low down and out of shot, allowing the shutter to be triggered at will

Exposure reading

To determine the exposure for these self portraits, the subject took a reading from the back of his hand while standing where the pictures were to be taken.

Self portrait setting, *below*
Using a timer allows you to position yourself some distance from the camera.

PHOTO SET-UP: Delayed-action timer

A test run timed with a stop watch determines that there is enough time for the subject to take up his position before the delayed-action timer triggers the shutter.

Viewfinder may have to be covered to keep stray light from affecting exposure

Colors in the scene are warmed up using a color-compensating filter

35mm camera with an 85mm lens is set on a delayed-action timer to release the shutter after 20 seconds

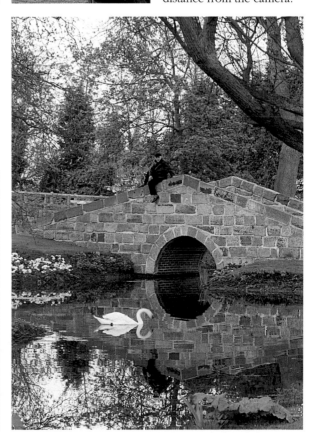

COMPOSING GROUP PORTRAITS

No matter what type of group portrait you are photographing, you need to show that all those involved are somehow associated with each other. This can be done by arranging the figures so that they all obviously relate.

ARRANGING A GROUP

When arranging a dynamic subject such as this modern-dance ensemble, aim to convey the sense of group movement. It is possible to use a slow shutter speed to record subject blur (*see page 114*), but this technique can be problematic in group portraits. The solution here is to place the dancers in active poses, carefully choreographed and integrated to create a very definite compositional shape. In all group portraiture, take plenty of shots of each variation of the pose so that there is at least one frame in which every individual is seen to best advantage.

Dynamic arrangements
Try experimenting with several group arrangements. Two different compositions work in different ways. The pyramid (*above*) has greater group cohesion, but the other arrangement (*right*) emphasizes movement.

Background canvas is painted to give a mottled green effect

6 x 6cm camera on a tripod with an 80mm standard lens

Undiffused flash lighting unit is angled down to lighten tonal value of floor surface and increase exposure on the dancers

Flash lighting unit and softbox reflector with front diffusing panel removed to increase the intensity of light

Power pack for main light

Undiffused flash unit lights background and subjects

Synchronization lead links camera to power pack

Cable release

PHOTO SET-UP: Lighting a group

The lighting for group portraits needs to be generalized to create a broad spread of light over a fairly large area. Here a matched pair of diffused flash units, one either side of the camera, ensures even lighting. Two undiffused flash units at the rear of the set help increase exposure on the dancers and so pull them out of the mottled green background.

Professional tips

● Aim for a broad spread of light, perhaps from wide-angle units.

● Soften directional lighting to prevent shadows falling on any member of the group.

Circular group, *opposite*
Careful attention to the shapes described by the dancers' bodies produced this circular composition. The group seems poised to explode into movement.

CREATING INFORMAL PORTRAITS

A good informal portrait relies on the photographer working unobtrusively. The presence of a camera may make some people self-conscious, and some subjects may not want their photograph taken. Ideally, the photographer and his camera should go unnoticed. Modern compact and SLR cameras are lightweight, discreet, and quick and easy to operate, and often ideal for this type of candid photography. However, it is always best to ask permission if you think that the person you want to photograph may object.

KEEPING YOUR DISTANCE

Successful photographs depend on awareness as well as being in the right place at the right time with your camera loaded and preset to the correct exposure. A compact camera or SLR fitted with a zoom lens allows you to distance yourself from your subject.

Natural reaction
At first glance, the model appears to be a casual passer-by. In fact, as the set-up picture shows, she is deliberately positioned level with the musician and is reacting for the camera.

PHOTO SET-UP: Dramatic expression
A bustling riverside setting is an ideal location to wait for the reactions of passers-by to this street entertainer's bizarre guitar-playing technique. This set-up picture shows how you can stage an expressive and amusing portrait with the cooperation of your subjects. The model is carefully positioned in the foreground to give the picture added humor and exaggerated theatricality.

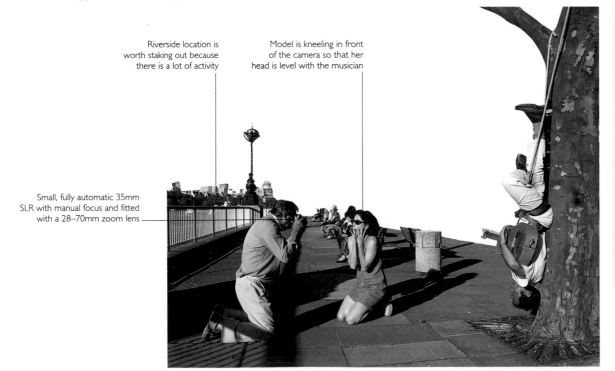

Riverside location is worth staking out because there is a lot of activity

Model is kneeling in front of the camera so that her head is level with the musician

Small, fully automatic 35mm SLR with manual focus and fitted with a 28–70mm zoom lens

Professional tips

● Candid portraits are easiest to take in public places where lots of people carry cameras.

● Zoom lenses allow fine-tune cropping and subject enlargement from one position.

● Pretend to take a shot of an accomplice in the foreground, but use a zoom to focus on your real subject in the background.

Advance planning
This picture is the result of careful advance planning. If you visit the location beforehand and choose your subject carefully you will be able to envisage precisely the type of image you want to recreate.

Storyboard sequence
Each image should work on its own, but when they are viewed together, all the pictures in a sequence tell a complete story and have greater impact.

Monochromatic light, *top*
With the air heavy with wood
smoke and the threat of rain, the
moody light gives atmosphere to
this scene of an elderly Romanian
couple holding their grandchild.
The light is so diffused that the
landscape appears monochromatic.
*35mm camera, 28mm lens,
Fujichrome 400, f8, 1/60 sec.*

Street life, *above*
The markets of Cairo are full of
photographic opportunities. This
candid portrait of a shopkeeper
with his hookah was taken using a
long lens. Always ask permission
before taking your picture if you
think that a person may object.
*35mm camera, 90mm lens,
Kodachrome 100, f16, 1/250 sec.*

Unposed perfection, *above*
Although completely unposed,
this portrait of a Romanian boy
seems to be in an environment
almost too painterly to be true.
Strong geometric squares and
rectangles and clearly defined
blocks of color comprise most
of the image. Snaking through
the center is the single, sinewy
shape of an ancient vine.
*35mm camera, 28mm lens,
Ektachrome 200 , f11, 1/250 sec.*

Ultra-violet light, *right*
The hazy effect of ultra-violet light can be clearly seen in this picture of young Indian tea pickers.
35mm camera, 80mm lens, Ektachrome 200, f11, 1/125 sec.

Tropical brightness, *far right*
Intense light and heat create specific photographic problems. Depth of field has been strictly limited here.
35mm camera, 135mm lens, Ektachrome 100, f5.6, 1/1000 sec.

PHOTOGRAPHING THE NUDE

In the same way as the study of the human figure in fine art is an exercise in drawing and painting technique, so the nude can be used to show the photographer's skill. Lighting the figure offers numerous ways to emphasize skin texture, form, and tone. Daylight from a window, or diffused sidelighting from a flash enhances form, whereas backlighting highlights shape rather than form to create a silhouette.

WORKING WITH A LIFE MODEL

Successful nude photographs depend upon there being a good relationship between the life model and photographer. The more you involve the model in the picture-taking process, the better the results are likely to be. Working indoors assures your subject of privacy and allows you to set up equipment in advance. Remember to keep the room warm and make sure the model feels relaxed.

Graphic profile, *above*
The heavily diffused light reflected from the gray backdrop gives it a mottled appearance. The figure is in total shadow and stands out as a bold, stark shape.

PHOTO SET-UP: Silhouette lighting
For a silhouette effect, the background must be much lighter than the subject. A large exposure difference between the two will produce a high-contrast result. With the exposure taken for the light background, the subject appears as an underexposed shape.

Gray background paper returns some of the light bounced from the umbrella reflectors

Adjustable lighting stand makes it possible to change the height and angle of the flash unit

Flash lighting unit (one either side of the set) with an umbrella reflector, throws broad, soft beams of light onto the background paper

Flat boards are placed either side of the set to stop stray light from the flash units reaching the camera side of the subject and weakening the effect

6 x 6cm camera on low tripod with a 120mm long-focus lens

Cable release

Synchronization lead runs from the camera to the main power pack; the second power pack is fitted with a slave unit that triggers its flash the instant the first one is fired

LIGHTING THE HUMAN FIGURE

Lighting for the human form usually needs to be not only diffused and softened, but also directional. If lighting is used in this way, some planes of the body are lit while others grade off into progressively deeper shadow. This suggests the contours and shapes of the whole, but leaves the form only partly revealed and thus abstracted. This type of lighting effect can be achieved relatively easily using natural daylight from a window covered with a large sheet of tracing paper. Harsh frontal lighting is usually inappropriate for the human figure. It often reveals too much detail, resulting in a clinical or an overly suggestive quality.

PHOTO SET-UP: Directional sidelighting
The background lights used for the silhouette on the opposite page remain the same, but a third flash is added. This flash unit has a snoot attachment and is pointed at a white reflector board to bounce a narrow beam of light onto the figure. The reflector softens the lighting effect.

Gray background paper

White reflector board bounces light onto front of the subject

Flash head with snoot attachment gives a narrow beam of light

Flash lighting unit with umbrella reflector lights

Board to prevent light from straying and weakening the effect

Power pack for main light

Synchronization lead runs from camera to main power pack

6 x 6cm camera on a low tripod with a 120mm long-focus lens is level with the seated model

Cable release

Professional tips

● For a silhouette, take your light reading from brightest part of frame.

● Brief the life model beforehand not to wear tight clothing that may leave marks on the skin.

Using a sidelight
The silhouette takes on a fuller, rounded form, as the play of light and shade helps flesh out the figure.

Enigmatic image
Using just the sidelight, the background drops away. The resulting increase in contrast produces an enigmatic, intimate image.

NATURAL LIGHTING FOR THE NUDE

The essential requirement for a photographic session with a life model is guaranteed privacy. This may be difficult if you wish to use an outdoor setting, but a secluded garden or quiet beach may make suitable locations if there are not too many curious onlookers.

Photographing a life model in an indoor setting does not mean that you have to use flash (*see page 96*). If you have access to a bright, sunny room with a large window or skylight, a wide range of subtle effects is possible using only natural daylight. Artists' studios are traditionally positioned so that they receive light from a bright, open sky rather than from direct sunlight, and this type of reflected light is the most sympathetic when photographing the human figure.

PHOTO SET-UP: Natural light source
This bright room benefits from a large window. Normally, the bigger the light source, the less contrasty the lighting effect. But by positioning the model in front of the glass, the exposure difference between the lit and unlit areas makes for dramatic pictures that emphasize form.

Model's gracefully curved body contrasts with the angularity of the window frame

6 x 6cm camera on a tripod with an 80mm lens

Low camera angle emphasizes the immediate foreground

Shadow reading, *above*
A wall of light floods past the model, softening her outline; exposure is judged from a dark area on her leg, and the highlights are allowed to burn out.

Bright reading, *opposite*
As well as lighting, aperture and shutter speed are also important. Exposure for this darker image is taken from the view outside. The model is now silhouetted.

Professional tips

● Explain your aims to the life model.

● Allow the model privacy to undress, and keep the room warm.

● A window facing north gives softer, more indirect lighting than a south-facing one.

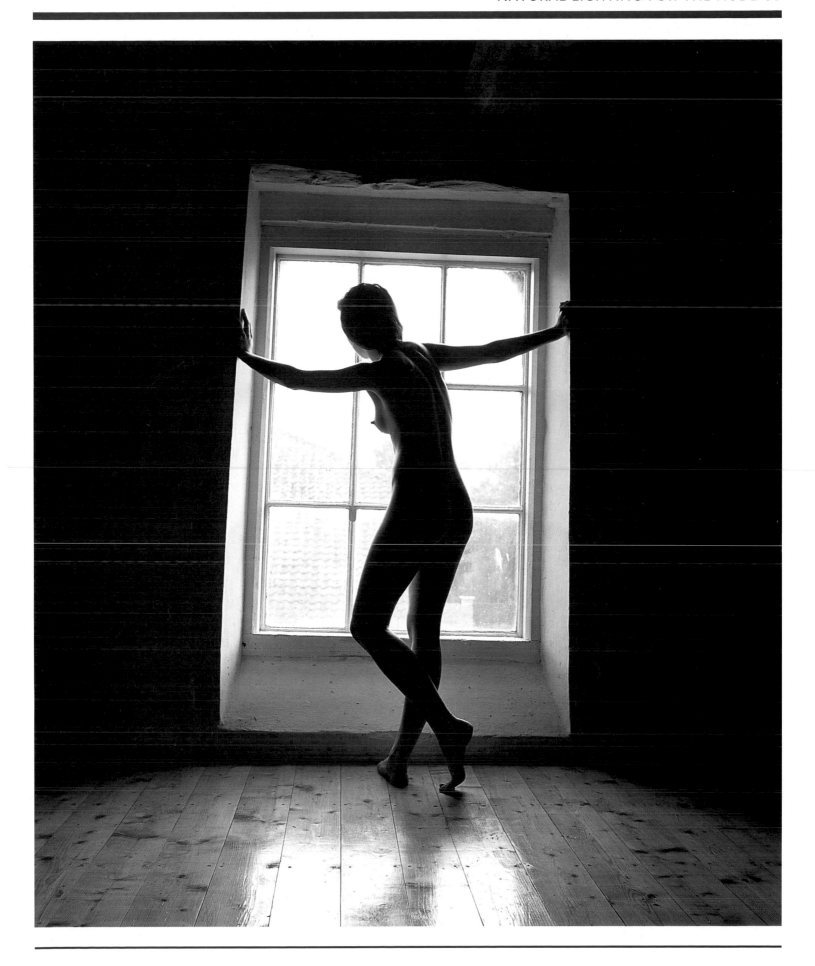

CREATING ABSTRACT NUDE IMAGES

When viewed through a camera, the human figure can be seen as a series of interacting abstract shapes. Variations in muscular tension in a model's body may seem minor when looking at the whole figure, but when filling the frame with a single area such as a torso or upper arm, every little detail is important.

LONG-FOCUS OR WIDE-ANGLE LENS

Choice of camera position and focal length are vital considerations. Long-focus lenses have a restricted angle of view and facilitate cropping. Extreme long-focus lenses flatten the subject, robbing it of clearly differentiated planes, while a wide-angle lens can cause curious distortions, exaggerating depth and distance.

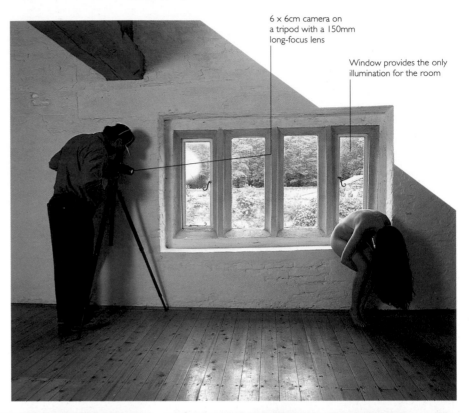

6 × 6cm camera on a tripod with a 150mm long-focus lens

Window provides the only illumination for the room

PHOTO SET-UP: Lighting for form
By positioning the model on the windowsill, the curve of her back and buttocks receives direct illumination. In contrast, her front and her lower body below the windowsill are all in heavy shadow and would require a longer exposure time to bring out additional detail.

Lighting contrast, *left*
This image uses lighting contrast, rather than lens focal length, to highlight parts of the model's body. Her hair is also hanging forward, casting her face into dark shadow.

Angular form
Asking the model to bring her arm across her body creates a sense of diagonal movement. Excluding the model's head focuses attention on the abstract angularity of the form.

Abstract form
As the life model leans against the wall, the contours of her arms, shoulders, and back create an effect that emphasizes abstract form and textural contrasts more than her nudity.

Lenses to isolate
Longer focal-length lenses are useful when you want to fill the frame with just a small aspect of the figure. In this picture a long-focus lens is used to isolate the model's back.

Diffused natural light, *left*
Daylight is diffused through a
blind to reveal both the texture
and form of this reclining nude.
*6 x 6cm camera, 80mm lens,
Tri X Pan, f16, 1/8 sec.*

Tonal definition, *below left*
Superb tonal range and definition
result from an overhead skylight.
*6 x 7cm camera, 80mm lens,
Tri-X Pan, f22, 1/60 sec.*

Selective light, *below*
A tungsten spotlight illuminates
the model's arm and side.
*6 x 6cm camera, 120mm lens,
Plus X, f32, 1/500 sec.*

Floodlit form, *bottom*
The lighting for this detail comes
from a 500 watt floodlight. Tungsten
lights allow you to see the highlights
and shadows before shooting.
*6 x 6cm camera, 150mm lens,
Tri-X Pan, f16, 1/60 sec.*

Candid nude, *opposite*
Lost in thought, the model seems
unaware of the camera. Natural
light gives a moody low-key result.
*6 x 7cm camera, 80mm lens,
HP5 Plus, f11, 1/125 sec.*

PORTRAYING A MOTHER AND CHILD

The bond that exists between a mother and her newborn child is an enduring theme for photographers. Capturing those feelings of trust and intimacy is easiest when you are photographing members of your own family. With patience you should be able to record natural, spontaneous images, especially if you stay alert to the baby's shifts in mood.

UNPOSED BABY PORTRAITS

Babies and young children cannot be directed or persuaded to stay still while you compose the shot in the viewfinder. Always enlist the help of the mother to keep the baby relaxed and happy and to divert its attention away from the camera. With portraits it is usual to take more pictures than you think you will need, but when working with babies you should show greater restraint. Constantly flashing lights, even when heavily diffused, are likely to upset a young baby.

Reflector returns light and keeps shadows from becoming dark

Draped, softly folded muslin is used as a backdrop to create an intimate setting

Wide-angle flash head is directed at backdrop

Main flash unit for the mother and child; its effect is softened by bouncing it from an umbrella reflector

6 x 6cm camera on a tripod with a 120mm lens

Individual power pack for each light minimizes the need for cables running across the set

Cable release

PHOTO SET-UP: Soft lighting
Bounced light from an umbrella reflector produces diffused light to emphasize the softness of the baby's skin. The simple background does not compete for the viewer's attention.

Synchronization lead links the power pack to the camera

Private moment, *above*
The reflector is used to brighten the shadows and create a gentle gradation of tones without losing detail.

Open affection, *below*
A happy and relaxed pose shows the mother's natural pride and is complemented by slightly subdued lighting.

Flash unit and umbrella reflector is lowered so as not to put too much toplighting on the seated figures

Draped muslin background

White cardboard reflector panel

6 x 6cm camera on a tripod with a 150mm long-focus lens

Power pack

Synchronization lead

Cable release

PHOTO SET-UP: Baby portraits
Using a long lens allows you to take close-up portraits without altering the camera position. The flash lights and reflectors are positioned to concentrate on the baby.

USING A LONG LENS

Although long lenses result in large images of small or distant subjects, they do not necessarily give you the feeling of standing up close to the person being photographed. The longer the lens, the more obvious this effect becomes. For an intimate picture, it is often best to move in closer, if the subject is easily accessible, and to use a standard lens (*see page 75*). With a young baby, however, moving in too close with a camera could seem threatening. You may, therefore, need to strike a balance between the ideal focal length and what a young subject seems most comfortable with.

LIGHTING AND FRAMING FLEXIBILITY

A bonus of working with a long lens is that since you are farther back from your subject, you have more flexibility in where you can place lights and reflectors. You can position lights close to the subject without danger of casting a shadow by partially blocking them. If you have a zoom lens, you will be able to adjust framing, without changing position, to ensure that unwanted parts of the set are excluded from the shot.

Professional tips

• A zoom lens gives you flexibility in framing shots.

• Keep sessions short to minimize possible distress, and allow time for breaks to rest the child.

• A slightly longer lens allows you to take detailed close-ups without intruding too close.

• Include the mother's hands in shots to highlight the difference in scale and skin texture between subjects.

• Soft, diffused lighting is best to capture the skin tones of both mother and child.

Close-ups of baby, *above*
These close-ups are linked by the repetition of gently rounded forms, the soft, directional lighting, and the contrast in scale provided by the mother's hands.

Intimate detail, *right*
For this scene, a long-focus lens produces a detailed close-up. The tight framing excludes unwanted details, and lighting is easier to control over a small area.

TAKING CHILDREN'S PORTRAITS

Photographing children requires patience and a sense of humor. In a studio, the space and equipment will all be new and fascinating, and children may well want to touch and ask questions about everything. For good results, try to make the photo session fun – let them look through the camera viewfinder, for example, and answer their questions about what you are doing and why as fully as possible, even while you are shooting.

CAMERA AND LIGHTING EQUIPMENT

Children rarely sit still, so do not try to restrict their movements too much or they may become bored and uncooperative. Flash lighting units should be set to give a broad area of even light, perhaps positioned either side of the set. You will have to be as mobile as your subjects, and a hand-held camera fitted with a telephoto zoom lens will allow you most freedom of movement.

Framing the shot
A long lens allows you to photograph your subject without moving in too close. A zoom lens offers even greater flexibility – you can fill the frame with a child's smiling expression (*above*) or achieve a more formal result as in the half-length portrait (*left*).

A wide background is created by draping a curtain of muslin at the back of the set

Wide-angle flash lighting units are positioned on either side of the set to give broad frontal illumination

Wide-angle flash lighting unit

Each light is powered by an individual power pack

Hand-held 35mm camera with a zoom lens

Synchronization lead

Power pack

PHOTO SET-UP: Lighting a large set
Wide-angle flash lighting units fitted with softbox diffusers give almost shadowless light over the whole set. The lights are positioned low down to suit the height of the subject and the camera viewpoint is set at the child's eye level.

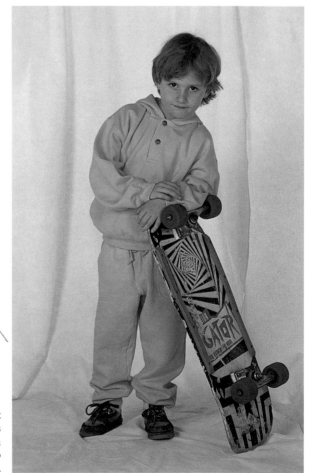

Full-length portrait
A battered skateboard gives the boy something to lean on and adds informality to this full-length portrait.

WORKING WITH CHILDREN

A 35mm camera is ideal for photographing
children since it is lightweight and easy to
operate. With a young subject you have to
work quickly, and there is little time to focus
or to adjust the exposure for each frame.
Count on using more film than normal to
cover inevitable framing and focusing errors.
Many children are great exhibitionists and
enjoy having their picture taken. However,
the presence of a parent or other adult family
member will give a child extra confidence.
A parent can also encourage or entertain a
child from behind the camera to provoke
laughter and smiles.

PROVIDING TOYS AND GAMES

A young child gets bored easily and has a
short attention span. You will need a supply
of toys or other props, such as books and
games, on hand. Provided with an interesting
toy or a colorful picture book, children soon
become absorbed in what they are doing and
forget about the presence of the camera.

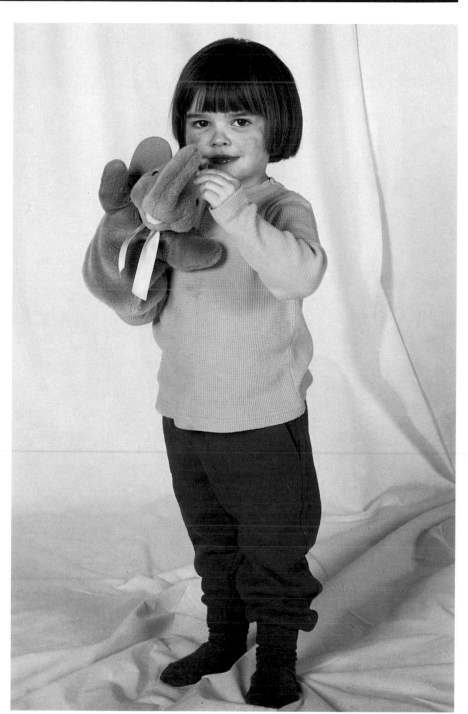

Professional tips

● Talk to the child constantly, taking an interest in
what he or she is saying to put the child at ease.

● Make sure cables, switches, and expensive camera
equipment are safely kept out of harm's way.

● Kneel so that the camera is at the child's eye level.

● Lights need to be positioned lower than normal.

Candid approach, *below*
You must be able to work
quickly since a child will
not stay still for very long.
Dancing to the music on
the radio, this three-year-
old girl soon forgot about
the lights and camera.

Center of attention, *right*
This child's debut in front
of the camera is facilitated
by her companion – an
elephant glove puppet.
With her prop, she spent
an enjoyable 15 minutes as
the center of attention.

PHOTOGRAPHING CHILDREN AT PLAY

Leave nearly any group of children to their own devices and within a few minutes they will have invented some sort of game to play. Young children make ideal subjects for informal, candid photographs, and older children can also make cooperative models if you want a more formal portrait (*see page 106*). The attraction of working with children is their boundless energy, enthusiasm, and constantly changing expressions and moods.

RECORDING CANDID IMAGES

Once the photo session starts, it is often best to keep well on the periphery of the children's activity. Children tend to behave more naturally if you are out of immediate sight. To avoid distant shots with the children very small in the frame, use a long-focus or zoom lens with a range that allows you to fill the frame with the entire group or to come in close on an individual. Use a fast shutter speed and fast film if you take shots of children on the move.

Sand castles, *above*
A high camera viewpoint keeps the children and the circle of sand castles from becoming confused with the breakwater visible in the set-up picture. The bright colors of the pails and spade give a color lift that helps to compensate for the flat lighting.

PHOTO SET-UP: Candid action
A quiet beach makes an ideal location for photographing children. By squatting down you can position the camera at the children's eye level (*below*), whereas by taking the shot from a standing position (*above*), you can show the children against a plain background.

Hand-held 35mm camera with an 85mm long-focus lens allows freedom of movement

Subjects are absorbed in play and pay no attention to the camera

Professional tips

● Fast shutter speeds with a long-focus lens help freeze movement and avoid camera shake.

● Keep apertures as small as possible to compensate for slight focusing errors with fast-moving subjects.

● Fast film gives you more flexibility with shutter speeds and apertures, especially if the weather is dull.

Sports sequence, *above*
These four pictures taken in rapid succession show a complete action sequence. The boy prepares to hit the ball, makes contact, swings the bat, and starts to run. Fast film was used because of the poor natural light.

Captured action, *right*
This shot captures the peak of action as the boy runs to first base. An aperture of f16 ensures sufficient depth of field, and a fast shutter speed of 1/500 is used to freeze most movement and overcome camera shake.

PHOTO SET-UP: Baseball game
The priority in photographing this baseball game is to find the best camera position to photograph the boy with the bat. It is important to keep far enough back so as not to interfere with the game. This means using a long-focus lens and selecting a fast shutter speed to freeze the action.

Hand-held 35mm camera with a 70–210mm zoom lens is not too bulky to carry and is also powerful enough to bring one figure up large in the frame

Boy with the bat is the main subject

Facial expression
Changing to a lower camera angle and close focusing with a zoom lens shows the children's excitement on finding a crab. The tight framing emphasizes the boys' friendly relationship.

FREEZING A MOVING FIGURE

When using flash lighting as your sole or principal source of illumination, you can take advantage of its movement-stopping characteristics to create unusual action portraits that are full of "frozen" energy.

ARRESTING MOVEMENT

If, for example, you were to use a flash-synchronization speed of 1/125 second at f8, your subject would be recorded by light from the flash alone (without flash, a shutter speed of 1/30 or 1/15 second would be necessary for correct exposure). The "freezing" power of this technique stems from the fact that flash units – studio units, add-on flashguns, or built-in types found on some SLRs and compact cameras – deliver a burst of light of short duration. The longest flash duration from a small unit might be only 1/1000 second, while larger units might deliver light in 1/10,000 second bursts – brief enough to stop any normal subject in its tracks.

Anticipating the action
To capture the dancer in mid-leap with his legs perfectly horizontal requires anticipation so you can release the shutter at exactly the right moment.

Plain white background does not detract attention from the subjects and is a good surface to bounce the light off

Subjects wear brightly colored clothing and are positioned toward the rear of the set

Front flash lighting unit with a large softbox diffuser provides direct, diffused illumination over the whole set

Synchronization lead

Rear flash lighting unit increases overall light levels and bounces light off the white backdrop to produce a bright background

Second flash lighting unit with large softbox diffuser provides additional soft light

Single power pack

Cable release

6 x 6cm camera with an 80mm standard lens set on a low tripod

PHOTO SET-UP: Capturing the moment
Four flash units are needed to light this large set, but it is possible to create similar effects using a single flash unit in a smaller room with neutral-colored walls and ceiling.

Professional tips

• Position flash close to subject to shorten light output duration.

• Fast film allows the flash to deliver a shorter burst of light and still achieve correct exposure.

• Use fastest flash-synchronization speed available to prevent blurred images.

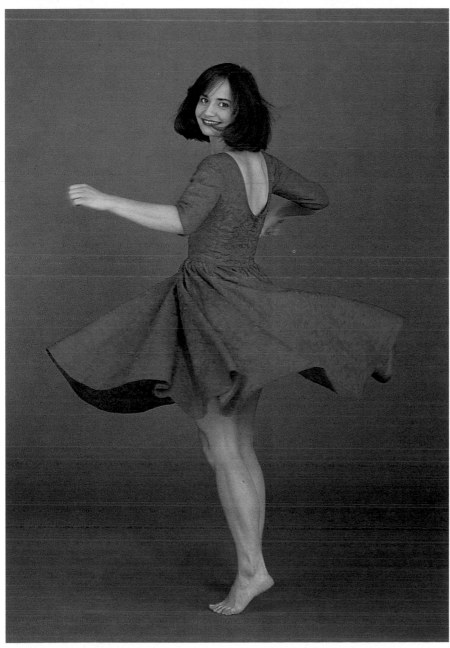

Dynamic portrait, *left*
The brief burst of flash lighting from the two units on either side of the set has perfectly captured the model – her hair is framing her face, her expression is good, and her skirt and posture convey interrupted, frozen movement.

Shooting rate, *above*
You need to shoot a lot of film since there is no way of predicting the results at the instant when the flash fires. A motor drive allows you to take a continuous sequence of exposures with a firing rate of several frames per second.

Colored backdrop for contrast with blue dress

Diffusing panels scatter light, creating a more subtle effect

Flash lighting unit with umbrella reflector

Power pack

6 x 6cm camera with an 80mm lens

Synchronization lead

PHOTO SET-UP: Freezing action
To create an even spread of light, the flash units on either side of the model are fitted with umbrella reflectors and placed in front of diffusing panels made of heavyweight tracing paper. The set above is smaller than the one on the opposite page, so fewer flash units are required.

EMPHASIZING MOVEMENT

Movement can be recorded in two ways. You can freeze a moving subject by using a fast shutter speed (*see page 110*), or you can record a more indistinct, blurred image to give a different impression of the action.

CREATING A GHOST IMAGE

To record blurred and frozen detail on the same frame, select an aperture and shutter speed combination (the recommended flash-synchronization speed or one slower) which would result in detail being recorded even if flash were not used. If, for example, you set an aperture of f11 and a shutter speed of 1/15 second, the flash would fire a burst of light lasting, say, 1/1000 second when you pressed the shutter release, but the subject would continue to move and be recorded on film for all of the 1/15 second exposure.

PHOTO SET-UP: Blurred image
If ambient lighting is sufficiently high at the slow shutter speeds used, a secondary image records after the flashes have fired. The slower the shutter speed, the more obvious the secondary ghost image becomes.

Flash unit fitted with barn-door attachment to highlight the dancer's skirt and arms

Plain white background is unlit so that subject blurring is more apparent

Single flash unit with a large softbox diffuser provides diffused illumination over the whole set

6 × 6cm camera on a low tripod with an 80mm standard lens

Cable release

Power pack

Professional tips

• Lights should be set to isolate the subject from the background.

• Ambient light levels must be kept high.

• Subtle blurring of an image may be lost if background is well lit.

• Try experimenting with different shutter speeds and exposures.

Evocative imagery
The first image of the dancer (*right*) was shot at f11 and 1/15 second, while the second (*far right*) was shot at f11 and 1/8 second.

Ghostly dancer, *opposite*
The ghostly image on the opposite page was shot at f16 and 1/4 second – the slowest shutter speed in the entire sequence.

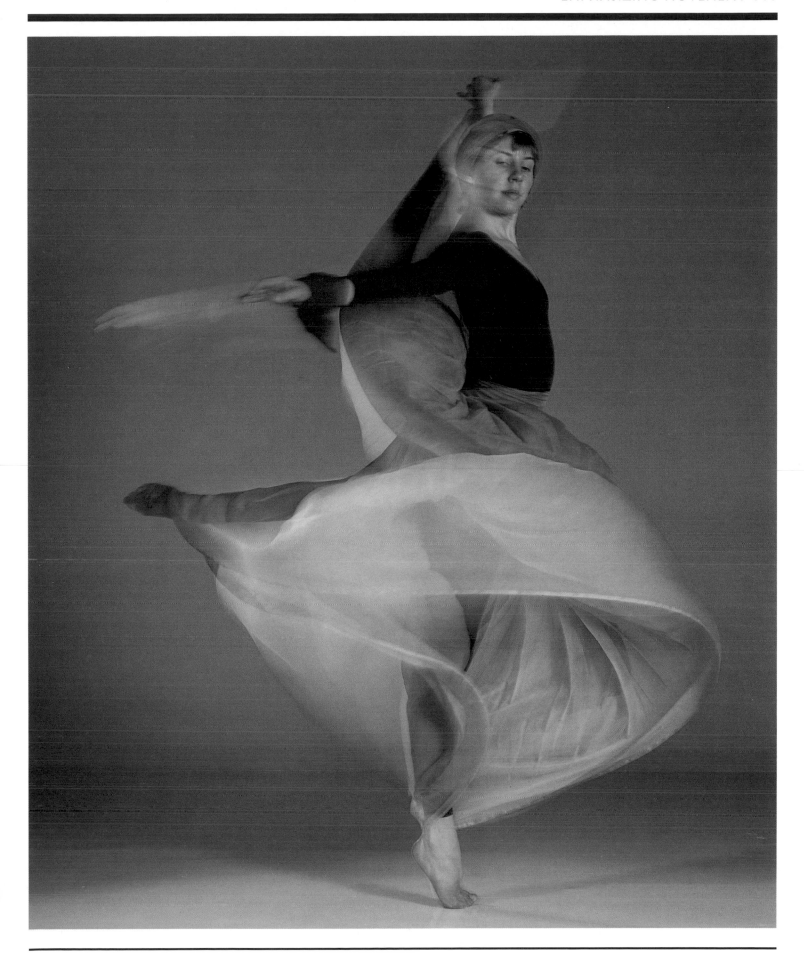

PHOTOGRAPHING SPORTS ACTION

The key to taking successful sports action photographs is anticipation. Find the most suitable camera position before the event starts and then try to interpret how the action will develop so that you can be ready with the camera. Good results are also more likely if you are familiar with the rules of play.

USING A LONG-FOCUS LENS

The most effective action shots are those in which the subject appears large in the frame; the impact will be lost if you can barely see the action. For most field events, a lens with a focal length of 200mm or longer is ideal, but for close-ups of players in mid-field, a 500mm lens may be necessary.

PHOTO SET-UP: American football
The photographer kneels at the sidelines, near the action. A motor drive attachment on the camera automatically advances the film at a rate of three to four frames per second, allowing shots to be taken in quick succession.

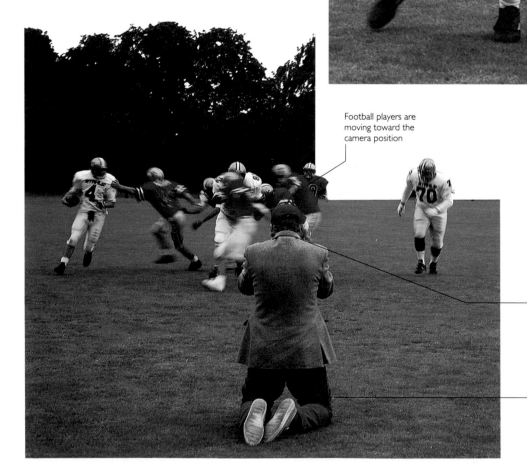

Football players are moving toward the camera position

35mm camera with 200mm long-focus lens and motor drive attachment

Kneeling position close to ground level gives a dramatic viewpoint

Fast action sequence, *above*
A camera with a motor drive attachment allows you to take dramatic shots, such as this image, which shows the football players running toward the camera. The small amount of blur due to subject movement imparts a sense of action. By using a motor drive you do not need to look away from the viewfinder to advance the film between frames and risk missing an important shot.

Motor drive

Shutter
release
button

Lens

Flash
hot
shoe

Detachable
motor
drive unit

Camera with motor drive unit

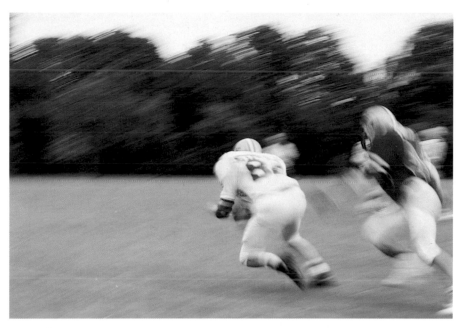

Many modern SLRs have autowinders or motor drives built in to the basic camera. Professional cameras, however, have separate units that are attached to the base of the camera. These sturdy units can be set simply to advance the film after each exposure or to take up to four frames a second, depending on the selected shutter speed. Some models can also be programed to take shots at preset intervals. Remember that at four frames per second a 36-exposure film wil last only nine seconds. Use continuous exposure settings in short bursts when shooting dramatic action sequences.

Panned action, *above*
You can increase the sense of excitement in an action photograph by panning the camera to produce streaks and blurs that exaggerate the impression of movement. This photograph conveys the urgency of the football player's situation as another player sprints to tackle him.

Frozen action, *below*
Although this frozen-action photograph presents the subject in a very unnatural way, it depicts the power and athleticism of the player who is frozen in mid-air. The plain background serves to emphasize the figures of the players and the two levels of action – in the air and on the ground.

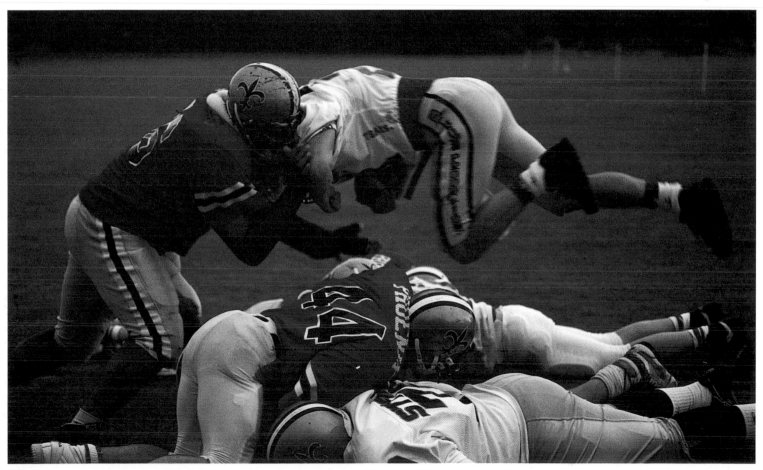

Timing
A poolside camera position and careful timing of the shot captures the swimmer's facial expression.
35mm camera, 135mm lens, Ektachrome 200, f8, 1/250 sec.

Peak of action
This boy is photographed at the top of his jump, before gravity takes over and he falls back to earth.
35mm camera, 70mm lens, Kodachrome 100, f22, 1/125 sec.

Viewpoint, *left*
The right viewpoint is often the vital ingredient of a good action photograph. If taken from the riverside, this canoeist would be obscured by spray. An overhead viewpoint shows his descent downstream in a dramatic fashion.
35mm camera, 135mm lens, Ektachrome 100, f8, 1/500 sec.

Roundup
When you are on vacation look for exciting action images that capture the spirit of the country you are visiting. This shot of a roundup of wild horses in the Australian outback is given atmosphere by the swirling dust.
6 x 6cm camera, 80mm lens, Ektachrome 200, f16, 1/250 sec.

Direction of movement
By adopting a camera position
head-on to the action, a relatively
slow shutter speed is used to
freeze movement. If the hurdler
had been photographed from the
side, a faster shutter speed of at
least 1/250 second would be
needed to get a sharp image.
*35mm camera, 250mm lens,
Kodachrome 200, f22, 1/125 sec.*

Panning
A plume of water, kicked up as
the water skier changes direction,
adds drama and excitement to
this shot. To keep the rapidly
moving subject in focus, it is
necessary to pan the camera,
resulting in the slight blurring of
the background scenery despite
the very brief shutter speed used.
*35mm camera, 500mm lens,
Ektachrome 100, f8, 1/500 sec.*

STILL LIFE

Photographing a still life can serve as an exercise in skill and creativity, honing your understanding of composition and the effects of lighting on objects. Like a painter, the photographer can use a still life picture to communicate ideas of color, form, tone, texture, and composition.

Lighting
See pages 122–123

Still life themes
See pages 124–125

Outside still life
See pages 126–127

Found still life
See pages 128–129

Arranging a still life

A still life is an object or group of objects, which is usually arranged as the subject for a picture. Because the subject is inanimate, you can concentrate more than is usually possible on the lighting and composition. Setting up your own still life can be rewarding, since you have total control over the selection and arrangement of the objects. It is advisable to begin with one object and gradually build up a composition in which the various parts relate to each other. The items used should not be selected arbitrarily, but should fit into a theme – for example, objects from a certain place or a particular period. The essential point is to collect as many props as possible. Gather everything you may want to incorporate and keep it on a table beside you while you work. This allows you to develop your composition carefully, one piece at a time.

Found still life

These are compositions that occur naturally around you, and "found" still life photographs will demonstrate your ability to see good pictures in day-to-day life. A collection of objects in a shop window, for example, may strike you because of their overall arrangement, or the unusual nature of the items. And the natural world abounds with found still life possibilities, from driftwood on a beach, to a pile of fallen apples.

Photographing food

Simple ingredients such as fresh vegetables and exotic fruits offer a sensuousness and a variety of color and texture not found in other inanimate objects. Food photography is a thriving area of commercial photography and professionals use special techniques for enhancing the appearance of food.

STILL LIFE SET-UP

The equipment shown here comprises an ideal set-up for photographing a still life subject. A single diffused light is sufficient to provide overall illumination, as all the shadows should fall in the same direction. Ideally, this single flash unit should be fitted with a softbox diffuser to soften the effect. Use a flash unit with a built-in modeling light, if possible, so you can see how the shadows fall. You will also need a reflector to bounce light into the shadows for overall illumination.

Light source
A single flash unit is the light source for this set-up. The flash head is positioned at about 90° to the still life.

Softbox diffuser
The front of the diffuser is covered with semi-transparent material, softening the light and diffusing it over a large area.

Light stand
Adjustable stand allows you to experiment with the light at different heights until you get the desired effect.

Power pack
The flash unit is powered by a 3,000-joule power pack. Light output can be varied in one-stop increments.

Synchronization lead
This links the camera and the flash unit's power pack, triggering the flash to fire in time with the shutter release.

Clamp
To support the background, you can use a clamp attached to a free-standing pole.

Background
This should harmonize with the still life without dominating it. The texture of this white board adds interest.

White card reflector
A simple reflector bounces light back into the shadowy areas. There should not be any accidental shadows.

Still life group
This still life is the result of the set-up below. Soft, directional light from the diffuser on the left-hand side suggests natural light from a window.

Still life surface
The surface on which you arrange the still life should be away from the walls so that you can position the lights to best advantage.

Overhead view

Light source

White card reflector

1½ft (49cm)

2ft (65cm)

Still life subject

Camera

Table with additional props

Equipment

- 6 x 6cm camera
- Roll film
- Range of standard, wide-angle, and long-focus lenses
- Adjustable tripod
- Cable release
- Flash lighting unit
- Softbox diffuser
- Power pack

Camera and film
6 x 6cm camera with a 120mm long-focus lens, loaded with ISO 100 film. It is set so that the lens is level with the still life.

Prop collection
A variety of objects allows you to experiment with several different arrangements.

Tripod
This allows you to check the composition in the viewfinder.

Cable release
This releases the shutter, reducing the risk of camera shake from hand contact.

COMPOSING A STILL LIFE

For a successful still life you have to establish some sort of link between the objects used in the composition. This link could be a theme – the objects on this page are all typical of a pastoral lifestyle and could have been found on a farmhouse pantry shelf.

BUILDING UP A COMPOSITION

Most still life pictures are built up element by element. Begin with the most important object, viewing it through the camera and adjusting its position until you are satisfied. Then add the second component, and again check the image through the viewfinder. In this way you can build up your arrangement piece by piece, making minor adjustments until you are satisfied with the result.

A wooden storage container is the starting point.

A blue bottle is positioned to provide balance.

A wire basket filled with eggs confers warmth.

A weathered lamp gives character to the composition.

Adding an old copper pot anchors the still life.

Finished still life, *below*
The final addition is a small wooden pestle. Its position keeps the gaze from being drawn to the gap at the bottom. It also reintroduces the warmth and texture of the wood of the storage container, which had become slightly obscured.

ANALYZING A STILL LIFE

A collection of still life objects arranged for the camera should have shared attributes such as shape, color, form, and texture. When you start to take note of these qualities as well as the more obvious thematic connections, your creative scope is widened immeasurably.

BALANCE AND HARMONY

The most difficult part of creating a still life arrangement is knowing when it is complete. A finished composition should have balance and harmony. The objects should be organized so that they emphasize, rather than detract from, the main focal point. Creating a balanced still life composition is instinctive, but you will recognize it when your eye is drawn from one object to the next, with the characteristics of each adding to your pleasure in the next.

Shape and pattern, *above*
The repeated shapes of fork and spade handles leaning against a fence create a strong pattern in this still life picture.

Triangular group, *left*
A group of bottles defines the apex of a triangle, a classic compositional shape. The bottle at the rear acts as a visual anchor, and the similar shapes and textures of all the bottles give the image unity.

Simple grouping, *above*
The appeal of this simple still life is the wealth of detail visible on the two wooden objects as well as their strong shapes.

Placement and balance
Although these bottles appear to be arranged in a haphazard fashion on the shelf, they have been deliberately placed so that the densest mass sits in the central portion of the picture frame.

LIGHTING A STILL LIFE

How you undertake the lighting for a still life depends largely on the elements making up the composition and the degree of translucency, solidity, or color saturation you want them to take on in the final photograph. Generally soft lighting coming directly from in front of the camera will have a form-flattening effect, and results may appear two-dimensional. In contrast, sidelighting tends to enhance the surface characteristics of objects, but shadows may be cast that obscure surface detail.

OVER- AND UNDERLIGHTING

Overlighting by directing a lot of harsh light at the subject lightens the "visual weight" of the subject elements, but it may also cause colors to appear less saturated and weak. Conversely, underlighting by restricting the amount of light reaching the subject may make objects appear heavier and more solid, and colors, too, may appear darker and stronger. By introducing secondary lights, reflectors, or diffusers, myriad subtle or dramatic lighting effects can be achieved.

PHOTO SET-UP: Directional light
A white-painted textured board directly behind the bottles makes a visually interesting backdrop. Lighting is provided by a single flash unit fitted with a softbox diffuser and positioned to one side of the glass bottles, pointing slightly downward. On the far side of the group a reflector throws back some of the light and so lessens the exposure difference between one side of the group and the other.

Form and modeling
Diffused sidelighting and a reflector, combined with a textured backdrop that also reflects some of the light, highlight the form and modeling to produce a subtle gradation of tone.

Textured white board makes an interesting yet simple background

Lighting head fitted with a diffuser ensures that reflections on the glass bottles are not intense enough to pick up reflections from the flash and other nearby objects

Power pack is used to power the single flash unit

Reflector positioned on the shadow side of the composition makes the exposure more even across the whole arrangement

6 x 6cm camera on a tripod with a long-focus 120mm lens, which makes it possible to shoot from farther back, lessening the chance of the image appearing as a reflection in the surfaces of the bottles

Table with selection of props to be added to the arrangement if required

Varying light, *left*
The textured board directly behind the glass bottles is removed for this sequence of three photographs. This leaves the white-painted walls at the back of the set as the effective background. Then, for each shot, the light output from the flash is gradually increased to produce progressively lighter images.

Color saturation, *far left*
In the darkest image in the sequence, you can see immediately that the glass bottles appear more solid and heavier than in lighter versions. Note, too, that as the image darkens the red stopper on the bottle on the right seems darker and the color more saturated.

PHOTO SET-UP: Transmitted light
Flash lighting is directed at the white background behind the glass bottles so that they are defined solely by the light transmitted through them (left and bottom left). The shape of the bottles becomes the principal element.

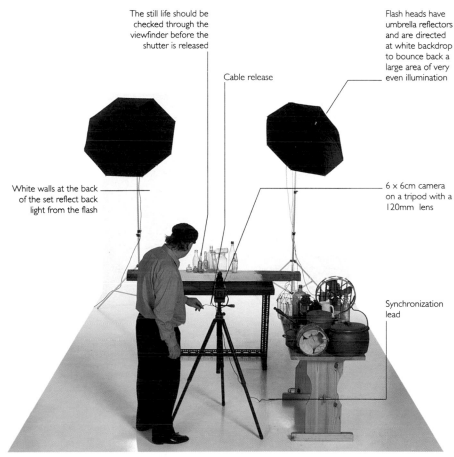

The still life should be checked through the viewfinder before the shutter is released

Flash heads have umbrella reflectors and are directed at white backdrop to bounce back a large area of very even illumination

Cable release

White walls at the back of the set reflect back light from the flash

6 x 6cm camera on a tripod with a 120mm lens

Synchronization lead

Backlighting, *top*
Lit from behind, the surface characteristics of the glass disappear. The silhouette of each bottle is defined by a dark line. The red stopper now appears nearly black.

Combined lighting, *above*
A flashgun fired from the camera position gives soft frontal illumination to the glass bottles. Backlighting predominates, but some form has been reinstated.

SELECTING STILL LIFE THEMES

Working with inanimate objects allows you time to select suitable subjects, to find the most appropriate background, to position the lights if using flash, and to make any subtle corrections to the composition. All of this can be carried out at your own pace, without having to worry about the comfort of a model.

CHOOSING ELEMENTS

Look for some aspect that unifies the items in a composition. This could be texture, function, color, shape, or age. A suitable background and sympathetic lighting are also important. In the pictures on these pages the high-key (light-toned) composition is lit by bright, reflected light, and the low-key (dark-toned) one is illuminated by daylight and fill-in flash.

Light composition
Although composed almost entirely of white, there is sufficient tonal variation to separate the enameled pots from their surroundings, while the black rims give balance and contrast.

PHOTO SET-UP: High-key still life
For this simple still life study, the color and reflective nature of the objects dictate the lighting used. To achieve the desired high-key effect, a broad spread of reflected, indirect light from a wide-angle flash head is angled toward the ceiling and another light is reflected by a white-painted board positioned to the left of the objects.

Wide-angled flash head points at the junction of the ceiling and back wall to give a variety of toplight angles

White, plastered wall does not compete for attention, but provides a contrast in texture with the smooth surface of the objects

Objects are linked by their white coloring, rounded shapes, and enameled texture

Single power pack is the power source for both lighting units

6 x 6cm camera with a 120mm long-focus lens

Secondary flash head is directed mainly at a reflector but its light also spills over and reflects onto the subject from the rear wall

Adjustable tripod can be positioned at appropriate height for still life

Professional tips

• Nearly all still life photography requires the use of a tripod. Use the viewfinder to check changes to the lighting and composition.

• For a high-key still life, provide sufficient illumination so that there is only about a one-stop difference between highlights and the deepest shadows.

• A hand-held flashgun can be fired manually during a long exposure and does not need to be synchronized with the shutter.

PHOTO SET-UP: Low-key still life

This antique kettle and range require additional illumination since there is not much natural daylight in the kitchen. This lighting is provided by a silver reflector on the object's shadow side (to reflect the available window light) and a boost of indirect light from a flashgun.

Hand-held flashgun directed at the wall bounces light onto the objects

35mm camera with a 100mm lens is set on a manually timed exposure

Adjustable tripod

Silver reflector is positioned opposite the window to reflect soft light onto the kettle's shadow side

Objects to be included in the next still life shot are ready and prepared nearby

Dark composition

An antique kettle and range make an ideal low-key still life subject. Lighting is also low-key, which suits the subject. Even with added light from a flashgun, an aperture of f16 requires a long shutter speed of two seconds.

TAKING OUTSIDE STILL LIFE

The main advantage of working outdoors lies in the range of backgrounds and settings you have at your disposal. Indoor settings tend to be cluttered and the decor may compete with the subject. Photographing a subject outside allows you more space to find a setting that makes a positive contribution to the shot.

WORKING IN NATURAL LIGHT

The disadvantage of photographing a still life outdoors lies in the diminished control you have over lighting. Working inside, you can position lights and reflectors at will, and bounce light off the walls and ceiling. Outside, however, you are reliant on natural light – either direct sunlight or, preferably, an overcast sky. You can influence the lighting quality by using reflectors to redirect light into the subject's shadows and so lessen contrast, or you can use a flashgun to add highlights or raise the level of exposure.

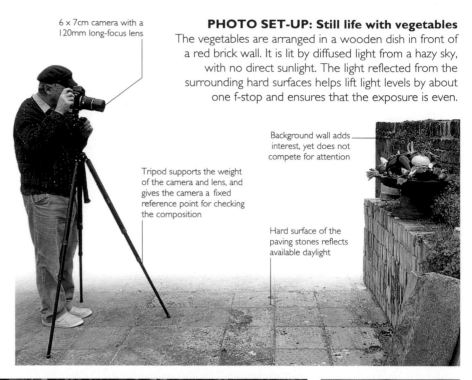

6 x 7cm camera with a 120mm long-focus lens

Tripod supports the weight of the camera and lens, and gives the camera a fixed reference point for checking the composition

PHOTO SET-UP: Still life with vegetables
The vegetables are arranged in a wooden dish in front of a red brick wall. It is lit by diffused light from a hazy sky, with no direct sunlight. The light reflected from the surrounding hard surfaces helps lift light levels by about one f-stop and ensures that the exposure is even.

Background wall adds interest, yet does not compete for attention

Hard surface of the paving stones reflects available daylight

Fruit arrangement
You can create a still life by confining yourself to one type of food, like this composition, which is made up of colorful fruits arranged in a glass vase.

Vegetable still life
In this well-balanced composition, the shapes, forms, textures, and colors of the vegetables were all carefully considered. Diffused rather than direct light is used because of the reflective surface of the eggplants and red onions.

Food still life
Daylight helps bring out
the color and texture of
the red and green pasta,
the pink crayfish, and the
slab of stone. The color
contrast and shadows give
an impression of depth.

Mirroring art
The inspiration for this
rustic tableau is a 19th-
century watercolor painting.
Although the scene looks
almost natural, the quail
eggs were bought and
placed in an artificial nest.

PHOTO SET-UP: Spring still life

Sunlight filtering through the tree canopy is the light source for
this still life of an artificially re-created bird's nest and eggs. The
use of a long-focus lens means that an aperture of f22 is
required to ensure sufficient depth of field, and this necessitates
a shutter speed of ¼ second. A windbreak prevents unwanted
subject movement.

Board is propped
against the tree to act as
a windbreak to prevent
subject movement

Appearance of the
subject is carefully
checked in the camera
viewfinder after every
minor adjustment

6 x 7cm camera with a
165mm long-focus lens

Tripod and cable release
are essential to prevent
any slight movement of
the camera during the
exposure

Professional tips

● For professional
food photography,
ingredients must have
no marks or bruising.

● Care and attention
to detail is critical.

● Objects with shiny,
reflective surfaces can
be polished to remove
finger marks.

● Start by positioning
the largest object in
the composition and
then build up the other
elements around it.

● Background color
can affect the mood of
a still life composition.

PHOTOGRAPHING FOUND STILL LIFE

Any arrangement of everyday objects that forms a pleasing composition, but that has not been put together specifically to be photographed, can be termed a found still life. The art of photographing found still life lies in finding the appropriate camera angle and using sympathetic lighting so that the final image you have in your mind's eye becomes the image captured on film.

NATURAL ORDER AND PATTERN

In one way or another, all of us tend to impose order on our surroundings – in our homes, in our places of work, and our gardens. Manifestations of this tendency are all around us. We organize ordinary cooking ingredients in the kitchen so that the ones we use most often are easy to find, or we change the position of everyday items on a shelf so that they make a more attractive grouping.

PHOTO SET-UP: Gardening tools

The sun is low and behind the shed for this shot, but there is still plenty of indirect illumination to brighten the scene. The line-up of tools propped against the shed door is fortuitous – they are in the process of being cleaned before being put away. The wheelbarrow is moved to the front of the picture frame because its shape and coloring make such a positive contribution to the foreground.

Still life theme
Tools designed for a similar purpose seem to have a natural affinity and harmony when grouped together.

Professional tips

• View a potential still life subject from all possible angles before deciding on the final camera position.

• Use your thumbs and index fingers to make a frame, to help previsualize how the image will appear in the viewfinder.

• Watch out for good photographic subject opportunities in the unlikeliest places.

Cluttered interior of the garden shed is excluded from the final picture

Tools neatly lined up before being put away

Painted wheelbarrow creates foreground interest

35mm camera with a 70–210mm zoom lens

Tripod is positioned so that the camera is at about the same height as the garden forks and spade

PHOTO SET-UP: Greenhouse detail

The sunlight filtering through the greenhouse creates a dappled lighting effect. The white wall behind the objects acts both as a textured background and as a reflector, raising light levels and relieving areas of shadow.

35mm camera on a tripod with a 70–210mm zoom lens

Collection of objects among the clutter on a garden work bench is isolated in the viewfinder

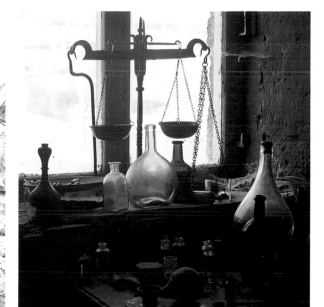

Nostalgic mood, *above*
Sunlight entering through the window behind adds to the mood of this picture. Strewn with cobwebs, the glass bottles and scales are a glimpse into the past.

Work bench, *below*
A collection of plant pots, garden tools, a weathered watering can, and drying bulbs, makes a harmonious still life with a unity of color, form, and purpose.

Repetition of shape

Finding a coherent theme for the objects making up a composition is one of the most difficult aspects of still life photography. In this collection of objects, it is the repetition of shape that forms the common link. Note, too, how the arrangement sets up a strong diagonal flow within the frame.
6 x 7cm camera, 120mm lens, Fujichrome 100, f11, 1/60 sec.

Natural sunlight

Soft, directional light coming from a window to the right of this still life is the only illumination. The sense of calm would be marred if the contrast between the shadows and highlights were too marked, so a white cardboard reflector has been added on the left-hand side.
35mm camera, 100mm lens, Kodachrome 200, f16, 1/30 sec.

Found objects, *top*

A still life does not have to be a collection of objects arranged for the camera. Use the viewfinder to isolate found objects, such as these old, discarded boots, to form a pleasing composition.
35mm camera, 120mm lens, Ektachrome 200, f11, 1/125 sec.

Shape and symmetry, *above*

The repeating shapes and symmetrical composition of these terra-cotta plant pots convey a sense of balance and harmony. The low camera angle introduces a depth that would be missing from an overhead viewpoint.
35mm camera, 50mm lens, Ektachrome 100, f5.6, 1/250 sec.

Multifaceted imagery

Although the components making up this still life are very simple, the combination of elements with the lighting and background results in a multifaceted image comprising shape, form, texture, and tone.
6 x 6cm camera, 80mm lens, Ektachrome 100, f16, 1/250 sec.

Dominant color

The two principal colors in this composition – the yellow of the sunflowers and the blue of the table top – represent a potentially discordant color combination. However, the intensity of the daylight spotlighting the flowers is such that the yellow relegates all other colors to supporting roles.
35mm camera, 28mm lens, Fujichrome 100, f8, 1/500 sec.

LANDSCAPES

Landscapes are constantly changing. Depending on the time of day, and weather conditions, they can take on many different personalities and moods. Learning to see and capture on film the potential in a scene is perhaps the hardest part of landscape photography.

Viewing a landscape
See pages 134–135

Water and light
See pages 148–149

Moving water
See pages 150–151

Dramatic skies
See pages 154–155

The light factor

Unlike an outdoor portrait, where a subject can be moved into position for the most beneficial lighting effect, with a landscape picture you must work with the prevailing light. This does not mean that you cannot influence how the subject will appear in the photograph. For example, from one angle, a pool lying at the bottom of a ravine may appear black and lifeless, while seen from another, the water may be a mirror holding a flawless reflection of blue sky and white clouds.

Compositional control

Before taking any pictures you should explore the surroundings to find the best viewpoint. A landscape may be dramatically improved by the inclusion of a feature in the foreground or when photographed in a particular light. Even if your camera angle is restricted to a single viewpoint, you should be able to move to the left and right to find the best perspective. The height from which you shoot is also critical. Squatting down tends to stress the foreground, while gaining extra height may allow you to exclude an unwanted foreground detail. Look at the scene through the viewfinder to see how landscape features relate as you move around.

Lenses for landscapes

A wide-angle lens is ideal for broad panoramas with a wide sky and plenty of foreground. If the sky is flat and dull, you can use a long-focus lens to restrict the angle of view to parts of the scene that have maximum impact. It is best to use a tripod and cable release to avoid camera shake, even if you are not working with slow shutter speeds. Remember that a landscape may look most dramatic toward dusk or in dark stormy light, conditions that make long exposures essential.

LANDSCAPE SET-UP

A 12th-century priory in the heart of the English countryside is the focal point of this landscape picture. The camera viewpoint and the position of the sun show some sides of the ruins in bright sunlight, while other sides of the building are in shadow. The camera angle does not show the reflections of any of the clouds in the pool of foreground water, but it does reveal the reflections of the higher parts of the building and the ancient tree to the left.

Overhead view

Direction of light

Landscape subject

300ft (90m)

Camera

Emphasizing elements
Using a wide-angle lens
emphasizes the pool of
water in the foreground
and allows more of the
blue sky and white clouds
to be included in the shot.

Equipment

- 6 x 6cm camera
and spare film

- Range of lenses

- Cable release
and tripod with
spiked feet

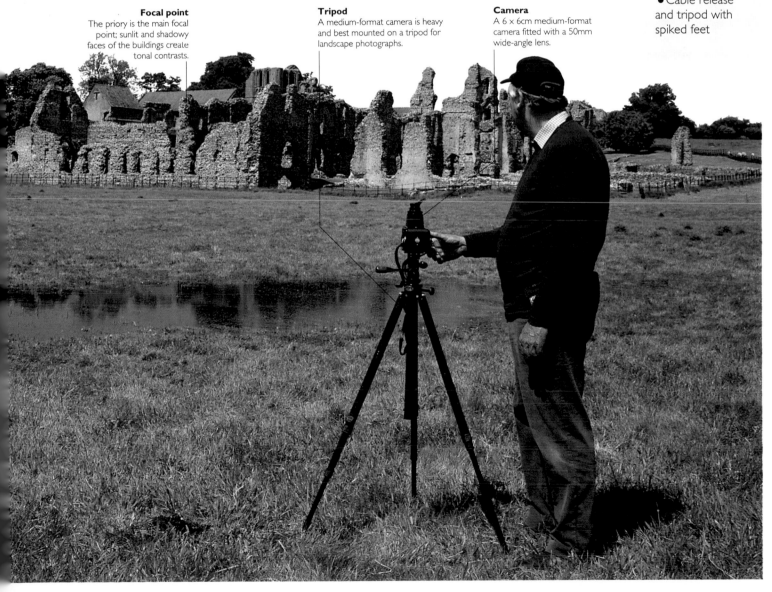

Focal point
The priory is the main focal
point; sunlit and shadowy
faces of the buildings create
tonal contrasts.

Tripod
A medium-format camera is heavy
and best mounted on a tripod for
landscape photographs.

Camera
A 6 x 6cm medium-format
camera fitted with a 50mm
wide-angle lens.

VIEWING A LANDSCAPE

Photographing a landscape is more difficult than it seems because it involves translating a three-dimensional panoramic scene complete with all its nuances into a flat image.

CHOOSING A DOMINANT ELEMENT

Any landscape is a complicated mixture of colors, tones, textures, forms, and perspectives. If you simply point the camera in a general way at such a potential jumble of subject matter it is likely to result in an uninspiring picture, so it is important to have a clear idea of how you want the elements to relate to each other. Try to be selective about what you include in the picture. By careful choice of viewpoint and lens focal length you can decide which elements are important and how you can best arrange them within the confines of the viewfinder. This task is often simplified if you can identify one element as being the main subject.

PHOTO SET-UP: High viewpoint

Relatively small differences in camera position can create huge shifts of emphasis in a photograph. The extra height afforded by shooting from the top of a four-wheel drive car lessens the effect of the field in the foreground and emphasizes the main subject – the windmill in the distance.

35mm camera with a 100mm long-focus lens

Distant windmill is made more prominent by the use of a long-focus lens

Platform on roof gives high viewpoint

Tripod ensures that the camera is level and steady

Distant viewpoint

A high camera viewpoint is essential to keep the green field from dominating this landscape. The 100mm long-focus lens with its narrow angle of view (*see page 24*) isolates the main subject and crops unwanted elements. This viewpoint also assigns the trees in the middleground a subsidiary role as an attractive frame for the windmill.

Professional tips

● If the light is not favorable, try to find a different viewpoint or wait until the light is in the right direction.

● Shooting from a high viewpoint minimizes the foreground.

● Shooting from a low viewpoint emphasizes the foreground.

● A landscape should have a principal feature.

PHOTO SET-UP: Changing the angle

Moving in closer to the windmill gives a different emphasis to the landscape. The merits of the camera viewpoint in terms of composition and lighting are considered in the viewfinder before pressing the shutter release button.

Foreground feature
Inclusion of the stream in the foreground adds shape and color. Its curve helps draw the eye to the mill.

Placing the horizon
A low horizon emphasizes the sky and introduces a feeling of space (*top*). A high horizon shifts the emphasis to the bottom of the frame (*above*). The landscape now seems more enclosed than previously.

Interesting cloud formations are an important element in this landscape

Windmill is the main focal point in this landscape view

Directional afternoon sun creates contrasting areas of light and shade

35mm camera with a 100mm lens is hand-held to allow greater freedom of movement

Extreme viewpoint
Moving in closer to the windmill and pointing the camera up results in an architectural shot that excludes any clue as to the landscape or surrounding elements.

RECORDING TIMES OF DAY

Light is the key ingredient in a successful landscape photograph. Its intensity and the angle at which it illuminates the subject play a vital role in conveying mood. Dawn light is of low intensity and has a gentleness that softens colors and definition. As the sun climbs, the angle of light accentuates texture and form. Toward noon the sun is overhead and the contrast between light and shade is intense. The light can be so strong that colors are bleached out and the landscape seems lifeless. In the afternoon as the sun descends, color intensity, form, and texture improve, and by dusk the scene has a rosy warmth.

Early afternoon
Light, color, form, and texture are evident in this scene, shot in the soft light of early afternoon.

Mid-morning
Although a clear morning, the sun is not yet high in the sky, and a grayness hangs over the beach.

PHOTO SET-UP: Time of day

One of the best ways to see how the mood of a landscape is influenced by different light is to take a series of pictures of the same subject throughout the course of a single day, perhaps at mid-morning, in the afternoon, and at sunset. To ensure the framing of all the shots is consistent, take a careful note of your camera position, camera height, and focal length, and line each shot up with a prominent landmark, such as this seaside pier.

Toward sunset
With the sun low, contrast is extreme. It is just possible to discern a hint of pink in the clouds close to the sun, an effect that will intensify as the sun dips below the horizon.

Position of the corner of the pier is carefully noted so that the framing of each picture is identical

35mm camera with a 28mm wide-angle lens

Low wall makes a handy support to lean on and ensures that all pictures in the sequence are shot from the same height and camera position

Day to night sequence
Dawn at Rio de Janeiro's Copacabana beach (*top row left and center*). Colors intensify as the sun climbs in the sky (*bottom row left*), until by late afternoon (*bottom row center*) the glass towers are in shadow with a blue sky behind. As night falls, the sky turns a warm reddish pink (*below*).

Highlight exposure
Scenes containing large areas of water tend to be brighter because they reflect available light – even the weak light from a twilight sky. Here the land is darkened by taking an exposure reading from the sky, which is the brightest part of the scene, leaving the rest of the image underexposed.
35mm camera, 135mm lens, Ektachrome 100, f8, 1/250 sec.

Afternoon light
The mirrorlike water of this Irish estuary is broken only by the boatman's oars. The wooden boat and finger of land provide contrast to the pastel pink-green scene.
6 x 6cm camera, 150mm lens, Ektachrome 200, f5.6, 1/250 sec.

Snow exposure
Snow reflects light, giving too high a light reading for the subject, which can result in underexposure. Here, the lens is opened by one f-stop. *35mm camera, 55mm lens, Kodachrome 64, f8, 1/60 sec.*

Sunset color, *below*
At sunset the landscape takes on an orange cast. Wavelengths of blue light are scattered, and longer red wavelengths illuminate the scene. *35mm camera, 80mm lens, Kodachrome 64, f11, 1/125 sec.*

Ultra-violet light, *above*
Large amounts of ultra-violet light contribute to the overall coloration and slight haziness of this scene. The fact that the landscape is illuminated by light from a deep blue sky rather than direct sunlight also influences the strong color-cast. *35mm camera, 135mm lens, Ektachrome 200, f16, 1/125 sec.*

Monochromatic landscape
This aerial composition consists almost exclusively of shades of green, relieved only by farm buildings, stone walls, and grazing cattle. The sun is low in the sky and throws long shadows across the fields, producing almost tangible surface textures. *35mm camera, 100mm lens, Fujichrome 100, f5.6, 1/250 sec.*

CHANGING LIGHT AND WEATHER

In unpredictable weather, light is variable, changing from second to second, and this presents specific problems when judging exposure. Wet weather does not necessarily lead to bad or uninteresting pictures, and it certainly does not need to keep you from taking photographs. Although you should always take precautions to protect the camera and lens from getting wet, a few drops of rain will not cause damage.

Storm light, misty conditions, and heavy rain can dramatically alter the appearance of a landscape, merging and simplifying colors, distorting perspective, and creating a varied vista. Landscapes do not have to be shot in fair weather – scenes shot in unfavorable conditions can result in spectacular pictures.

PHOTO SET-UP: Wet weather conditions
Although it is not raining, the air is saturated with sea mist and spray at this location overlooking steep cliffs. A clear ultra-violet filter (also known as a UV filter) is used to protect the lens, which must be wiped with a soft, clean cloth to keep the glass completely clear of moisture. A UV filter has no effect on the exposure.

Sturdy tripod is essential in windy conditions because it is impossible to hold the camera steady

Clean cloth is used to keep the UV filter clear of moisture

35mm camera with 35mm wide-angle and 135mm long-focus lenses

Worsening weather
The time difference between the first picture (*left*), shot with a 35mm wide-angle lens, and the second (*above*), shot with a 135mm long-focus lens, is only a few minutes, but the worsening weather conditions have completely changed the character of the landscape scene. This is especially noticeable in the background detail, which has almost disappeared in the long-focus shot.

EXPOSURE FOR VARIABLE LIGHT

Areas of bright highlight with clear detail immediately stand out in a landscape picture, and appear visually stronger in the frame compared to the shadowy parts of a scene. In order to record an accurate impression of a landscape, you should be able to set the exposure manually and to understand how the light metering system of your camera responds to changeable light. For example, if you want to record a small area of highlight in an otherwise shadowy scene, it may be necessary to override the light meter and expose for the highlight to keep the shot from being dominated by the area of shadow.

Light levels, *above*
Overall the light level is the same in these two images; but the meter showed a
half-stop fall-off in light for the version with the central shadow, and the exposure had to be manually set.

PHOTO SET-UP: Shadows on the landscape

The three photographs on this page were shot over a period of just a few minutes. A fence post acted as a camera support in place of a tripod. The shifting patterns of clouds moving across different areas of the sky divide the landscape up into distinct areas of light and shade.

Selective lighting
The most successful of the three landscape pictures shows the far distance in deep shadow, giving it less impact on the scene.

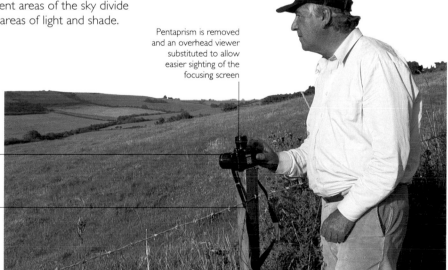

Pentaprism is removed and an overhead viewer substituted to allow easier sighting of the focusing screen

35mm camera with a 55mm standard lens

Fence post is used to steady the camera and align it accurately for the three different exposures

Professional tips

● In changeable weather, light varies rapidly, and you will need to shoot a lot of film in order to have enough images for a good final selection.

● An ultra-violet filter protects the lens from rain and mist, and minimizes the effects of UV light in coastal and mountain scenes.

BLACK AND WHITE VERSUS COLOR

If you try to take landscape shots using black and white film in the same way you would use color film, the resulting photographs are likely to be disappointing. Often, it is the color content of a landscape scene that creates an exciting picture – the bright yellow of a cornfield, the myriad shades of green in a forest panorama, the autumnal reds and golds of a woodland carpeted with fallen leaves.

SIMPLIFIED TONES

In black and white photographs, however, it is the contrast of light and shade and the tonal gradations of white through black that dominate the picture. What might appear distinct and obvious in color often becomes more ambiguous once the color content is removed, resulting in a more subtle picture open to a different interpretation.

PHOTO SET-UP: Black and white landscape
The photographs shown on this page illustrate the difference between a landscape scene shot in color and one shot in black and white. These images were shot within a few minutes of one another from the same camera position. A tripod is useful to maintain the same framing of shots while cameras loaded with black and white and color film are switched.

Color versus pattern
The most striking feature of the color version of the landscape (*left*) is the colorful russet hues of the rust on the old barn's roof and sides. In the black and white version (*below*) that same area of the picture is dominated by strong pattern and texture. The graphic effect of the black and white landscape is emphasized by the directional early evening sunlight.

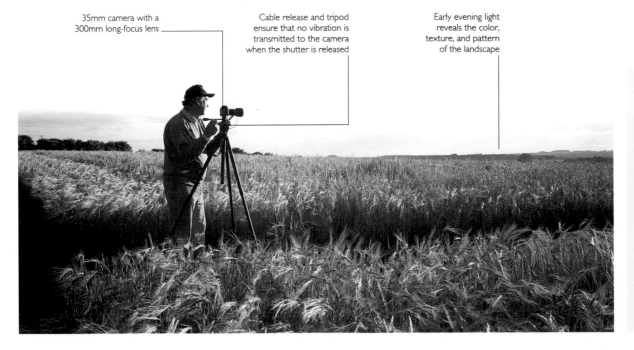

35mm camera with a 300mm long-focus lens

Cable release and tripod ensure that no vibration is transmitted to the camera when the shutter is released

Early evening light reveals the color, texture, and pattern of the landscape

Professional tips

- Contrasty lighting conditions are more effectively rendered in black and white images than color images.

- Bold, simple shapes are effective in black and white pictures.

- Different color lens filters create clear tonal distinctions between certain colors in landscape scenes.

Color versus shape
Comparing these landscape pictures, it is the bold shape of the semi-silhouetted tree that dominates the black and white version (*top*). In the color picture (*above*) it is the foreground stubble and plowed field that attract immediate attention.

Infra-red film, *right*
Objects appear to have different colors because they absorb and reflect different wavelengths of light. Infra-red sensitive film can capture light that is invisible to the eye, transforming images into unusual tones and shades.

Unreal effect, *top*
Black and white infra-red film gives
almost unreal tonal appearances.
*6 x 6cm camera, 80mm lens,
Kodak IR, f8, 1/125 sec.*

Tonal range, *above*
Delicate shades of white through
gray make up this tranquil scene.
*6 x 6cm camera, 50mm lens,
Pan F, f11, 1/60 sec.*

Storm light, *right*
Low clouds, failing light, and falling
rain might restrict some scenes
taken on color film to just a few
indistinct hues. The same scene
photographed on black and
white film reveals a wide range
of tones from deep black to
nearly pure white.
*6 x 6cm camera, 80mm lens,
Plus-X, f16, 1/60 sec.*

RECORDING THE CHANGING SEASONS

It is in the temperate regions that seasonal variations in the weather are most distinct. In tropical regions the sun stays high above the horizon and seasonal changes are between wet and dry rather than hot and cold.

THE CHANGING LANDSCAPE

The photographic potential of a landscape can be transformed by seasonal changes in light and weather. In temperate regions, the sun stays low in winter and high in summer, which affects the quality of light. It is best to shoot summer landscapes when the sun is low in the sky, which restricts photography to mornings and afternoons. Remember that latitude affects the color of the sky, so that it appears a deeper blue at high latitudes.

PHOTO SET-UP: Woodland scene
A woodland clearing is the setting for this early summer scene. A wide-angle shift lens (see page 27) is used to avoid distorting perspective by tilting the camera upward.

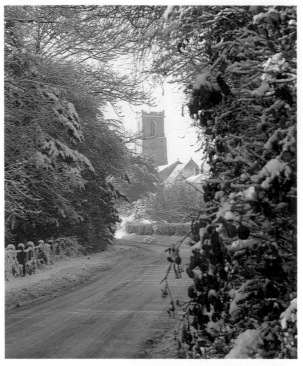

Winter landscape
A snow-covered hedgerow and icy country lane have produced a wintry scene of monochromatic simplicity. Snow scenes often need slight overexposure to keep the whites free from any appearance of dirtiness.

Early summer
The light filtering through the tree canopy makes exposure difficult, and overexposure by just one f-stop could rob the scene of its color and density of shadow. The scene is shot using several shutter speeds to avoid any miscalculation of the exposure.

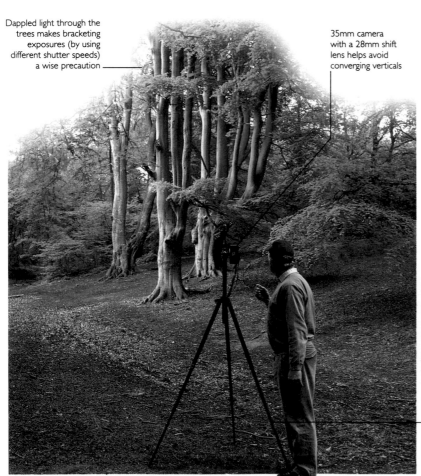

Dappled light through the trees makes bracketing exposures (by using different shutter speeds) a wise precaution

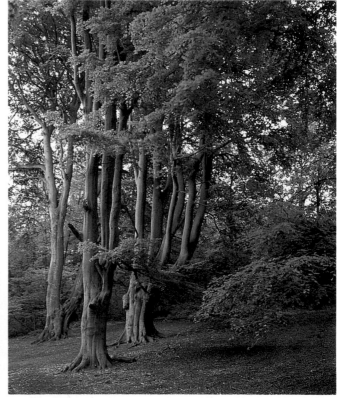

35mm camera with a 28mm shift lens helps avoid converging verticals

Cable release and tripod are essential to avoid camera shake when using slow shutter speeds

Spring landscape, *left*
Wild forest flowers such as these bluebells are one of the harbingers of spring. By keeping the camera angle low, just enough of the trees can be seen to give the picture context. Lighting is even across the scene because the tree canopy is not yet fully grown. Note that the color is more saturated in the shaded foreground.

Summer landscape
Viewed against the yellow field, the old tree appears almost silhouetted. The fully saturated green at the bottom of the frame and the intense blue sky above epitomize summer colors.

Fall landscape
With no foliage to obscure its path to the ground, a fall sun infuses this leafy carpet with a fiery bronze.

PHOTOGRAPHING WATER AND LIGHT

Light reflected from a lake, river, or pond can enhance an otherwise uninteresting landscape scene. An expanse of water in itself often makes an obvious focal point around which to build your landscape composition.

It is also important that you view the scene from different angles and heights. Seen from one particular angle, an area of water may appear emerald green as it reflects light from foliage on nearby hillsides. When viewed from a different angle, the surface of the water may sparkle with bright blue highlights as it mirrors the sky directly above it.

When light strikes the water's surface, the intensity of the reflection provides extra illumination, radically altering the exposure. To record reflected light in water you will probably have to take exposure readings for both the highlight and the shadow and select an aperture somewhere in between.

PHOTO SET-UP: Calm water reflections

Looking across this landscaped pond it is obvious that the brightest highlight in the frame is the reflection of the distant trees, vegetation, and blue sky on the water's calm surface. The lighting is bright and even, coming from a mid-afternoon sky unobscured by clouds.

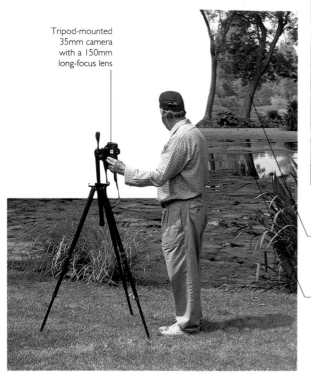

Tripod-mounted 35mm camera with a 150mm long-focus lens

Distant trees are the principal subject of the photograph

Reflections of the trees and the bright sky appear on the water's surface

Long-focus lens view
In this close-up of the far bank, shot with a long-focus lens, the backlit foliage has taken on a delicate translucency, while light reflecting off the water's surface looks like a sheet of shimmering silver. The strong afternoon light filters through the trees to create a calm, tranquil image.

PHOTO SET-UP: Sunset reflections

Spectacular reflections can be seen looking across a seascape at sunset. A range of different color effects is possible depending on the exposure selected, the most intense resulting from a highlight exposure reading.

Subject is rendered as a silhouette due to highlight exposure reading

Setting sun on the horizon casts a bright reflection on the water

Sunset silhouette
By selecting a low camera angle, the seated figure is aligned with the finger of reflected light. A higher camera position would lessen the graphic impact.

Hand-held 35mm camera with 28–70mm zoom lens

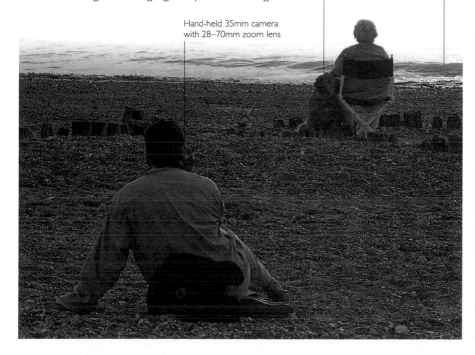

Color-enhancing filters

Filters can be used to improve colors or eliminate unwanted reflections. Polarizing filters remove reflections from water surfaces and intensify blue skies. For a warm effect, use a light red skylight filter. A light blue filter, in contrast, cools colors down.

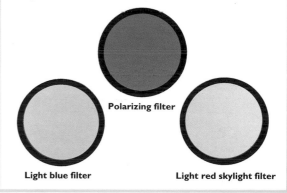

Polarizing filter

Light blue filter

Light red skylight filter

CREATING IMAGES OF MOVING WATER

Landscape scenes with moving water have a special charm for photographers. A small area of fast-moving water in an otherwise placid landscape scene introduces a strong contrast – white against blue, turbulence against smoothness and mirrorlike calm.

Moving water in a landscape scene allows you to experiment with a variety of shutter speed effects. A rapidly moving mountain stream shot in close-up needs a shutter speed of at least 1/500 or 1/1000 second to capture its motion. If you shoot it at 1/15 second, or even slower, film speed and light levels permitting, you will find that the moving water takes on an entirely different character.

PHOTO SET-UP: Water movement
Even very minor changes in camera position can create very different photographs of the same subject. Compare, for example, the appearance of the sea spray in this set-up picture with the version opposite, in which a lower viewpoint is taken. Careful selection of exposure and a fast shutter speed are needed to capture and highlight the way in which the light dances on the breaking waves.

Frozen movement
A fast shutter speed of about 1/500 second is used to freeze the movement of water over the stony bed of this fast-flowing stream. A shutter speed this brief often requires the use of fast film and a wide maximum aperture.

Blurred movement
A slower shutter speed results in the water appearing soft and blurred. This picture of the stream was shot at 1/4 second. Use a tripod (which keeps the camera steady) and a small aperture to compensate for this length of exposure time.

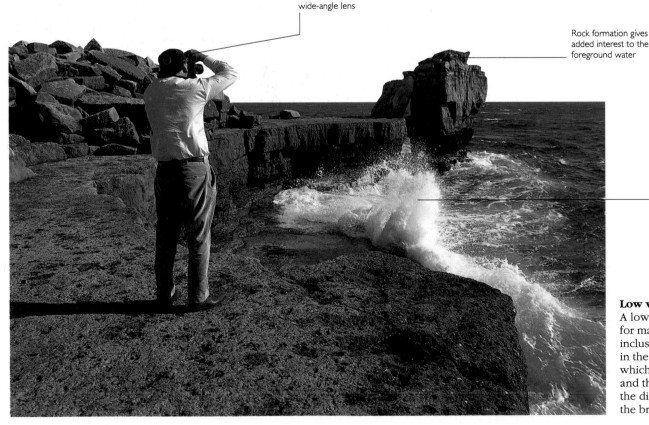

35mm with a 28mm wide-angle lens

Rock formation gives added interest to the foreground water

Brief shutter speed effectively stops the movement of the spray and allows a hand-held exposure

Low viewpoint, *opposite*
A low viewpoint is selected for maximum impact. The inclusion of the shoreline in the foreground, around which the water is boiling, and the menacing rock in the distance add drama to the breaking waves.

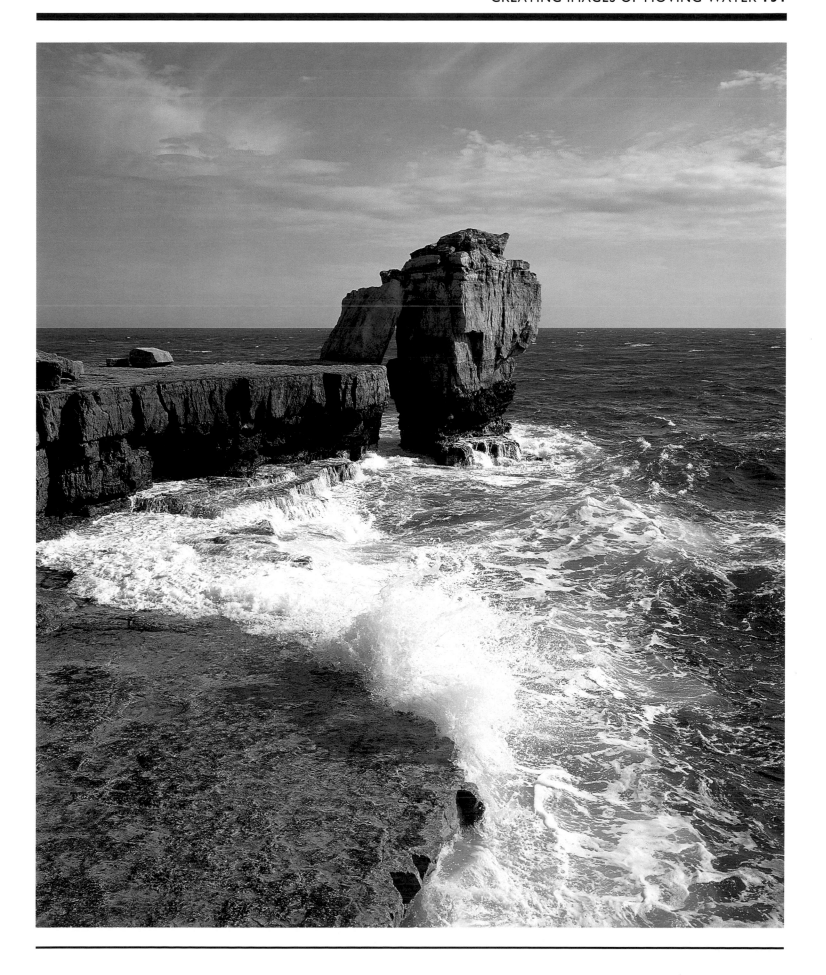

PHOTOGRAPHING SEASCAPES

Capturing the sea and its many moods is a constant challenge to the photographer. The extreme variations in appearance associated with the sea are due to the fact that the water not only mirrors the changing moods of the weather, but also magnifies them many times over. Coastal conditions can be very different from the weather just a few miles inland, so it is advisable to check on local conditions by telephoning the local coastguard beforehand.

When photographing coastal scenes, time of day is important, since this may dictate the state of the tide, which affects the appearance and accessiblity of the coast you want to photograph. Remember to protect your camera against damage from salt water and sand by cleaning it with a dry cloth after use.

PHOTO SET-UP: Moods of the sea
The inclusion of a prominent coastal feature adds interest to what would otherwise be a picture of just the sea and sky. In this photo set-up a majestic arch of limestone rock makes a perfect backdrop for the breaking waves.

Shutter speed, *above*
Selection of a fast or slow shutter speed determines how the movement of the waves will appear. Although the coast here is calm, a shutter speed of 1/250 second still leaves some wave areas blurred.

Sculpted rock formation is the obvious focal point of this seascape, punctuating the division between sea and sky

35mm camera on a tripod with a 28mm wide-angle lens

SPECIAL-EFFECT FILTERS

Polarizing, gradated, neutral density, and light-balancing filters are intended to cut down reflections and correct variations in lighting without changing the overall color. There are also filters that produce strong color-casts for dramatic effect. Red, yellow, and orange are the most popular filters for use with black and white film. These filters can darken a blue sky to emphasize the white of the clouds. Color filters can also be used with color film to enliven an otherwise uninteresting landscape. Remember that all filters absorb some light, so you must allow for a longer exposure time.

Filter effects
Strongly colored filters are designed for special effects and can radically alter our perception of a scene. The deep blue filter used with this seascape produces the most normal-looking image and the orange filter results in the most dramatic image.

Landscape without filter

Landscape with orange filter

Landscape with yellow filter

Landscape with blue filter

Color filters

Color filters are available in a range of hues and strengths for creating special effects with color film. All filters subtract some of the light that strikes the glass, making slower shutter speeds and/or wider apertures necessary to achieve a correct exposure as the filter color becomes darker. The more the image is underexposed, the stronger the color.

Green	Orange
Red	Yellow
Yellow/green	Blue

CAPTURING DRAMATIC SKIES

The sky, which may be an important element in a landscape photograph, can also make a fascinating pictorial subject in its own right. Not only does the sky have an almost endless capacity for color change – from the deepest blues to vibrant gold and crimson – but the variety of cloud formations visible from one location in the course of a single day may be breathtakingly wide, especially when the weather is changeable.

SUN AND CLOUD EFFECTS

The most dramatic photographic opportunities are when the sun illuminates banks of clouds at an angle or when small, billowing clouds are partially obscuring the sun. Dawn and sunset are the times of day when the colors of the sky are at their most variable and dramatic, and usually most photogenic.

PHOTO SET-UP: Sky at sunset

In order to photograph the sky at sunset, set up your camera on a tripod in advance and wait for the sun to dip below the horizon. Shooting the sun itself may create flare spots so it is better to wait until the sun is partly obscured by clouds. The exposure reading is taken for the brightest part of the sky so that the landscape appears black.

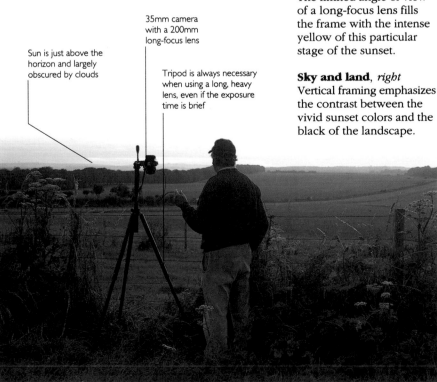

Sun is just above the horizon and largely obscured by clouds

35mm camera with a 200mm long-focus lens

Tripod is always necessary when using a long, heavy lens, even if the exposure time is brief

Close-up view
The limited angle of view of a long-focus lens fills the frame with the intense yellow of this particular stage of the sunset.

Sky and land, *right*
Vertical framing emphasizes the contrast between the vivid sunset colors and the black of the landscape.

Obscured sun
When the sun is obscured by clouds, those closest to the camera position appear dark and menacing, while dramatic shafts of light penetrate the gaps beyond and illuminate the peaks of the clouds farther away.

Stormy sky
In this picture, high banks of thunderous cumulus clouds are gathering over the hills flanking a city, signalling the onset of a rainstorm. Storm cloud formations can change from second to second.

Professional tips

● To accentuate the colors of a sunset sky, take your light reading from the brightest part of the sky.

● Keep the horizon low in the frame to give the sky greater compositional weight.

● A polarizing filter may help strengthen the contrast between sky and clouds.

● If the sun is in the shot, be careful not to damage your eyes, especially if you are using a long lens.

Scale and interest
A dramatic sunset scene illustrates just how effectively water or, in this case, wet sand, mirrors and reflects the colors of the sky. Note, too, how the lone figure walking on the beach adds an important element of scale and interest to the composition.
6 x 6cm camera, 80mm lens, Ektachrome 100, f11, 1/125 sec.

Wide-angle view, *below left*
Dramatic clumps of cumulus clouds, with cirrus formations above, transform this sunset sky into a poem of shape, form, texture, and color. A wide-angle lens gives a sense of depth and perspective to the photograph.
35mm camera, 19mm lens, Ektachrome 100, f8, 1/125 sec.

Hidden light, *below right*
Timing is critical when there are banks of moving clouds and the sun itself is in the shot. From the angle that this picture was taken, the cloud shields the camera from the intensity of the sun.
35mm camera, 135mm lens, Kodachrome 200, f16, 1/1000 sec.

Silhouette lighting
For this spectacular view of
St. Michael's Mount in Cornwall,
England, a light reading was first
taken from the brightest part of
the sky. The camera was then
redirected and the scene
photographed. The result is a stark
silhouette dominating the horizon.
*6 x 6cm camera, 50mm lens,
Ektachrome 100, f8, 1/125 sec.*

Rainbow hues
Rainbows occur when droplets of
moisture refract the sun's rays and
split them into their constituent
wavelengths. To intensify the
strength of a rainbow's colors, this
shot is underexposed by between
a half and one full f-stop.
*6 x 7cm camera, 80mm lens,
Ektachrome 100, f22, 1/125 sec.*

PHOTOGRAPHING URBAN LANDSCAPES

One of the most visually rich photographic resources we have readily at hand is the city. City centers, dominated by towering glass and steel structures, can be a fascinating mix of architectural statements, especially when contrasted with more traditional building styles, or when seen in the context of urban areas awaiting renewal. Watch for repeating patterns, dramatic shapes, contrasts of natural and artificial features, the use of color, even the written word on billboards, the sides of delivery vans, and neon signs.

PHOTO SET-UP: London Embankment
A personal view of urban life could include landmarks that typify a city for you. The location for this picture set-up is the Embankment beside the River Thames in London, and the view takes in St. Paul's Cathedral.

Brand color bias
The early evening summer light casts shadows over waterfront buildings in dramatic contrast to the lit area behind. Color can vary depending on the film brand used (*see page 31*). For example,

these two images were both taken from the camera position shown in the photo set-up under identical lighting conditions. Whereas one picture (*above*) has a strong green cast and is lighter, the other picture (*left*) has a blue cast and is much darker.

Hand-held 35mm camera fitted with a 70–210mm zoom lens

Choose a city landmark as the focal point of the picture

Railings make a convenient place to lean against to steady the camera

Early evening light casts strong shadows on the water's surface

Professional tips

● Choose a camera position that will give a good overall view of the city.

● Contrast between old and new buildings may make an interesting subject for photographs.

● Use a tripod and a long exposure to record subject detail at dusk.

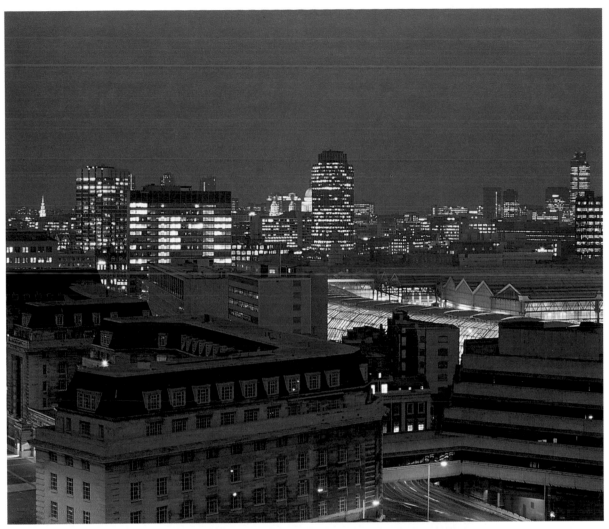

Time of day
Cityscapes change radically when viewed at different times of day. In this shot, taken just after dusk, there is enough daylight to reveal details in the buildings and streets, yet there is also sufficient artificial light to add extra color and interest

Dramatic sky, *below left*
Framing to give a low horizon imparts great emphasis to the sky in this cityscape. The storm-laden clouds are dramatic in themselves, but the composition is full of tension, as if the forces of nature are gathering to assault the city below.

Selected viewpoint, *below*
Finding a high viewpoint from which to shoot is an excellent way of showing tall buildings without the intrusion of converging verticals typical of ground-level shots. Here, the high viewpoint shows another aspect of urban topography – the contrast between recently built skyscrapers and lower, older buildings.

PHOTOGRAPHING THE CITY AT NIGHT

As night draws near, a whole range of picture-taking opportunities opens up. One of the best times to take night pictures is at dusk. At this time there is still sufficient ambient light to define subject details, and the presence of early street lighting, lighted store windows, and car headlights all combine to create a fairytale image of bright and distorted colors.

EXPERIMENTING WITH EXPOSURE

As the sky becomes darker, exposure times increase dramatically, but with a tripod or some other form of camera-steadying device this should not present a problem. Bracketing shots by experimenting with several different exposures is essential for night photography. Make a note of your exposure times and compare these with your processed results. If you do this regularly you will soon start to build up an instinct for nighttime exposures under a range of different lighting conditions.

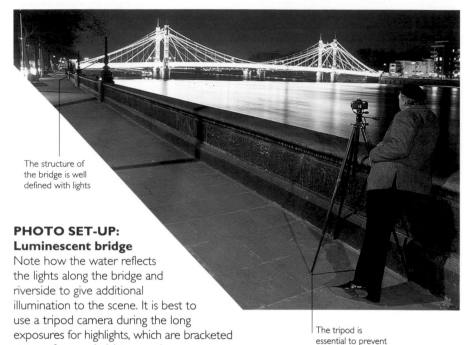

The structure of the bridge is well defined with lights

PHOTO SET-UP:
Luminescent bridge
Note how the water reflects the lights along the bridge and riverside to give additional illumination to the scene. It is best to use a tripod camera during the long exposures for highlights, which are bracketed at two, four, and eight seconds.

The tripod is essential to prevent camera shake

Colored filters
These three pictures were all taken from the position shown in the set-up picture. Different colored filters were used for dramatic effect. For the first picture of the illuminated bridge no lens filter was used (*top*). The color is not entirely natural, however, because of the effect of the tungsten lights on the daylight film. For the subsequent images, yellow (*above*) and orange filters (*left*) were used.

MOVING LIGHTS

One of the most impressive lighting effects is produced when you include moving lights in the frame combined with long exposure times. Car headlights and taillights are a good subject for this technique. Set up your camera on a tripod adjacent to a busy road or on a high vantage point overlooking the roadway. Using a long exposure, the white beam of the oncoming headlights and the red taillights of the cars traveling in the opposite direction will be drawn out into streaks in the resulting image. The length of the streaks of light is determined by the exposure.

PHOTO SET-UP: Colored light trails
The camera and tripod are positioned on the roof of a building overlooking London's Houses of Parliament. The resulting picture (*right*) has many streaks of colored light, but taillights are recognizable when the cars slow down at traffic lights. Static light sources, such as lighted windows and street lights, tend to burn out during the long exposure.

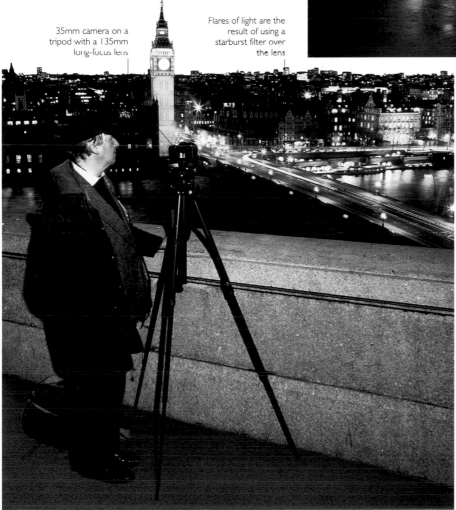

35mm camera on a tripod with a 135mm long-focus lens

Flares of light are the result of using a starburst filter over the lens

Overview, *above*
The high viewpoint shown in the set-up picture gives an unobstructed view of London at night. The clock tower of Big Ben makes a recognizable landmark.

Tunnel vision
A car dashboard is used to support the camera for this shot taken inside a tunnel in New York. The roof tiles reflect the red taillights of the cars.

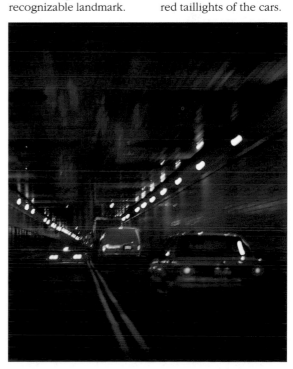

ARCHITECTURE

Architecture is a very broad subject area, encompassing both modern, state-of-the-art developments and traditional buildings; places of work and industry; religious centers; homes both suburban and stately; and bridges and dams, as well as interiors and decorative details.

Viewing a building
See pages 164–165

Using a shift lens
See pages 166–167

Large interiors
See pages 174–175

Simple interiors
See pages 176–177

Viewpoint and perspective

Some professional cameras allow the normal focusing screen to be removed and replaced by an architectural screen – a grid of parallel vertical and horizontal lines. This screen is used as a guide to ensure that your framing shows the subject square and perfectly upright.

Practical considerations

Outdoor architectural photography is largely dependent on available light. Take the time to see how the light reacts with the features you want to emphasize. Is the angle of the light from direct sun casting shadows over the detailing you want to see, or do you regard those same shadows as a positive asset in your picture, creating interesting patterns of light and shade? If the lighting is not right on one side of the building, then it may be better on the other, or you may have to come back at a different time of day. The sky is also a major consideration when photographing buildings. Dramatic pictures can result from cloudless or stormy skies, but overcast gray skies should be avoided if at all possible. Extreme weather conditions, such as mist or fog, will add a new dimension to your photographs.

Working in confined space

If space outside or inside a building is tight, then a wide-angle lens (and sometimes a shift, or perspective-control, lens) will be invaluable for including all of the subject in the frame. Often it will be a detail or an isolated feature of the building that catches your eye, and to record this a long-focus lens may be the answer. For lighting a small interior (or a small area of a large one), a hand-held flash unit may be useful, but you will also need to use fast film and long exposures that require a tripod or some other camera-steadying device.

ARCHITECTURE SET-UP

This newly built shopping mall is surrounded by tall metal railings, which make it problematic to photograph. The only way to achieve an unobstructed view of the building is to stand as close to the railings as possible and shoot over the top of them. From this angle it is not possible to include the whole of the building, so it had to be decided at the outset which part of the building to emphasize. It would also have been possible to shoot down from the pathway above, but from that angle views of the adjacent street would have been unavoidably included in the shot.

Camera
A 35mm camera with a 28mm wide-angle shift lens is used to include the domelike roof of the building without tilting the camera up and causing the vertical lines to converge. The camera is loaded with medium-speed ISO 200 film.

Overhead view

Direction of light

Architectural subject

18ft (6m)

Camera

High-contrast lighting
A highlight exposure reading from the strong, directional sunlight results in this contrasty image. The camera angle is such that the railings behind form arcs on either side of the dome.

Equipment

- 35mm SLR camera and spare film
- Range of lenses
- Adjustable tripod
- Flashgun
- Reflector

VIEWING A BUILDING

Most buildings, unless they are slab-sided and featureless towers, have countless different angles, faces, moods, and features to offer the camera. As you move around the building you are interested in photographing, keep a careful watch for architectural details both above and below your usual eyeline. Look for the flow or rhythm that the building projects and see how you might enhance these characteristics on film, or even suppress them for a more personal interpretation.

Look, too, at how the angle of light strikes the building, and decide when the optimum time of day is in terms of lighting for your photographs. Lenses of varying focal lengths, or different settings on a zoom, can influence the appearance of a building dramatically. Try viewing the subject through the camera with a series of different lenses attached before you start to take any pictures.

PHOTO SET-UP: Lloyds of London
A visually complex building such as the Lloyds Building in London provides innumerable photographic opportunities. The overall shape of the structure makes a powerful design statement and the geometric arrangement of steel pipes and girders is striking.

Design of building allows plenty of opportunity for picking out interesting architectural details

Glass reflects the blue sky and white clouds — a polarizing filter could be used to cut down these reflections

Hand-held 35mm camera with a 28mm wide-angle lens

Light coming from directly behind the photographer casts a strong forward-pointing shadow

Usual viewpoint, *far left*
This picture is taken from slightly farther back than the position shown in the photo set-up. There is some convergence of the parallel lines, but the distortion effect is minimal.

Extreme viewpoint, *left*
The dizzying convergence of vertical lines is produced by an extreme camera angle, near ground level and shooting upward. This approach imparts a sense of exaggerated height.

Implied movement
The camera viewpoint in this shot emphasizes the vertical nature of the architecture and introduces movement in the frame.

Abstract pattern
A striking way to portray this modern building is to emphasize the abstract pattern produced by the gleaming steel pipes.

Tilting the camera
An interpretative approach has been achieved here by photographing the building from an unusual angle. This effect is created by tilting the camera at an angle to the subject.

USING A SHIFT LENS

The apparent convergence of vertical lines at the top of a picture frame is most noticeable when a camera is tilted up to include the top of a tall building. This is caused because the back of the camera, and the film plane, are no longer parallel with the subject. The base of the structure is closer to the film and seems larger; the top is farther away and appears smaller. This results in the sides of the building appearing to converge at the top. By moving back from the subject, you may be able to get all the building in without tilting the camera, but details might then look small. Using a shift lens is the solution to this problem.

Shift lens

A shift, or perspective control, lens alters the appearance of vertical lines. By turning a knob or ring on the lens you can make the front of the lens shift upward, downward, or sideways. So instead of tilting the camera to include the top of a building, simply shift the lens upward until the top of the building comes into view on the focusing screen. Shift lenses are costly, however, and are usually only made with 28mm and 35mm focal lengths for 35mm cameras.

PHOTO SET-UP: Perspective problems

This 17th-century customs house on a quayside in Kings Lynn, England, illustrates the problems of distorted perspective. If shot from close-up with a wide-angle lens, the building would appear to fall away and topple backward.

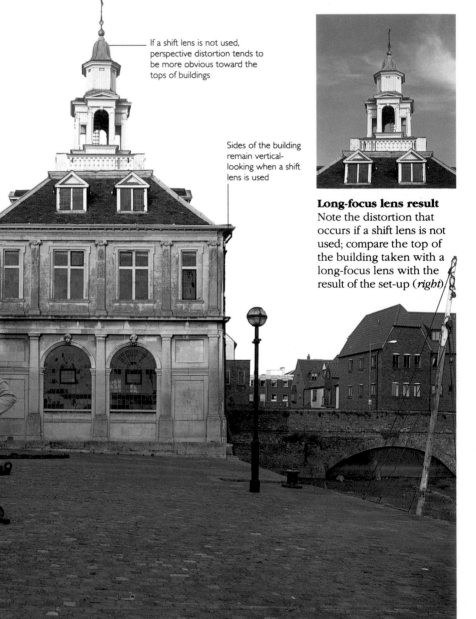

If a shift lens is not used, perspective distortion tends to be more obvious toward the tops of buildings

Sides of the building remain vertical-looking when a shift lens is used

35mm camera with a 28mm shift lens

Long-focus lens result
Note the distortion that occurs if a shift lens is not used; compare the top of the building taken with a long-focus lens with the result of the set-up (*right*)

Before and after
These pictures of a
building photographed
from the same position
with a shift lens (*above*)
and without (*top*) show
how this lens corrects the
appearance of converging
vertical lines. Once shifted
off-center, the back of the
lens is no longer pointing
directly at the middle of
the film frame, so a shift
lens has greater covering
power than a normal optic.

Shift lens result
This picture is the result of
the photo set-up opposite,
but now the sides of the
building appear perfectly
square. The shift control
has been used to raise the
front part of the camera
lens, which straightens
vertical lines and corrects
any perspective distortion.

PHOTOGRAPHING EXTERIOR DETAILS

The details on the outside of a building can sometimes tell you more about the building than the whole structure. An entire building, especially a large one, would appear so small in the frame that much of interest could be lost or overlooked. Another point to consider is that the lighting might be ideal for features such as a doorway, colonnade, or windows, but unsuitable for the building as a whole.

The focal length of the lens required for exterior details is dependent on the size of the feature to be photographed and how close you can get to it. For example, a gargoyle under the eaves of a cathedral roof may require a lens of at least 300mm for a reasonably sized image, while to include all of the main entrance of that same building, a 28mm wide-angle lens will be needed.

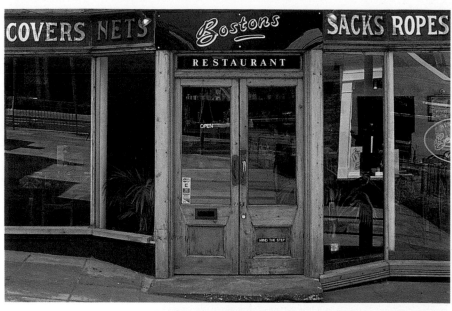

PHOTO SET-UP: Focusing on details

Architectural details, even on ordinary buildings such as private homes, offices, or shops, can make interesting photographic subjects. In this picture the gilt lettering above the shop door is picked out using a long-focus lens.

Gilt lettering over shop doorway is an interesting detail

Hand-held 35mm camera with a 90mm long-focus lens

Paving stones reflect light and make a shorter exposure possible

Problems with glass
The major difficulty when photographing glass-fronted buildings is unwanted reflections, such as that of the photographer (*above*). Think how you can position yourself out of view – for example, the photographer has so placed himself (*top*) that he is shielded by the uprights of the door frame.

Professional tips

● A polarizing filter helps minimize reflections.

● Instead of shooting from ground level, details high up on buildings can be tackled by finding a nearby building and shooting at the same level as the subject.

● To get vertical lines straight, line up the edge of the viewfinder frame with an important subject element.

PHOTO SET-UP: Architectural details

The subject of this set-up picture is the carved stonework of a church doorway and surround. A 28mm wide-angle shift lens is used to make sure there is no perspective distortion caused by converging vertical lines (*see page 166*). The doorway is lit by diffused, directional daylight from a bright sky, but with no direct sunlight falling within the picture area.

Doorway and surround are lit by diffused daylight that emphasizes the texture of the stonework

35mm camera on a tripod with a 28mm wide-angle shift lens

Textural emphasis, *above*
The doorway in the set-up picture is lit by diffused daylight that brings out the texture of the stone. Bright sunlight would result in dark shadows that might mask important detail.

Long lens details
Using an extreme long-focus lens allows you to record architectural details that you might easily miss when using a standard lens. Shot with a 250mm lens, the elaborate carving on the columns (*far left*) and the grotesque face of the gargoyle (*left*) fill the picture frame and so can be studied in detail.

Introducing drama, *top*
An intense sun and low camera viewpoint highlight the walls of this Canadian granary, producing dramatic contrast against the deep shadows of the unlit surfaces.
35mm camera, 28mm lens, Ektachrome 64, f16, 1/125 sec.

Time of day
Photographs of ancient sites, such as this of the Ramesseum (the mortuary temple of Ramesses II on the west bank of the Nile at Luxor in Egypt) are often best taken at midday when the sun is overhead, creating strong contrast between highlights and shadows.
35mm camera, 35mm lens, Kodachrome 25, f22, 1/250 sec.

Foreground addition
The space in front of this mosque in Istanbul is relieved by placing a figure in the foreground.
6 x 6cm camera, 50mm lens, Ektachrome 64, f11, 1/125 sec.

Intentional distortion, *right*
By moving in close to the base
of this building and tilting the
camera back, the towering glass
edifice appears almost to be
toppling over, as if giving up its
struggle against gravity. The
curved gridwork adds dynamic
pattern to the composition.
*35mm camera, 24mm lens,
Ektachrome 200, f22, 1/60 sec.*

Polarizing filter, *top*
The impact of this stark, white
building would have been
diminished without the use of a
polarizing filter, which darkens
the blue of the slightly stormy sky.
*35mm camera, 35mm lens,
Ektachrome 200, f8, 1/250 sec.*

Lead-in lines, *above*
A shadowy wall guides the eye
toward the main subject of this
scene, a church on a Greek island.
*35mm camera, 50mm lens,
Ektachrome 200, f16, 1/250 sec.*

Color content, *left*
Even when the architectural merits
of a building are dubious, its color
content may still make it an eye-
catching subject for a photograph.
In the drab surroundings of a
Moroccan backstreet, the birthday-
cake pink, green, and blue color
scheme of this building has
immediate impact.
*35mm camera, 85mm lens,
Ektachrome 100, f22, 1/60 sec.*

PHOTOGRAPHING INTERIORS

Photographing the interiors of buildings has its limitations, primarily associated with working in a confined space and the quality and intensity of the lighting. Relying on natural light can result in strong contrasts, with beams of light entering through well-defined window areas and casting distant parts of the room into shadow. If this is not the effect you want to achieve, use a white cardboard reflector or mirror to bounce light into dark corners or supplement the available light using an add-on flash unit.

USING A WIDE-ANGLE LENS

Unless you want shots of specific details that require the use of a long-focus lens, a 28mm or 35mm wide-angle lens is best for limited spaces if your aim is to include as much of the room as possible in the shot. You will still need to select the most appropriate angle and rearrange furniture if it is a vital element.

PHOTO SET-UP: Using a fisheye lens

Photographing this old-fashioned kitchen would be difficult without an extreme wide-angle lens. A 15mm fisheye lens fits in as much of the room as possible. This results in extreme distortion – most noticeable at the front of the frame. The front-to-back distance is also very exaggerated.

Fisheye lens

Fisheye lenses for 35mm format cameras include focal lengths of 15–18mm, which give full-frame images, and lenses of 6–8mm, which produce circular images in the center of the film area (see *page 27*). The angles of view of fisheye lenses are enormous, with the widest taking in 220° of the scene – this is actually so wide that the lens "sees" behind the camera.

Extreme views, *above*
The bowing of all vertical lines positioned near the frame edges – evident in this picture – is typical of images taken with extreme wide-angle lenses. Depth of field at every aperture is so great with a 15mm fisheye lens that there is virtually no need to focus.

35mm camera with a 15mm fisheye lens

Tripod is required to hold camera steady during long exposure of two seconds

Objects are positioned at the front of the frame to emphasize the distortion effect of this extreme wide-angle lens

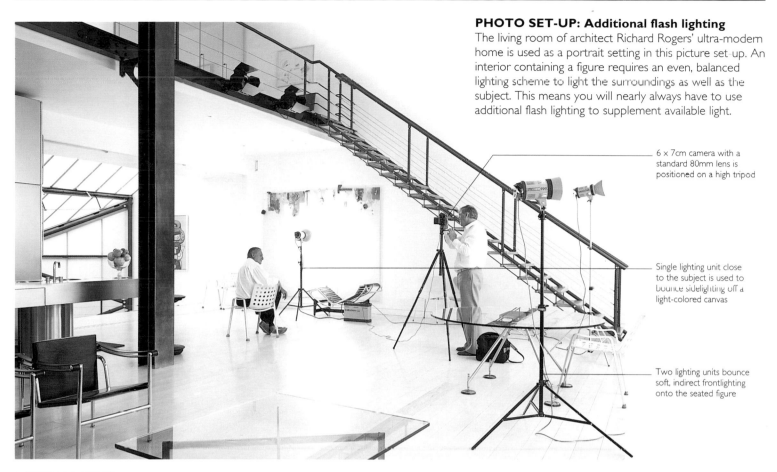

PHOTO SET-UP: Additional flash lighting

The living room of architect Richard Rogers' ultra-modern home is used as a portrait setting in this picture set-up. An interior containing a figure requires an even, balanced lighting scheme to light the surroundings as well as the subject. This means you will nearly always have to use additional flash lighting to supplement available light.

6 x 7cm camera with a standard 80mm lens is positioned on a high tripod

Single lighting unit close to the subject is used to bounce sidelighting off a light-colored canvas

Two lighting units bounce soft, indirect frontlighting onto the seated figure

Standing figure

By positioning the subject away from the skylight, the potential lighting problems are at once lessened. The flash lights become more important, but there is now no need to balance them with the natural light.

Seated figure

Positioning the subject off-center is a useful device when both the figure and the interior are important. The figure is backlit by natural light and the flash is just used as a fill-in.

WORKING IN LARGE INTERIORS

Working inside a large interior usually means being selective about what you include in the picture and what you leave out. If you cannot accommodate everything in the frame even by using your widest lens, then look for the angle that shows the most revealing or impressive aspects of the particular location.

Often you will find that the best camera position is directly in front of the windows, with the camera looking into the interior. In this way the light will be behind you and the interior features will be lit from the front or side. If there are windows in both flanking walls, then a more central camera position may result in the most flexible lighting.

High viewpoint
This shot of the entrance hall is taken from a higher angle than the photo set-up. Taken from a standard viewpoint, the ceiling is excluded from the picture.

Low viewpoint
This dramatic picture results from the low camera angle in the set-up photo. The pillars appear to converge, directing the viewer's gaze to the ceiling. The staircase seems far steeper from this position and the foreground area has been minimized.

PHOTO SET-UP: Camera viewpoint
The marble hall of this stately home, with a grand staircase leading up past ornamental pillars to a galleried landing, is best viewed from the center of the ground floor to take full advantage of the daylight entering through the windows in the side walls above and behind the camera.

Low camera viewpoint and use of a wide-angle lens includes the ornate ceiling in shot

35mm camera with a 15mm wide-angle lens is positioned on a short tripod

FLASH TECHNIQUES

A single burst of light from a hand-held flash unit does not make much of a difference in terms of lighting a large interior, especially one with a high ceiling like the church shown in this photo set-up. Rather than firing the flash just once, try setting the camera's shutter to T (time), then press the cable release to lock it open and fire the flash manually as many times as you think you need for a correct exposure. A tripod is essential if you use this technique during an exposure of many seconds. You may need the help of an assistant to shield the lens while you move between flash positions.

With and without flash
The first picture (*below*) was taken without flash. An exposure of six seconds gives detail where the light falls, but the roof area is lost in shadow. For the next shot (*below right*), the shutter was held open while a hand-held flash was fired at different parts of the roof.

PHOTO SET-UP: Painting with light
To light the high ceiling in this church, a flash unit is fired from a variety of positions around the interior to direct the light at different parts of the roof.

Each burst of flash is fired from a different position

Camera shutter is held open throughout the exposure using a locking cable release

35mm camera on a tripod with a 28mm shift lens

LIGHTING SIMPLE INTERIORS

Simple interiors can make fascinating subjects for the camera. Whereas large public buildings are designed to project an impersonal public image, people's homes are full of private, intimate touches that can reveal much about those who live there.

NATURAL LIGHTING

When shooting an interior you must decide whether to rely on natural daylight from windows, doors, or skylights, or to use artificial lighting such as flash or tungsten lights. The color temperature of daylight and flash are the same, so color-casts are not a problem on ordinary, daylight-balanced film. Do not, however, turn on any of the room lights unless you want an orange cast.

PHOTO SET-UP: Directional daylight
This kitchen is lit solely by light entering through the large windows on the right. Contrast could have been a problem were it not for the white walls, which reflect light and so keep the shadows from becoming too dense.

35mm camera with a 28mm wide-angle lens is positioned on a tripod in one corner of the room

Directional daylight from the windows is the only source of illumination

Country kitchen
This shot is composed in the camera viewfinder to exclude unwanted details. The high camera position looks over the top of the sink unit and the framing is tight in on the cabinets to avoid the edge of the door frame appearing in the shot.

Church interior
Directional daylight from windows on the left of the frame is the chief illumination for this simple church interior. Natural daylight casts shadows into the central aisle, adding to the mood and atmosphere of the tranquil scene.

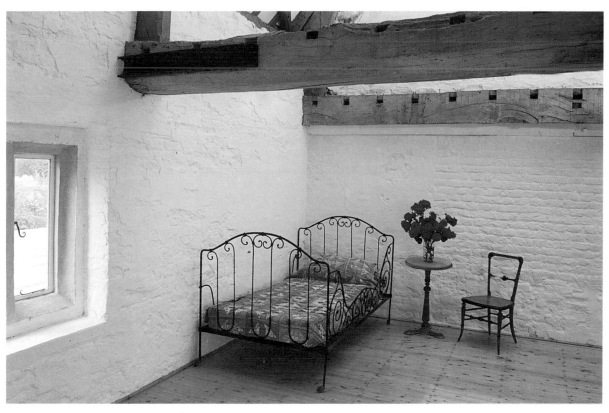

Lit by flash
Note how evenly the scene is illuminated using fill-in flash. However, in this flash version some of the mood has been lost and the absence of shadows removes the sense of depth.

Professional tips

• Meticulous attention to detail is vital.

• Direct flash units to precisely the areas where light is required.

• Look at the image in the viewfinder before taking the shot to make sure that there are no extraneous details in the frame.

Lit by daylight
This picture is taken in natural daylight without using flash. In comparison with the shot taken using flash (*top*), the scene looks more natural and has an intimate atmosphere.

White-painted wall and ceiling make ideal surfaces off which to bounce light

Flash lighting head is angled upward to produce indirect, reflected illumination

Cable release

35mm camera with a 28mm wide-angle lens is positioned on a high tripod

PHOTO SET-UP: Supplementing light
Although supplementary flash can be used to light an interior when daylight is not sufficient, the effect of even lighting is difficult to achieve and can ruin the atmosphere of a room. To illuminate this entire bedroom with flash would require a minimum of three lighting units. One flash unit is used here to light a corner of the room.

PHOTOGRAPHING INTERIOR DETAILS

Stairwells, windows, and doorways are just some of the interior details that often make a far more revealing and interesting subject for a photograph than the setting as a whole.

DETAILS IN PUBLIC BUILDINGS

If you are shooting in a large public building, such as a church, museum, or stately home, you may need a long-focus lens to enlarge the detail in the frame. In addition, camera angles may be restricted; a 70–210mm zoom allows you the flexibility to adjust the size of the subject in the frame without changing position. However, zoom lenses have small maximum apertures, limiting their use in poor light. It is best to use a fast film to avoid blurred pictures caused by slow shutter speeds and to overcome problems of shallow depth of field due to shooting at maximum aperture. Remember that you may need to ask permission to use a tripod in a public building.

PHOTO SET-UP: Stairway detail
Although flash could be used for a small interior detail such as this stairway, it is preferable to rely on daylight whenever possible (see *page 177*). Natural light lends a moody and atmospheric quality that is almost impossible to achieve with flash or tungsten. Although the levels of ambient light appear high, a long four-second exposure using fast film makes the use of a tripod essential.

35mm camera with a wide-angle 28mm shift lens

Tripod is essential if you are shooting a long exposure, and it is also useful for keeping the camera in precisely the position you want

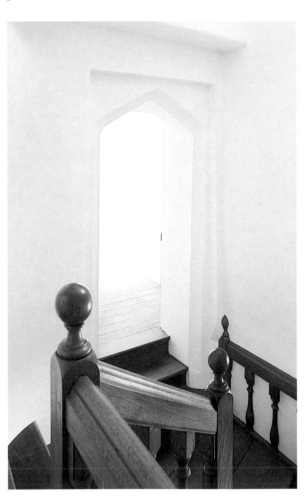

Framing of detail, *left*
Space is very restricted on the upper landing of this oak stairway, making it difficult to position the tripod and to frame the shot correctly. In order to keep the lens level and avoid any perspective distortion, a 28mm wide-angle shift lens is used.

Professional tips

• If using an ordinary wide-angle lens, keep the camera back parallel with the subject to avoid unwanted distortion of perspective.

• Interiors lit by natural window light alone can be contrasty; use a simple reflector to lighten shadows.

STAINED GLASS WINDOWS

Although most often seen in churches, stained glass windows are also found in some secular buildings. For successful results, try to get as close as possible to the window and level with the detail you want to record. If the windows are high up, use a long-focus lens. The light coming through the glass is best from an evenly lit, overcast sky. The lower the light levels, the deeper the color of the glass will appear. Always use a tripod and allow long exposure times.

PHOTO SET-UP: Stained glass detail
It is best to position the camera as level with the window as possible, so that it is neither pointing up nor down. Because of the height of the window being photographed in this photo set-up, the tripod is raised higher than normal by placing its legs on three identical chairs.

35mm camera with a 28–70mm wide-angle zoom lens

Tripod is needed to support the camera since low light levels require a long exposure

Chairs are used to raise the camera level with the windows

Subdued lighting
Light from a bright but overcast sky usually gives the best results when photographing stained glass. In these pictures (*above*) there is an even intensity of color over the glass. Positioning the windows in the viewfinder so that the black metal borders serve to frame the scenes strengthens the resulting effect.

Powerful symmetry
Some of the finest architectural features in churches are to be found high above the heads of the worshippers and visitors below: majestic arches, delicate stained-glass windows, and intricately detailed columns and ceilings.
6 x 6cm camera, 120mm lens, Ektachrome 200, f22, 1/15 sec.

Harmony of tone, *below*
Overcast light is often the least flattering for architectural work. The lack of contrast in this detail, however, has created an image composed of harmonious tones. The only black that can be seen is the view into the interior, framing the window on the other side.
35mm camera, 50mm lens, Ektachrome 100, f11, 1/60 sec.

Indirect lighting, *far left*
The ornately carved stonework and marble floor of this building are seen to best advantage when the sun bounces off the walls of the courtyard and indirectly reaches the interior depicted here.
35mm camera, 35mm lens, Ektachrome 100, f22, 1/125 sec.

Focusing on detail, *left*
By selecting the appropriate focal length lens, or focal setting on a zoom lens, you can isolate a single detail of architectural merit, such as this ancient wooden door and surround, in an otherwise uninteresting scene.
35mm camera, 100mm lens, Kodachrome 200, f8, 1/125 sec.

Selective focus
The choice of a relatively large aperture to focus on the opaque glass and ironwork of this light fixture renders the background slightly out of focus so that it does not compete for attention.
35mm camera, 90mm lens, Kodachrome 64, f5.6, 1/60 sec.

Graphic imagery
By omitting the doors, windows, and other features of this Tudor house, the black of the timbers seen against the white of the infill makes for a strong, graphic image.
35mm camera, 50mm lens, Kodachrome 64, f8, 1/125 sec.

Domestic tungsten, *above*
When shooting an interior, you will often have to rely on the available light. This scene of a stairway is lit by a mixture of natural daylight and domestic tungsten bulbs. Where the tungsten lighting is strongest, a warm orange color-cast is noticeable.
35mm camera, 28mm lens, Ektachrome 200, f8, 1/60 sec.

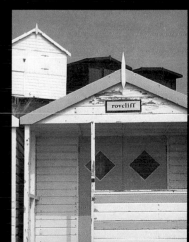

Venetian detail
These candy-striped mooring poles make the location of the image (Venice) immediately obvious to the viewer. There is no need for a wider angle to communicate more clues as to the identity of the locale.
35mm camera, 135mm lens, Kodachrome 200, f11, 1/60 sec.

Interpretative result
For this interior view of the Guggenheim Museum, New York, which has a series of spiraling galleries, the exposure is set for the brightest parts of the scene. The result is an abstract study rather than a descriptive depiction.
35mm camera, 28mm lens, Kodachrome 64, f16, 1/125 sec.

Selective geometry, *right*
All types of architectural styles provide interesting details for the camera lens. In this picture, the view has been carefully chosen so that the image is composed of geometric shapes – squares, rectangles, and triangles.
35mm camera, 85mm lens, Fujichrome 100, f16, 1/250 sec.

NATURE

Photography has an increasingly important role to play in recording the natural world. As human habitation spreads ever deeper into the landscape, submerging meadows and forests, photography can reveal a unique beauty of form, color, and texture that might otherwise pass unnoticed.

Nature in close-up
See pages 184–185

Macrophotography
See pages 186–187

Macro lighting
See pages 188–189

Flowers and shrubs
See pages 194–195

A question of scale

The key to successful nature photography is to move in close to capture the many guises of nature. Close-up photography no longer represents a technical problem. Many modern cameras allow close focusing with ordinary lenses and many zoom lenses also have macro mode settings that let you shoot with the front element almost touching the subject.

Close-up equipment

Additional close-up equipment such as bellows units and extension tubes allow you to get extremely close to your subject. Successful nature photography relies to a large degree on you, the photographer, adjusting your sense of scale. Viewed from a distance, a bluebell patch is a subtle wash of color, but you can move in closer so that your view is of a single plant, and then closer still so that a single flower fills the frame, and then perhaps even closer so that a detail of a single flower is revealed.

Confined view

Although your view is more restricted when working with natural history subjects than when you are photographing landscapes, the basic disciplines that are needed to make good pictures in any field of interest still apply. First, use your judgment to find the most appropriate camera angle from which to photograph your subject. Second, think about the best possible composition and adjust framing to maximize the distribution of color and tone within the frame. Third, experiment with horizontal and vertical framing: even try framing the subject diagonally if that seems best. Finally, consider the lighting for your subject and if it is not appropriate, think about returning at another time of day when the lighting direction and quality are more favorable.

NATURE SET-UP

Photographing this lily pond requires careful framing with a zoom lens to avoid unwanted details. The lighting is diffused, with the sun hidden behind clouds. An overhanging tree also reduces available light. Note how the green of the lily pads seems to be intensified by the heavy shade, while the white lilies show up starkly in comparison. However, conditions change rapidly, and later in the day the sun broke through the clouds to bathe the lilies with direct light and completely change the atmosphere of the scene.

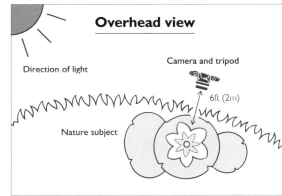

Overhead view

Direction of light

Camera and tripod

6ft (2m)

Nature subject

Effect of sunlight
Direct sunlight lessens the contrast between the lily pads and flowers, but highlights the difference between the plant and the dark, reflective surface of the surrounding water.

Equipment

- 35mm SLR camera and spare film

- Range of lenses including a 100mm macro lens, bellows, and extension tubes

- Adjustable tripod

Camera
A 35mm camera with a 70–210mm zoom lens set at about 90mm and positioned on a tripod. The camera is loaded with medium-speed ISO 200 film.

Lighting
Dappled light from overhanging tree casts shadows over part of the water and intensifies the color saturation of the leaves and flowers beneath.

REVEALING NATURE IN CLOSE-UP

Natural history photography is not restricted to those who have specialized macro lenses. All of the images shown on these pages were taken using a 35mm camera with a 150mm long-focus lens. Many modern zoom lenses also have a macro mode setting, which is useful for smaller subjects (*see page 188*).

The principal problem with close-up shots using either a long-focus or macro lens is the restricted zone of sharp focus, known as the depth of field. This problem is made worse because depth of field is even more restricted at close focusing distances. Small apertures are needed to make sure everything is in focus, and this often results in long shutter speeds, which can introduce problems of camera shake or subject movement. To avoid camera shake, use a tripod and cable release and choose fast film to speed up exposure.

PHOTO SET-UP: Close-up on flowers

Although the subject is lit by bright daylight, a small aperture of f22 results in a shutter speed of 1/60 second. Remember that even at this shutter speed you should wait for any breeze to die down before taking the picture so that subject movement does not spoil the shot.

Viewpoint is chosen so that the camera looks down into the open flowers

35mm camera fixed on a tripod with a 150mm long-focus lens

Natural pattern
The camera looks into the open trumpets of the lilies. The angle of view of the 150mm lens excludes all other details, creating a strong composition of color, pattern, and form.

Professional tips

● Any problems with depth of field can be minimized by finding a straight-on angle that shows all of the subject at the same distance from the camera.

● If photographing live animals, handle them carefully and as little as possible, work quickly, and return them to the same spot that you found them in.

PHOTO SET-UP: Mobile subject
When photographing a mobile subject such as this toad, it is important to confine the animal within an area of its natural habitat. Make sure that the enclosure is sufficiently large and try not to handle the subject too much or keep it confined for longer than necessary.

35mm camera with a 150mm long-focus lens

Tripod is necessary to prevent camera shake during a long exposure

Natural setting provides a camouflaged background for the toad

Large enclosure to keep the toad from escaping

Subject and setting
Successful natural history shots require patience and perseverance. It is always preferable to photograph a subject in a natural setting (*top*). Finding your subject in the right surroundings may take a little time but the results make it well worth the effort (*above*).

Depth of field
The light for this shot is slightly overcast, and this, linked with an aperture of f32 to ensure sufficient depth of field for subject and background, means using a slow shutter speed of 1/30 second. Careful timing of the shot so that the toad is sitting still on the stone results in a sharp image (*left*), whereas even a tiny movement of the toad will cause the picture to be slightly blurred (*above*).

MACROPHOTOGRAPHY

Look at a lens when it is focusing on a close-up subject and you will see that as it moves away from the camera body, the closer the focusing distance becomes. Many zoom lenses have a macro setting that extends the lens beyond its normal range.

MACRO TECHNIQUES

Macro lenses have greatly extended focusing ranges and they are used for high-definition, close-up photography. Other close-up techniques involve using extension tubes or bellows between the camera body and lens. Lighting for macro shots can be difficult since the camera, lens, and tripod are so close that they may cast unwanted shadows. This problem can be partly overcome by using a longer 100mm lens rather than a standard 50mm lens on a 35mm camera. Ring flash offers the most controllable form of lighting for close-up subjects (*see box opposite*).

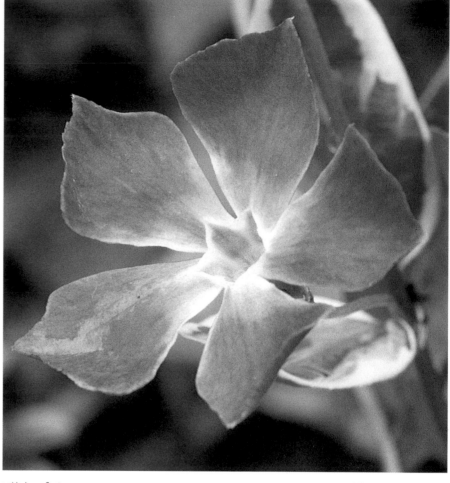

PHOTO SET-UP: Macro lens

When working at very close distances, even the most minute degree of subject movement will result in a very blurred image. To prevent any movement of the flower in this set-up, a white cardboard reflector is propped up on one side to act as a windbreak. The stem of the flower can also be secured using a piece of wire (*see inset*).

35mm camera on a tripod
with a 100mm macro lens

White cardboard helps reflect
light onto the subject and shield
the subject from any air currents

Cable release allows you to fire the
shutter without touching the camera
and perhaps causing vibrations that
would spoil the picture

Length of wire
attached to the rear
wall is used to hold
the flower steady

Periwinkle
The blue flower is separated from the background by selecting a wide aperture. Depth of field for close-up shots is shallow, making accurate focusing critical.

Professional tips

● Lighting the subject solely with flash will give you a sharp image if all subject movement cannot be eliminated.

● If you have a choice, use the longest focal length macro available. A 100mm lens gives greater magnification, allowing more space between the camera and the subject.

Water lily, *above*
Restricted depth of field emphasizes the flower and gives a sense of depth.

Pale rose, *left*
Ring flash produces an almost shadowless result and creates an exposure difference that shows the background subdued by slight underexposure.

Rose and dew, *far left*
The beads of dew add extra interest to this picture of a rose. The effect is easily achieved by misting the flower with a water spray.

Macro and close-up equipment

The term macrophotography describes film images that are life-sized or larger. For 35mm SLRs and the various medium-format roll-film cameras, the most flexible systems for macro and general close-up work include macro lenses, bellows, and extension tubes.

Macro lenses

Macro lenses for 35mm SLRs range from 50mm to 200mm. Although they can be used for ordinary work, they are designed to give best resolution for subjects very close to the lens. Sharpness is slightly poorer for distant subjects in comparison with an ordinary lens. A macro lens is expensive and should be considered only for specialized close-up work.

60mm macro lens

100mm macro lens

Bellows unit

Fitting a bellows onto your camera gives you a wide range of possible image magnifications. One end of the bellows fits into the camera while the other accepts a normal lens. Moving the bellows along its track takes the lens closer to or farther away from the subject to alter magnification.

Standard bellows

27.5mm extension   **14mm extension**

105mm extension

Extension tubes

Extension tubes, usually available in sets of three, can be used individually or in combination to alter lens-to-film distance, and so produce fixed degrees of subject magnification.

Ring flash

This specialized unit has a circular flash tube that fits around the front element of the lens. Designed for use with small close-up subjects, it gives an almost shadowless light effect.

Ring flash for 35mm camera

LIGHTING FOR INDOOR MACRO

In order to take close-ups of small subjects such as butterflies, insects, coins, or jewelry, you often need to position the camera lens extremely close to your subject. This can result in problems, since the camera and lens are so close that it may be difficult to get sufficient light where it is needed. A 100mm macro lens makes lighting easier since it allows you to work farther away from your subject.

Enhancing the subject
It is important to use the right lighting to enhance your subject's form, color, or other characteristics. The differences in these pictures are startling, with sidelighting used for the first image (*far left*), and diffused toplighting for the second image (*left*).

Directional light
Strong, directional light from the right-hand side of this small red butterfly emphasizes the texture and color contrasts. Sidelighting also highlights the deeply grooved surface of the wood on which the insect has been placed.

PHOTO SET-UP: Directional lighting
A single flash lighting unit is used in this set-up. The light is positioned low down to give a strongly directional effect. The snoot attachment ensures that a concentrated beam of light falls onto the subject.

Adjustable lighting stand

Flash lighting unit with a snoot attachment

35mm camera with a 100mm macro lens

Cable release

Power pack

Synchronization lead

Soft lighting
This time the small red butterfly has been lit with soft light from above. Its color and shape are now more obviously the subject of the photograph, the wood background is less intrusive, and the effect of the toplighting is warmer.

PHOTO SET-UP: Diffused toplighting
Toplighting is provided by a flash unit fitted with a softbox diffuser. Although this amount of light may seem overpowering for a small subject, much of the light is lost due to the proximity of the camera, lens, and tripod.

Flash lighting unit with a softbox diffuser

Cable release

35mm camera with a 100mm macro lens

Adjustable lighting stand

Power pack

Synchronization lead

Blue butterfly
With some subjects, the direction of the lighting will have a profound effect on the way their color is recorded. For this image, diffused toplighting was used so the brilliant blue and black-edged coloration of the butterfly's wings is highlighted.

Gray butterfly
Although the subject is the same blue butterfly (*left*), strong sidelighting produces a very different picture. Here the insect is illuminated by light reflected up through its translucent wings from the surface of the stone, rather than from above.

Professional tips

• If you do not have a snoot, cut a hole in the center of a piece of card to create a narrow beam of light.

• Lighting is easier using a long lens and bellows since you are able to work farther away from the subject.

• Extremely shallow depth of field associated with close-ups means working with a small aperture.

• A ring flash is useful for lighting a small subject.

Light and texture, *far left*
In this shot, intense sunlight falls
at an angle that accentuates the
rich color of the fungus and the
texture of the supporting bark.
*35mm camera, 90mm lens,
Fujichrome 100, f16, 1/125 sec.*

Abstract effect, *left*
At first glance, this picture seems to
be an abstract pattern of shapes in
the long grass. In fact, the subject is
a field of fallen apples.
*35mm camera, 50mm lens,
Ektachrome 100, f11, 1/60 sec.*

Wide aperture
A large flower can be photographed
without specialized equipment. To
keep the background from being
too prominent, use a wide aperture.
*6 x 6cm camera, 150mm lens,
Ektachrome 200, f4, 1/60 sec.*

New life

A few days before being photographed, this fern barely showed above the soil. Part of the fascination of nature photography is the awareness it gives you of the natural cycle of growth and decay.
35mm camera, 80mm lens, Fujichrome 100, f8, 1/30 sec.

Color rendition

The color of the toadstools varies subtly, from near white to blue, according to where the sunlight and shadows fall.
35mm camera, 135mm lens (plus extension tube), Kodachrome 64, f16, 1/15 sec.

Supplementary lighting

With a tightly framed subject, it is possible to supplement lighting with a flashgun. The angles of the flash and natural light must correspond to prevent a double set of shadows.
35mm camera, 100mm macro lens, Ektachrome 100, f22, 1/60 sec.

Early morning

Crisp, clear, winter sunshine has a particular steely clarity not found at other times of the year. To record the frost still clinging to evergreen leaves, however, you need to photograph your subject early in the morning before the sun has warmed the surrounding air.
35mm camera, 135mm lens, Ektachrome 200, f5.6, 1/30 sec.

PHOTOGRAPHING GARDENS

When taking a picture of a garden setting, the details of the location are less important than the way in which they interact with each other to create a unified whole. A standard and a wide-angle lens are generally more useful than longer focal lengths, though this depends on the size of the garden and the vantage points its design and layout allow.

THE GARDEN AT ITS BEST

Gardens are at their best at different times of the year, depending on the plants – some are spectacular in early summer when in full bloom, while others may be spring or fall gardens. The time of day is also important. To the naked eye, a garden may look most impressive in bright, midday sunlight; on film, however, early morning and late afternoon light usually produce the best results.

House and garden, *above*
The vantage point shown in the photo set-up results in this charming image of an idyllic country house surrounded by its garden.

PHOTO SET-UP: Garden as a setting
This is a mature garden, and the house is an integral part of the overall setting. By positioning the camera on the riverbank opposite the house, it is possible to convey some of the atmosphere of the scene.

Fast moving water adds vitality to the scene

Direction of the shadows indicates afternoon sunlight, which tends to be better for recording the color and texture of plants

6 x 7cm camera on a tripod with a 90mm standard lens

Use of color
At first glance, this formal garden setting at Villandry, France, appears to be a riot of random color separated by trimmed and shaped hedges. However, the repetition of colors, notably the yellow, leads the gaze back toward the château.

Leading the eye
Many devices can be used to direct attention to a specific area of the picture frame. It could be the repetitive use of color or, as here, a statue that seems to compel you to follow its gaze into a sheltered corner of a much larger garden setting.

PHOTOGRAPHING FLOWERS AND SHRUBS

Unless carefully considered, photographs of flowerbeds and planted borders can be a disappointing amalgam of discordant color with no particular center of interest, form, or structure. Avoid this pitfall by finding an individual plant or group of plants around which to build your composition. Once you have this focal point, look for angles that show other parts of the garden in supporting roles to give your picture a coherent structure.

EQUIPMENT AND CONDITIONS

The selective angle of view of a long-focus lens is best for filling the frame with an individual plant. Wind is the main problem when photographing flowers. Gusty conditions require a fast shutter speed to avoid subject movement, and this in turn requires a wide aperture, resulting in shallow depth of field.

PHOTO SET-UP: Coordinating color

By concentrating on flowerbed and planting details you can create an interesting picture, even if the garden as a whole does not have photographic potential. The chief attraction of the flowerbed shown in this photo set-up is the coordinated color theme. The flowerbed is in shade, which accounts for the slight intensifying of the color.

Flowerbed detail, *above*
A harmonious theme of lilacs, mauves, pinks, and reds unites this flowerbed detail, with the whites and greens acting to cool the warmth of the other colors.

Kneeling down on one knee creates a steady camera position

Hand-held 35mm camera with a 90mm long-focus lens

Area of flowerbed in direct sunlight contrasts well with the shadowy areas

Intensity of color in the front part of flowerbed is due to the angle of light

Still image
Any slight movement will be noticeable when you take photographs of flowers and plants. If you do not use a windbreak to prevent movement, wait for the wind to die down, or use a fast shutter speed.

Traditional garden
A landscaped garden is often designed to be seen with the house it surrounds. The stately appearance of this 16th-century house is reinforced by the climbing roses following the outline of the arched windows, and the perennials planted in the foreground.

Frame-filling form

Large flower heads, such as that of this sunflower, allow you to take detailed, frame-filling close-ups without going to the expense of using specialized macro equipment. Here the bloom dominates the frame, even though it was taken using only a moderately long lens. *35mm camera, 90mm lens, Kodachrome 64, f11, 1/125 sec.*

Indoor light levels

An exotic *clivia* photographed in a large, glass-covered conservatory requires a slow shutter speed. A wide aperture ensures correct exposure for the dim conditions, since the flower is surrounded by other plants and lit only by daylight filtering through the glass. *6 x 6cm camera, 80mm lens, Ektachrome 100, f4, 1/15 sec.*

Controlled imagery, *above*
A combination of aperture, focal length, and camera distance produces this image of a brilliant red hibiscus flower. The green leaves are softened and out of focus but add extra information and interest to the picture. *35mm camera, 70mm lens, Fujichrome 100, f5.6, 1/60 sec.*

Ring flash, *opposite*
By fitting a ring flash to the lens, exposure on the orchid bloom alone is increased, making the background appear much darker in comparison. The ring flash gives almost shadowless illumination of the orchid itself. *35mm camera, 100mm lens, Ektachrome 100, f11, 1/60 sec.*

PHOTOGRAPHING GARDEN ARCHITECTURE

It is quite common to find ornate structures, such as dovecotes, summerhouses, follies, and even classical temples in large gardens. The best way to photograph garden architecture does not differ from that used for any other outdoor architecture, except that the setting – the garden itself – should be an integral part of the photograph. For a harmonious composition, try to imagine how the landscape designer planned the garden to be viewed, and visit it at different times of the day to capture the best lighting effect.

Before shooting, try to find the vantage point that shows the garden to best advantage. The garden may vary from different viewpoints, at particular times of the day, in certain seasons, or when seen from a distance.

PHOTO SET-UP: Afternoon light

A low, bright afternoon sun in a sky strewn with white clouds provides the perfect illumination and backdrop for this building – a large dovecote, with box hedges and an ornamental fish pond in the foreground.

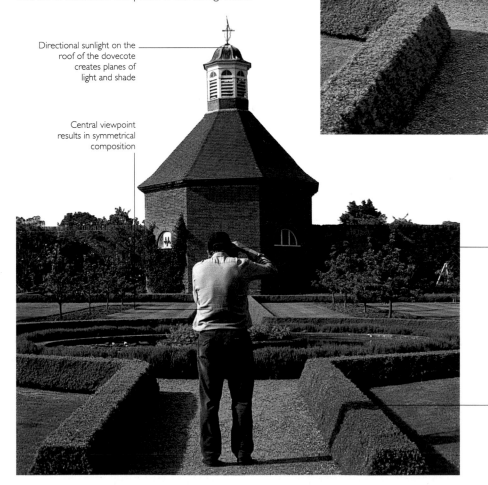

Directional sunlight on the roof of the dovecote creates planes of light and shade

Central viewpoint results in symmetrical composition

Hand-held 35mm camera with a 28mm wide-angle lens

Long shadows indicate that the sun is low in the sky

Symmetry, *above*
This viewpoint records the symmetrical arrangement of clipped box hedges, the circular fish pond, and the avenue of trees leading to the large brick dovecote.

Professional tips

● Avoid shooting when the sun is high in the sky, since this tends to produce excessive contrast and poor color saturation.

● Look for a camera angle that corresponds to the way the garden was originally intended to be viewed.

Romantic image, *left*
This image successfully captures the romantic and secluded atmosphere evoked by the ruined, medieval-type folly.

Silent grotto, *above*
Framed by lavender and roses, this folly is the perfect backdrop for this small garden. The angle of the light creates added impact.

PHOTO SET-UP: Ruined folly
The position of this folly in a quiet, shady corner of the garden makes a slow shutter speed and the use of a tripod essential. Although the day is bright, much of the light is obscured by the overhanging foliage. The need for a small aperture to ensure adequate depth of field results in a long exposure time.

Overhanging foliage casts dappled shade over the folly

Flower colors help brighten the resulting image

Tripod-mounted 35mm camera with a 50mm standard lens

RECORDING GARDEN FEATURES

The finishing touches to a landscaped garden are the ornaments used and the focal points created by them. Statues, urns, garden seats, pergolas, rose arches, and similar devices are the nonorganic features intended by the garden designer to enhance the beauty of the setting, and they can make ideal subjects.

For small garden features and close-ups of larger ones, a 35mm SLR camera fitted with a 100mm lens is useful. This lens allows you to exclude extraneous detail, but the angle of view is not so narrow that it removes all traces of the setting.

PHOTO SET-UP: Garden statue

To photograph this garden statue, it is important to wait until the sun is low in the sky so that the bust is lit from an angle of about 45°. This lighting direction is best suited to show the bust's texture and form, which are emphasized by the interaction of light and shade (see *page 46*).

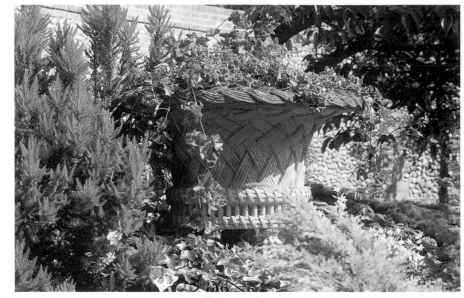

Decorative urn, *above*
A low camera angle is essential to show the decorative basketweave molding on this garden urn.

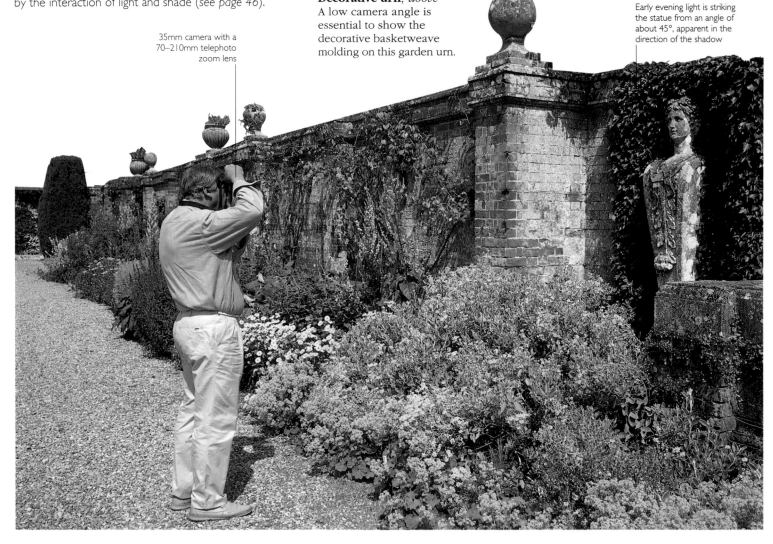

35mm camera with a
70–210mm telephoto
zoom lens

Early evening light is striking the statue from an angle of about 45°, apparent in the direction of the shadow

Garden statue
The lichen-covered garden statue in the photo set-up is made to stand out from the surrounding greenery by using a long lens with a restricted angle of view.

Selecting a detail
A telephoto zoom is useful for isolating a garden detail and finely adjusting subject framing without changing the camera position.

Informal planting

A rich and varied planting theme using a mixed color palette has been created by the designer of this garden. The yellow rose bushes in the background create a feeling of depth and distance.
35mm camera, 35mm lens, Fujichrome 100, f16, 1/250 sec.

Sculpted beauty

The formal topiary shapes in this garden create large blocks of dense, hard-edged greenery, unlike the softer, more organic shapes normally associated with garden photography. A carefully chosen camera angle allows a tunnel-like view through to the rear of the garden.
35mm camera, 50mm lens, Ektachrome 200, f16, 1/30 sec.

Water view
The early morning light shows up perfectly the shades of green and still water in this shot of the gardens at Stourhead, England.
35mm camera, 35mm lens.

ANIMALS

Animals have long held a fascination for the photographer. While luck can play a part in taking a successful wildlife photograph, a knowledge of animal behavior is essential, as are patience and perseverance. When the opportunity for a good shot arises, you should be prepared to act quickly.

Wild animals
See pages 206–207

Birds
See pages 208–209

Pet portraits
See pages 210–211

Pets on location
See pages 210–211

Early cameras and lenses

Until the early years of the twentieth century, the only pictures you were likely to see of wild animals were of dead specimens. Cameras and lenses were bulky and film so insensitive and slow that long exposures of several minutes were common. Rather than seeing a picture of a bird in flight, you were more likely to be confronted by a photograph of a stuffed collector's specimen behind a protective glass dome. Today, with cameras a fraction of their former size, and lenses and film hundreds of times faster, the scope for photographing wild animals in their natural habitat is vast.

Wild animals

Most of us normally see wild animals only in zoos, nature reserves, wildlife and safari parks, and animal sanctuaries, but the spread of human habitation into the countryside and wilderness areas has brought humans into closer contact with many animal species. Even if accustomed to the presence of people, wild animals should always be approached with caution. Long-focus lenses allow you to stand back from your subject, and fast film permits a brief shutter speed or small lens aperture for freezing subject movement or creating the necessary depth of field.

Domestic animals

The most readily available animal subjects for photography are, of course, pets. Since most pets, especially dogs and cats, are not at all camera shy, you will be able to move in much closer and use a shorter lens. Try for portraits that show your pet's facial expression, and remember that shots taken from the animal's eye level usually work better than ones taken from standing height. Be prepared to shoot a lot of film and select the best shots afterward.

ANIMAL SET-UP

The location for this set-up picture is the reptile house in a safari park. Light levels are not high in the glazed building due to the dense vegetation. The rail surrounding the observation platform makes an ideal surface on which to steady the camera during the long exposure.

Overhead view

Direction of light

Camera

12ft (3.5m) camera-to-subject distance

Animal subject

Surroundings
Overhanging palm leaves and other vegetation shade the subject and reduce light levels.

Camera
Hand-held 35mm camera fitted with a 70–210mm zoom lens. The camera is loaded with fast ISO 400 film.

Tight framing
Using a zoom lens allows you to adjust framing to exclude unwanted detail. Low ambient light levels result in a slow shutter speed of only 1/60 second.

Camera support
Safety rails surrounding the platform make a suitable surface for steadying the camera.

Animal subject
Crocodile is asleep and oblivious to the camera so subject movement is not a problem, allowing a slow exposure.

Equipment

- 35mm SLR camera and fast film

- Tripod if necessary

- Range of lenses including long-focus lenses and converters

PHOTOGRAPHING WILD ANIMALS

Although bars and wire fences can present a problem when photographing wild animals in captivity, modern enclosures with high observation walkways offer superb picture-taking opportunities. As with all animal photography, the most important attributes required are patience and timing.

ELIMINATING UNWANTED ELEMENTS

A high camera position can often eliminate an unattractive background by showing the animal subject against a backdrop of grass or stone. If this is not possible, use a long-focus or zoom lens and a wide aperture to restrict angle of view and depth of field. A motor drive is useful since you do not have to look up from the viewfinder to advance the film.

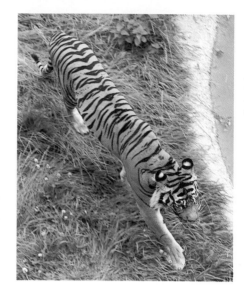

Overhead viewpoint
The viewpoint shown in the photo set-up results in these photographs in which the subject is seen against a background of grass and foliage. The diffused sunlight is excellent, because it ensures that the rich color of the tiger's coat is well recorded.

PHOTO SET-UP: Wildlife park
The high walkway at a wildlife park is the perfect vantage point for this photo set-up overlooking a large enclosure of Sumatran tigers. A long-focus lens with a x2 converter ensures that the framing is tight on the tiger and that none of the resulting shots reveals the encircling safety fences.

Hand-held 35mm camera with a 135mm long-focus lens and x 2 converter

Patience is required to wait for the subject to adopt a suitable pose

Safety rail makes a convenient support to steady the hand-held camera – camera shake, even at fast shutter speeds, is always a risk when using a long-focus lens

Timing, *opposite*
A slight change in the tiger's posture or facial expression can make all the difference between an ordinary or an outstanding shot. Working with an unpredictable subject means that you have to keep your finger on the shutter release at all times. In this shot the tiger momentarily looks back toward the camera.

Background is excluded from resulting picture by tight framing of animal subject

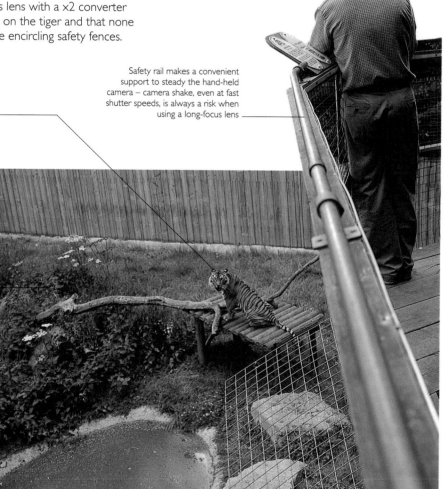

Professional tips

- In a wildlife park, obey all the safety rules and take no risks.

- Take the minimum equipment if you are stalking wildlife.

- A motor drive may disturb the animals.

- Bring out the color of your animal subject by including contrasting vegetation in the shot.

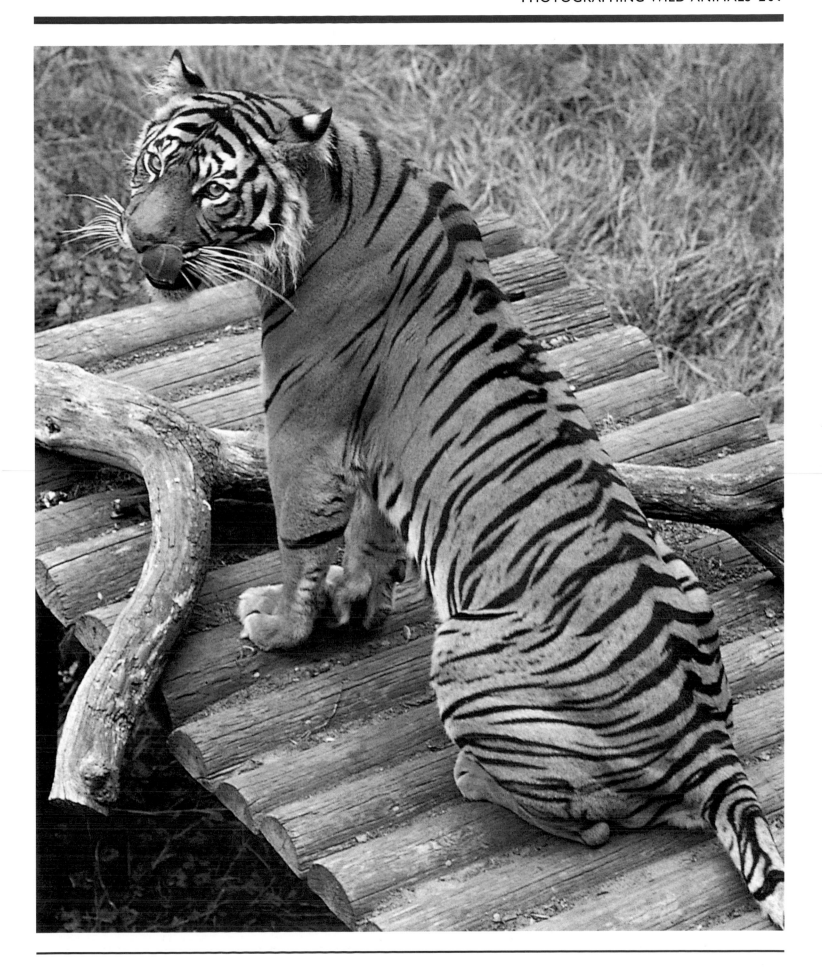

PHOTOGRAPHING BIRDS

With their senses of hearing and sight far sharper than our own, wild birds can be difficult subjects to observe and to photograph. Whether or not your intended subjects will let you come within camera range often depends on whether they regard you as a potential threat or just as a harmless observer.

OBSERVING BIRDS

Many birds, such as common garden visitors, and others found in parks, sanctuaries, and lakesides have developed a tolerance of people and can be easily approached. However, it is best to assume that all wild birds will be cautious, making a long-focus lens and tripod essential for detailed close-ups. To avoid scaring birds, keep out of sight, using natural cover or a manmade shelter if available, and make as little noise as possible.

PHOTO SET-UP: Nesting birds
You cannot approach too close to nesting birds since they may damage the eggs or even abandon the nest. A long-focus lens and converter is useful for recording detailed images of the birds without causing unnecessary stress.

Canada goose's nest is well hidden in tall grass, with the bird keeping very still

35mm camera with a 300mm lens and fitted with a x2 converter, which increases the focal length to 600mm

Tripod is essential for sharp images because of the slow shutter speed and the weight of the long-focus lens

White swan
Surrounded by tall reeds, this swan's nest is sunlit for only a short period each day. Without this direct sunlight, the swan's white plumage would take on a gray coloration, and the surrounding plants would lose their vibrancy of color.

Canada goose
Although in a sleeping position, with its head resting on its back, this goose is alert to danger. A 300mm long-focus lens with a x2 converter is used to avoid getting too close to the subject and possibly frightening it.

PHOTO SET-UP: Natural camouflage

The less obvious your presence, the more natural the behavior of the birds that you want to photograph will be. These geese are aware of the intruder, but with the lake nearby for a quick escape they are not too concerned. A 500mm long-focus lens makes it possible to use natural cover and to be positioned some distance from the subject.

Family outing, *above*
This family scene shows a clutch of goslings under the guardianship of two adult geese. Depth of field with the 500mm lens is shallow and isolates the birds from the surroundings.

Lighting direction, *above*
Patient observation results in natural-looking pictures. Here a concealed camera position is used to record the same goose family swimming on the lake.

Conveniently located tree provides cover

35mm camera with a 500mm lens

Tripod is essential to avoid camera shake because of the combined weight of the camera and lens

Geese congregate near the water for a swift escape if necessary

PHOTOGRAPHING PETS

Many people regard their pet as one of the family, so it is not surprising that owners often want an animal portrait and that this is a popular area of photography. The main difficulty is persuading the animal to stay still long enough to be photographed.

DECIDING ON A SETTING

The controlled environment of an indoor setting is ideal if you want a detailed, well-illuminated, and carefully composed image of your pet. However, if you are working with an animal that you do not know, make sure the owner is present and that it is well trained and not of a nervous disposition. For more informal portraits you can choose an outdoor location. Depending on the animal being photographed, your back yard, a local park, or a beach could make a perfect setting.

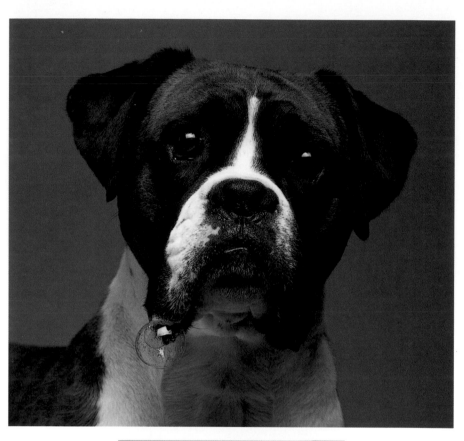

Full-length portrait
This portrait of a Boxer shows the dog's stance and facial expression, as well as its distinctive markings and coloring.

Close-up portrait
An endearing image is achieved by closing in on the dog's face. The bubble at the corner of his mouth makes the portrait amusing.

White reflector board is positioned to return light from the flash opposite

Single lighting head fitted with a softbox diffuser produces soft, even illumination on the table

Cloth covering the table helps reflect additional illumination

Owner makes sure the dog is looking in the right direction for each shot

6 x 6cm camera with a 120mm long-focus lens

Power pack

PHOTO SET-UP: Working with pets
Animals can be very difficult to photograph in an unfamiliar environment and may need to be restrained. A large dog can be a danger to those around it if it becomes frightened, and it could also damage equipment. A useful tip is to remember that most pets respond to their owner. In this set-up, the dog's attention is focused on its owner, who is standing out of shot, and on the rubber ball she is holding.

A boy and his dog, *left*
This close-up image of the boy and dog was taken using a long-focus zoom lens to alter framing without having to change the camera position, which might distract the dog.

Dog on the move, *above*
The Dalmatian's high spirits are illustrated in the first image, as the dog pulls against the leash. The boy lets the dog run along the sand, the surface of which throws back reflections.

PHOTO SET-UP: Pets on location

Early morning is chosen for the photographic session because at this time of day the beach is nearly deserted. The dog's young owner helps to keep his pet's high spirits in check, and a low camera angle ensures that both faces can be clearly seen. A long-focus zoom lens is especially useful when the dog is off the leash and running freely.

35mm camera with a 70–210mm long-focus zoom lens allows a range of framing options

Boy squats down beside the dog to restrain him, bringing their faces level

Wet surface of the sand acts as a mirror, reflecting the images of the boy and the spotted dog

Professional tips

• Be ready to react quickly to an animal's changeable and unpredictable moods.

• Using an autofocus and autoexposure camera, you can give your complete attention to the animal.

• Use a long-focus zoom lens for shots taken in rapid succession.

Exposure override, *above*
To prevent overexposure of this toucan perched in sunlight with the dark forest behind, the exposure reading is overridden by increasing the recommended shutter speed by one f-stop.
35mm camera, 135mm lens, Ektachrome 200, f 60 sec.

Shooting through glass, *left*
Some zoos and wildlife parks provide observation windows so that the public can see a different view of the animals, such as this pair of seals. The water is clear and shallow enough to allow sufficient light to filter through from the surface for a hand-held exposure using medium-fast film.
35mm camera, 135mm lens, Fujichrome 400, f8, 1/125 sec.

Shooting through mesh, *far left*
The mesh surrounding this tiger's zoo enclosure is rendered invisible by placing the front of the camera lens close to the wire and then selecting a wide aperture.
35mm camera, 300mm lens, Ektachrome 200, f8, 1/60 sec.

Camera angle, *left*
An unusual camera angle can often hide an unwanted background. To disguise its zoo enclosure, a high vantage point is used for this shot of a swimming tiger.
35 mm camera, 100 mm lens, Ektachrome 200, f4, 1/30 sec.

Choice of aperture

A wide lens aperture is selected for this shot of a tree frog. The shallow depth of field resulting from the aperture separates the small creature from a similarly colored background. A very fast shutter speed is used to arrest any sudden movement of the subject or hand-held camera.

35mm camera, 135mm lens, Ektachrome 200, f2.8, 1/2000 sec.

Backlighting

When any subject is backlit, such as this puma sunning itself on a log platform, you need to select a wide aperture (or use a slow shutter speed) to avoid any risk of underexposing the subject.

35mm camera, 210mm lens, Fujichrome 100, f5.6, 1/125 sec.

IMAGE MANIPULATION

A wide range of photographic techniques can be used to create special effect photographs that are far removed from normal images. This section shows effects that can be achieved by using special films, by darkroom manipulations of both color and black and white originals, and by combining traditional photographic chemistry with the wizardry of modern computers.

SPECIAL FILMS

Using special films is a simple way to create unusual imagery. Special films include black and white and color infra-red-sensitive emulsions and high-contrast recording film.

Infra-red film is sensitive to the infra-red region of the electromagnetic spectrum and can therefore record images by light that is normally invisible. The film is usually used in conjunction with an infra-red-transmitting filter over the camera lens, which blocks all visible lightwaves. Infra-red radiation comes into focus on a slightly different plane than visible light, so you may need to adjust your lens according to the infra-red focusing index (a red or orange line engraved next to the ordinary focus index on the lens barrel).

Special recording film mainly registers black and white, rather than the intervening shades of gray. To achieve a similar effect, use regular black and white emulsion film, then use high-contrast film developer and print onto high-contrast lith paper.

Color infra-red
This film can be used in conjunction with colored filters for a range of special effects. The result will depend on how much individual elements in a scene reflect infra-red radiation, as illustrated (*left*) and (*above left*). Some elements reflect no infra-red, appearing near-black.

Striking tones, *above*
Atmospheric haze is invisible to black and white infra-red film, so images taken with it are often rendered with great clarity. In addition, striking tones are made apparent, notably the snowy white foliage in this scene, which seems to give the image an almost surreal appearance.

Grain effect, *right*
Film manufacturers go to great lengths to produce ultra-fast emulsions with the minimum amount of graininess. However, if you want to achieve the type of impressionistic result shown here, use a fast ISO 3200 emulsion and then develop the film in a grain-enhancing developer.

Streaky light effect
The atmosphere of this carnival scene at dusk was enhanced by using artificial-light film. There is still enough natural daylight present to give the canvas tops a distinct blue cast, while using a slow shutter speed has recorded the fairground lights as colorful blurred streaks.

High-contrast treatment
A scene that is inherently contrasty provides the best starting point for this technique. Photographed on ordinary black and white emulsion, this image of a horse and young rider in the burned ruins of a barn was developed in a high-contrast developer to suppress most of the half-tones and then printed onto lith paper. The final image, although stark, has a rich sense of pattern.

MULTIPLE IMAGES

There are many ways to create multiple images on film. One simple method is to use a mini-strobe flashgun, which fires a rapid burst of flashes during a single exposure. A moving subject will be caught in a different position every time the flash goes off. However, too much ambient lighting will cause blurring in the final image. On some cameras it is possible to reset the shutter without advancing the film; you can then make repeat exposures either on top of each image or in selected areas.

SANDWICHING

The traditional and easiest technique for creating multiple images is to sandwich film originals together in a single slide mount and project the result onto a screen. This can then be rephotographed directly. Alternatively, the film sandwich can simply be loaded into an enlarger and printed in the normal fashion.

Seeing double
Dress your model in black clothes and place him in a darkened room. Take a series of flash-lit shots with the shutter held open on setting B. Get your model to shift position for each shot. When superimposed, the final images can make a dramatic composition.

Slide sandwich
A slide of Greek windmills and one of reflections in water were sandwiched to make this image. To create a sandwich, first experiment by combining different slides on a light box, then mount your chosen slides for projection or reshooting, or to use in the enlarger for printing.

Strobed action, *above*
The flash used to take
this multiple image of a
boxer is an amateur unit
capable of only six rapid
flashes. Professional
plug-in strobe units are
also used by athletes to
make detailed photographic
records of their events,
which are then used to
analyze how slight changes
in technique could improve
their performance.

Dancing leaf
To achieve this intriguing
shot, an assistant dressed
in black clothes waved
around a leaf on a length
of dark wire within a
predetermined space. The
leaf was lit throughout the
6-second exposure with
tungsten lamps, while a
flash was manually fired
four times to create a
mixture of frozen detail
and blurred movement.

BLACK AND WHITE DARKROOM TECHNIQUES

There are many techniques available for working in black and white; the few radical effects here are just a sample. These include printing a negative in combination with a patterned screen to break up the image, or introducing color into a print by hand or by chemical toning.

Changes you may want to make to an image include rectifying tonal imbalances. The sky in a landscape, for example, may have been overexposed if the land required extra exposure to define enough detail. In this case, give the sky on the negative extra exposure under the enlarger to balance the picture.

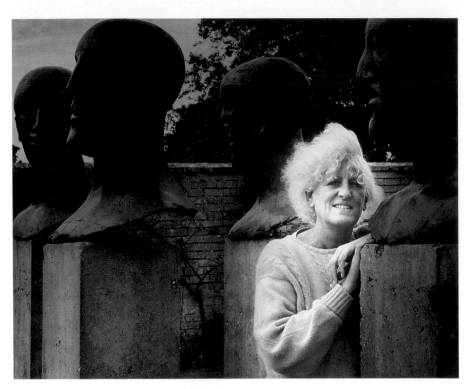

Patterned screens
Various effects are possible by printing with patterned screens. The chimneys (*below*) were printed with a linear screen and the ponies with a mezzotint (*below right*). Screens can also be used for color.

Local density, *right*
A shaped piece of dark cardboard known as a dodger was held over the the image of the sculptor Elisabeth Frink on the printing paper for the last quarter of the exposure time under the enlarger.

Color toning
In this darkroom process, the black metallic silver of black and white printing paper or film is dyed different colors. A normal print or film image is first immersed in a special chemical bleaching agent and then in a toning solution. The color toners used in these three images are sepia, copper, and blue, respectively.

Hand coloring, *opposite*
Any normal black and white print produced on fiber-based paper can be the starting point for artificial coloring. The density of the black metallic silver making up the image is first reduced using a chemical bleaching agent, either partially or all over. Color is then applied using a brush and watercolor, acrylic, or oil paints.

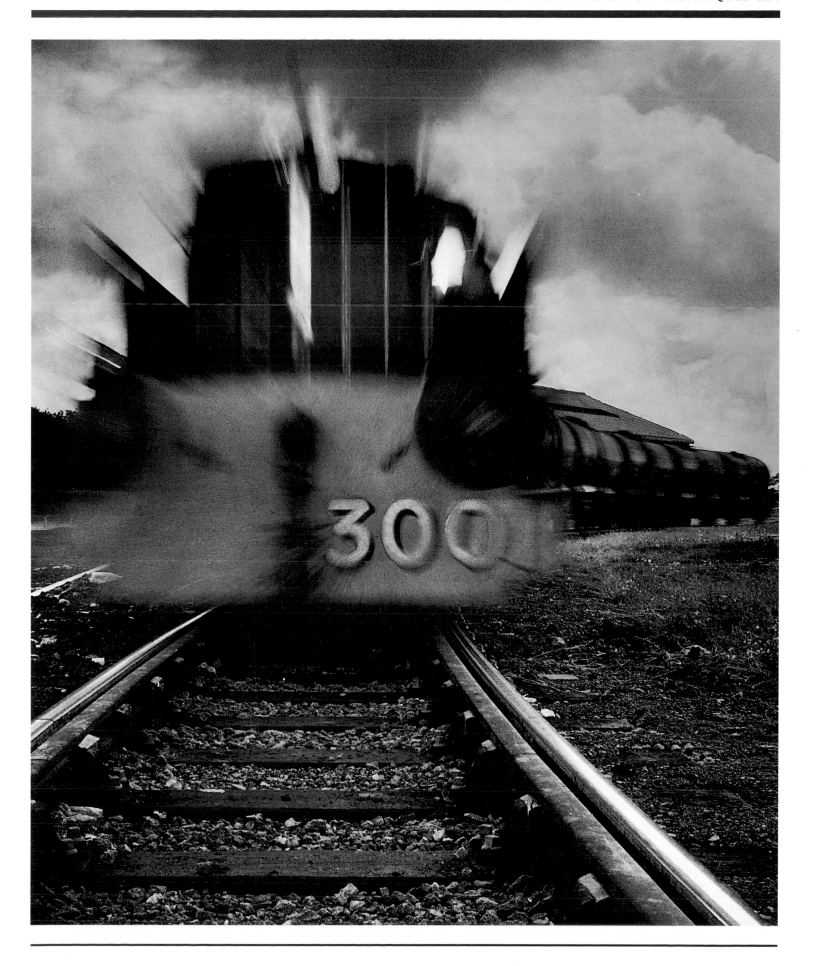

SOLARIZATION AND LITH FILM SANDWICHING

Solarization (also called the Sabattier effect) is a technique for producing a black and white or color image that is part positive, part negative. This is done by exposing the partially developed image (on paper or film) to white light. For the best results, a contrasty image should be used, because the re-exposure flattens contrast considerably.

To solarize, introduce light selectively when a print is partially developed in a tray – using a small flashlight is a handy way to do this. A more advanced technique is to solarize a film negative or positive. You can then make as many prints as you want.

Lith film sandwiches are made by contact printing a lith film negative to form a lith film positive, then placing the two together in register. You can then make prints from this sandwich onto either black and white or color printing paper, with good results.

Black and white effect
A normal black and white print was the starting point for this image. A black and white copy negative was then made from it. The negative was then solarized and used to make a print on regular black and white printing paper.

Color solarization
For this striking image, a copy negative was made from a 35mm transparency, then solarized using a color head enlarger. The color of a film image can be altered by adjusting the filtration of the light used for solarization.

Black and white lith
To produce this print, a lith film positive was first made, then contact printed to make a lith film negative. The negative and positive were finally sandwiched in register. Print developer was used for processing, because it softens the high-contrast effect of lith film.

Color lith
For this color result, the negative/positive lith film sandwich described above was used together with color printing paper. A wide range of color variations is possible by making appropriate adjustments to the filtration controls on the enlarger.

COLOR MASKING TECHNIQUES

All the images shown here were printed from slides onto positive/positive color printing paper, which is designed to produce a positive print from a positive original. The color response of the prints was manipulated using different types of mask.

A highlight mask is made by contact printing a slide onto high-contrast lith film. The slide and lith mask are then combined in register and printed. The highlight areas of the slide print as black or gray depending on the density of the lith; other areas appear normal. To adjust the colors of the shadow areas, first make print-sized negative and positive masks from the slide. With the slide in the enlarger and the positive mask in contact with the printing paper, make a first exposure. Remove the positive and register the negative mask in contact with the paper, then expose to light to tint the shadows.

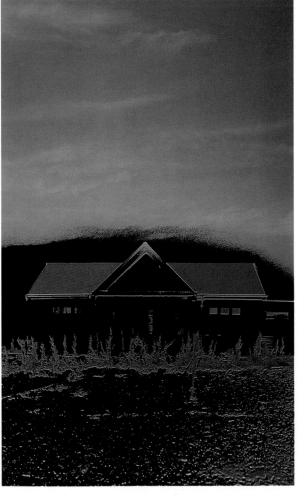

Shadow mask, *above*
The shadow colors here were created by first using a positive mask in contact with the printing paper. This covered the shadow areas, but the rest of the print was normally exposed. Another exposure was made with a negative mask, and the enlarger filtration controls set appropriately.

Flat area mask, *far left*
A negative and a positive mask were contact printed in register to produce this effect. With the slide in the enlarger, the paper was exposed for three-quarters of the correct exposure time. The positive mask was then removed and the exposure completed.

Solarization effect, *left*
This print was made in the same manner described above, but the enlarger lens aperture was increased by one f-stop, so doubling the amount of light reaching the paper and creating a pseudo-solarization effect. A colored filter was also used to produce an eerie, surreal result.

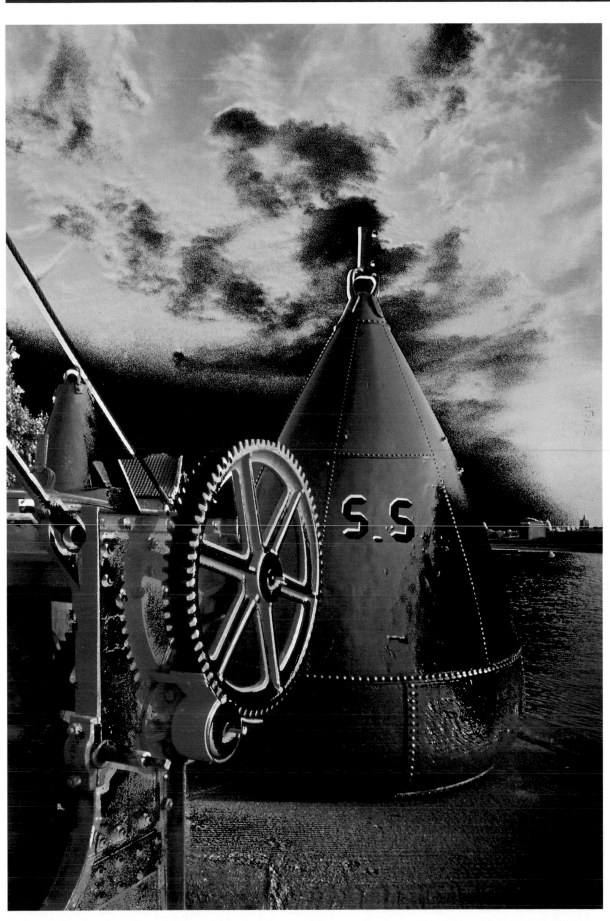

Highlight masking
This technique involves a lith film negative mask being printed in register with the slide original. Depending on the density of tone, the mask keeps a certain amount of light from shining through the highlight areas of the slide. However, if the mask is tinted rather than left as a gray tone, as it was here, dramatic prints with a mixture of real and unreal colors can be produced.

Superimposition

This surreal-looking image is the result of superimposing three different images. The figure is first photographed on infra-red film, using different color filters. Two of the resulting images are then combined with a transparency of the window that was shot on ordinary daylight-balanced film. *6 x 6cm camera, 80mm lens, infra-red and daylight-balanced film, f5.6, 1/60 sec.*

Front projection, *below left*

This dramatic image is created by projecting a slide of abstract black and white lines onto the torso of a model. The shape of the model's shadow visible on the wall behind is as important as the pattern itself. *35mm camera, 100mm lens, Ektachrome 160T, f11, 1/60 sec.*

Solarization, *below*

Color transparency film can be exposed to colored light halfway through its first development. The color of the light, the strength and length of exposure, and the stage at which the film is exposed affect the results. The remaining processing is the same as for normal film. *6 x 6cm camera, 80mm lens, Ektachrome 100, f11, 1/125 sec.*

Dual-color filter
A glass dual-colored filter is used here to produce an unusual image. The top half of this filter is yellow and the bottom is purple. You can position the filter to produce a vertical, horizontal, or diagonal color split.
35mm camera, 50mm lens, Ektachrome 100, f5.6, 1/125 sec.

Special effects filter, *below*
A diffraction filter is colorless, but its surface is engraved with a series of fine lines, the pattern of which diffracts light reflected from the subject in various ways. This filter produces a series of repeating images, shifted both horizontally and vertically.
35mm camera, 28mm lens, Ektachrome 100, f8, 2 sec.

Combining media
This picture of a car is first shot on ordinary daylight-balanced transparency film. The image is then recorded on a video camera and the color controls used to distort and scramble the color signals. Finally it is photographed again from a television screen.
6 x 6cm camera, 50mm lens. Ektachrome 100. f8 1/4 sec

COMPUTER FILTER EFFECTS

A new generation of desktop computers with multi-megabyte memories and rapid processors has opened up new avenues of experimentation in the world of image manipulation. The first step in the process is to import an original transparency, negative, or print into the computer using a laser scanner. The scanner produces an electronic reproduction of the original, recording its color distribution and intensity, and contrast.

USING FILTERS

Once a scanned image has been imported, it can be manipulated on screen using a CAD (computer-aided design) software application. The range of effects illustrated on these pages is well within the capability of many CAD packages. The effects were produced by overlaying the scanned image (see page 40 for the original) with various "filters," which electronically distort the pixels (basic units of optical information) making up the screen. Some programs allow you to custom design filters or to use imported filter tools.

Pointillize filter
So named because the colors of the original image are broken up into dots of pure color, creating an effect not unlike that of a pointillist painting.

Displacement map filter
This uses a displacement map, whereby a translucent image or pattern already contained in the computer memory is superimposed over the scanned image.

Zigzag filter
This skews the color data of the original around a central point, producing an image that resembles a reflection on the surface of gently rippling water.

Watercolor filter
A definite sense of depth is the most striking feature of this image. The fence wire, as well as the outline of the flower itself, appears much more defined than in the other filter images. The overall effect is not unlike a watercolor painting on textured paper.

Pencil stroke filter, *below*
This produces a vibrant and mobile image that mimics the strokes of an artist's pencil. Similar filters give crayon or charcoal stroke effects.

Crystallize filter, *right*
This filter synthesizes pixels of similar color into polygons of pure color. The sum of pixels making up a polygon varies; some incorporate up to 999.

Extrude filter, *right*
This combines pixels into pyramidal shapes that seem to leap out at you. The sense of angularity produced makes a very striking image.

Mosaic filter, *far right*
This filter is similar in principle to the crystallize filter, except that it synthesizes the pixels into small mosaic squares of pure color.

COMPUTER RETOUCHING

Once a photograph, transparency, or negative has been scanned into a computer, it is possible to alter its appearance and enhance details in very subtle ways and in localized areas. These techniques are one step beyond the broad-based manipulations achieved using filters (*see pages 228–229*) and include color alteration, engineering the composition of an image, and devices to increase the sense of movement or realism.

COLOR CHANGES

Color alteration computer options include the ability to change the color of an image as well as to modify selected areas, such as changing the color of the background against which a subject is set. Once an area to be changed has been highlighted, an extensive color hue and saturation menu can be accessed and pulled down onto the screen.

Mixed techniques
In this image the backdrop color has been changed and the sense of movement increased with a blur effect. Compare the image with the original (*see page 111.*)

Compositional change
The original image (*see page 213*) has been reversed, and the frog cut and repositioned; its jump has been emphasized by the addition of blur lines.

Color retouching
The ability to change local areas of color is illustrated effectively in this series of four images. The original (*top far left*) has a strong blue sky, but the colors of the beach huts are rather drab. This was overcome by strengthening the colors of the huts in a variety of ways to different effect. A range of subtle to extreme color changes is possible.

Surreal effect, *below*
For a less-than-realistic effect you can choose unexpected colors. The results can be amusing, or sometimes quite unusual. Color retouching is opening up a whole new world of creative and visually exciting possibilities.

COMBINING IMAGES ON COMPUTER

The prevalence of image manipulation using computer software surrounds us – virtually every advertising picture on posters and billboards, and in magazines and newspapers, has probably been doctored in this way. The results are often impressive and sometimes surreal, grabbing our attention and sealing the associated brand name in our minds.

Other computer enhancements are more subtle – the perfect skin tone of the legs of a model advertising nylons, for example, is achieved by copying an area of flawless skin and pasting it over any blemishes. This technique, whereby parts of an image can be highlighted and repositioned on the computer screen, was also used to create the images shown on this page. The "cheat" is obvious in the first, while the second mirrors reality more closely. Image combination can be used to even greater effect in metamorphosis sequences like that on the page opposite.

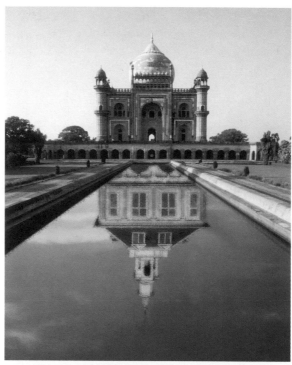

Trick of reflection
In this image combination made using the cut-and-paste technique, perhaps the best-known visual icon of India – the Taj Mahal – has as its reflection in the ornamental pool in the foreground the image of a traditional English customs house against an overcast sky (see page 167 for the original).

Wildlife scene
Here, the base image of a rocky waterfall was shot at a slow shutter speed to blur the movement of the water. The tigers were pasted on from another source. For added realism, a branch overlaps one tiger's tail. The outlines of both animals are not too sharp, so conveying a sense of movement.

Metamorphosis sequence
The computer technique used to achieve this sequence is surprisingly simple: first, the key features of an image (in this case, the dog's face) are pinpointed with fixed editing points. These points then appear automatically on a second image (the cat's face), and are adjusted slightly to fall on the corresponding key features, such as ears and eyes. Using these features as guides, the computer then superimposes the two images over a given number of frames.

Transposed surroundings

The mighty Sphinx and Great Pyramid, located in the desert on the outskirts of Cairo, Egypt, here appear out of place and incongruous, yet nevertheless fairly realistic, in a lush cultivated field of a more temperate region. This computer-aided image combination employed the cut-and-paste technique (*see page 232*).

Attention to detail

The dancer in this computer-generated image was originally photographed in a studio set-up, then cut and pasted onto the base image of a poppy field. Attention to detail, such as the natural falling of the shadows and harmony of colors, combines to give the finished image a sense of realism and authenticity.

Sunset sky, *above*
If the color of the sky in a
photograph is not to your liking,
find another one in which the
sky is preferable and paste it
onto the other image in the
computer. These beach huts
were originally shot against a
bright blue sky, but here a sunset
was pasted in and shadows added.
(*See also page 231.*)

Color palette
Image manipulation software
includes a color option and
intensity palette, which makes
it possible to change the color
of selected areas within a
photograph. So the fact that
nature did not make poppies in
bright green and purple is no
longer a problem, as illustrated
in this series of images.

STUDIO AND DARKROOM EQUIPMENT

In a studio environment you have complete control over the lighting, which allows you to concentrate on producing precisely the type of image you want. Taking the picture is only half the creative process, however. It is in the darkroom that you can exercise ultimate control over the final appearance of the image. This section shows all the basic equipment you need to set up a home darkroom. Also included is useful information on systems for viewing and storing slides, negatives, and prints.

THE HOME STUDIO

Many amateur photographers would like to create their own studio but are discouraged from doing so because they mistakenly believe that a studio necessarily requires a lot of space and that this area would have to be permanently set aside.

SPACE REQUIREMENTS

The size of a home studio depends on what types of subject you intend to photograph. If most of your photography involves table-top subjects, such as small still life objects, then an area measuring about 8 x 8ft (2.5 x 2.5m) will usually be sufficient. For portraits, however, especially full-length shots, you will probably need an area about twice that size at least. Generally, square rooms are best, since they give you the greatest flexibility in positioning lights and reflectors.

A spare bedroom is excellent for setting up a studio because you can leave camera, tripod, lights, reflectors, and background papers permanently in place. If this is not possible, equipment can be stored in a large closet and assembled in about 30 minutes when required.

WINDOWS AND LIGHTING

In a room with large windows (and ideally a skylight for additional lighting), you may not need to use flash or other lights if you restrict yourself to working during daylight. If possible, a home studio should have a good-sized window to supplement any lights used. A darkening shade or blinds can be used to exclude all window light when necessary.

Studio requirements

• White walls and ceiling to maximize ambient lighting levels and to double as reflectors without creating unwanted color-casts.

• Storage shelves or closets to store accessories and equipment when not in use, so that the working part of the studio can be kept free of clutter.

• A solid floor to stop vibrations being transmitted through the tripod to the camera.

• A ceiling high enough to allow you to position lighting units above the height of a standing figure.

Neutral-colored walls
Walls and ceiling should be painted either white or a pale neutral color so that they reflect light without introducing an unwanted color-cast.

Make-up mirror
The camera is critical of imperfections, so a well-lit make-up mirror is essential.

Storage shelves
Extra storage areas are always useful for camera and lens accessories, props, clamps, tape, reflectors, and numerous other items.

Make-up table
Table for cosmetics, hair accessories, and brushes is useful for portraiture and all shots involving life models.

Floor
Solid floor is essential to keep movement on the set from causing vibrations that might affect the camera.

Flash unit
Main light is positioned about 45° to the subject.

Synchronization lead
Links camera to the power pack so that the flash fires at the same time as the shutter is released.

Background paper
Selection of different-colored background papers is essential.

Subject on adjustable table
A stand or table on which height can be readily adjusted is useful for small-scale subjects.

Background supports
Telescopic metal supports hold the roll of background paper at various heights.

Other items

- Strong clamps for positioning small lights on shelves and backs of chairs, etc.

- Dulling spray for minimizing reflections from shiny objects.

- Different-length flash synchronization leads and shutter cable releases for different set-ups.

- Double or multiplug adaptors for additional power points.

Blind
An adjustable blind gives a range of lighting options. It also excludes daylight altogether if necessary.

Window
This gives you the option of using daylight alone or combining daylight and flash.

Snoot
Conical snoot fits over the lighting head and restricts the spread of light to a narrow beam.

Colored gels
Large sheets of colored gels are useful for special lighting effects and for filtering daylight to match any tungsten lighting being used.

Reflector boards
Different-sized reflector boards and surfaces give flexibility.

Compressed air
Can with compressed air is useful for cleaning filters and lenses, and for removing any dust from the surface of still life objects before shooting.

Spare lighting head
Range of spare heads allows you to adjust the lighting for each subject.

Tape
Masking or black tape can be used to attach filter gels to lights or windows and to adjust the position of background paper.

Umbrella diffuser
Light is reflected from the inner surface of the umbrella.

Camera and tripod
The camera should, whenever possible, be mounted on a sturdy, adjustable tripod.

Flash meter
If possible, choose a light meter that can also be used as a flash meter.

Power pack
Heavy-duty power source is required for the high output and rapid recycling times required of studio flash units.

THE HOME DARKROOM

All you need to set up a home darkroom is a windowless area, such as a walk-in closet or a spare room that can be sealed against outside light. The essential equipment required is shown on these pages. Arrange your darkroom to separate the wet and dry darkroom processes as much as possible. The wet side of the room is where all the film and paper processing and washing takes place and the dry side is where unprocessed and processed film and printing paper are handled, and where the enlarger is found.

It is best to have running water, but you can use a room that does not have a sink if you use a pail to move processed prints for washing elsewhere. The walls and ceiling of your darkroom can be a light color except for the area around the enlarger, which should be black. Proper ventilation, so that there is a flow of air through the darkroom, is essential.

FILM AND PRINT PROCESSING

Total darkness is required when removing an exposed film from its cassette and loading it onto a spiral. Once the spiral is inside a processing tank and the lid is firmly in place, the room lights can then be turned on.

The chemicals used in film and print processing must be diluted in exactly the proportions stated, and solutions must be brought to the correct temperature, and kept in contact with the film or printing paper for exactly the right time. Consistency of time and temperature ensures standardized results.

Practical advice

● All light sources in the darkroom should be operated by pull-cords. Ordinary light switches used with wet hands are potentially dangerous.

● Use correct strength bulbs in safelights to prevent film fogging.

● All ventilation units should be sealed to keep outside light from entering the darkroom.

DARKROOM PROCESSING SIDE

Storage bottles
Concertina bottles can be compressed to exclude air; this helps extend the life of the chemicals.

Processing tanks
Exposed film is loaded onto spirals before being put in processing tanks.

Measuring beaker

Chemicals

Mixing pitcher

Plastic funnels

Spirals

Measuring cylinders

Timer
Essential for timing processing stages.

Processing tongs
Used for lifting paper between trays.

Thermometer
To check solution temperatures.

Mixing rod
Ensures solutions are properly mixed.

Safelight
Placed above processing trays.

Film dryer
This unit has a thermostatically controlled heating element, and a long plastic tube that surrounds the film after processing.

Color processing unit
This thermostatically controlled unit has slots for processing chemicals as well as a motor to keep the film tank or print drum rotating.

Work top
Surface should be resistant to chemical spills.

Spare processing trays
Keep a supply of different-sized processing trays to suit various printing paper sizes.

Processing trays
These are used for black and white prints. Try not to splash chemicals onto surrounding surfaces.

Squeegee tongs
For removing water from film after washing. Tongs must be kept very clean.

Large sink with taps
For washing film, prints, and equipment.

Hose attachment
For washing prints.

Storage space
Large cabinets for accessories and equipment.

Heated print dryer
This greatly speeds up the print drying process.

DARKROOM PRINTING SIDE

Enlarger column
The enlarger head can be moved up and down on the column to make different-sized enlargements.

Enlarger head
This contains the light source and mixes the light before it reaches the film original and the lens. It also houses colored printing filters of varying strengths.

Timer
Easy-to-read timer to check the length of exposure of the printing paper.

Light
Wall-mounted white light with string pull-cord.

Wall color
The dry side of the darkroom where the enlarger is located should be painted black.

Compressed air
Useful for removing dust and hairs from negatives and for cleaning the enlarger lens.

Focus magnifier
Magnifies a small section of the projected image from the enlarger to ensure focus is accurate.

Bench
Work top should have an easy-to-clean surface.

Color analyzer sensor
This is held under the lens when a color original is being projected by the enlarger. It analyzes the color content of the image and recommends exposure times and filter settings.

Printing papers
Different sizes of printing paper are required and, for black and white printing, different contrast grades.

Printing easel
This holds the paper flat on the enlarger's baseboard during exposure; the metal arms can be adjusted to give different-width white borders around the finished print.

Contact printing frame
Strips of negatives are loaded into slots on the glass cover and then brought into contact with a sheet of printing paper on the base.

Negative carrier
Individual negatives, or short strips of negatives, are held in position between the enlarger's light source and the lens.

Additional printing papers
Store little-used or large-sized papers on shelves out of the way.

Floor
Hard wearing, easy-to-clean floor made of a nonslip material.

Print trimming equipment
Gives a straight, clean edge; a sharp craft knife can also be used.

VIEWING AND STORING IMAGES

As your interest in photography develops, you will need to create an effective system for storing and cataloging your increasing number of slides, negatives, and prints.

Slides generally come from the processing laboratory ready-mounted and packed in convenient plastic boxes to protect them from dust. If you want to be able to see all of them at a glance, file them in clear plastic sleeves. Slides can also be conveniently stored in projector trays, but these tend to be expensive and they take up a lot of space.

Keep negatives in acid-free paper sleeves in a file, and, for quick reference, file the negative contact sheets alongside. Prints are best displayed in albums, mounts, or frames.

SLIDE CHECKING, SELECTION, STORAGE, AND PROJECTION

Checking and selecting
Although subject colors and tones are unlikely to have been altered during processing, it is best to check all slides with a magnifying glass for image quality. The best way to compare and select slides is on a light box.

Mounted slide — Durable plastic mount

Magnifying glass — Glass lens

Light box — On/off switch — Opaque surface

Storage
Mounted and unmounted slides can be stored in plastic sleeves, which, for 35mm slides, usually have about 20–25 pockets. By inserting a metal hanger through the top, sleeves can be put in a suspension file system. For display, mount slides in black card.

Slides in plastic viewpack — Individual sleeve — 35mm color negative strip

35mm color slide — 2¼in color slide — Window for each transparency — Slides mounted in black card

Projection
Projection is the only way to get maximum impact from your slides. Projectors accept either round magazines (holding about 100 slides) or straight ones (holding about 40 slides). Some take both.

Slide projector — Lens — Circular slide tray in place

Circular slide tray — Slots for up to 100 slides — Standard slide tray — Slots for up to 50 slides

Compact disk storage

Photographs can now be stored on compact disk (CD), an innovation that is growing in popularity. Color or black and white film originals are digitally transferred onto CD and, via a special CD player, displayed on a television screen.

Compact disk — Laser-readable surface

Compact disk player — Slot for disk — Control panels

VIEWING AND STORING NEGATIVES

Viewing negatives

Even with careful scrutiny it is often difficult to make out the details of an image on a negative, and almost impossible to compare image quality. Contact sheets are very useful for selecting the best image, as they give an approximate idea of what your negatives will look like when printed and they can be stored adjacent to the negatives in an ordinary ring binder.

Contact sheets of miniature prints can be filed alongside their corresponding negatives

Each paper negative sleeve can accommodate a strip of six negatives; the paper is acid-free, so will not damage the film emulsion

Individual sleeve

Negative strip

Color negatives in paper sleeve

Hard ring binder protects the contact sheets and negative sleeves; mark each page with a date or reference number so that all the images can be readily identified

Ring binder with paper negative sleeves and contact sheet

Storing negatives

Negatives should always be handled and stored very carefully. To keep them from getting dirty or damaged, special acid-free paper sleeves are available.

VIEWING AND FRAMING PRINTS

Viewing prints

Albums for standard-sized prints include those with sticky pages to hold prints in place, in which every page is covered with a plastic overlay. Others require adhesive "corners" to hold prints in place.

Prints are held in place by a thin plastic overlay in this spiral-bound album; the dark album pages enhance the photographs

Lightweight glass frame is secured onto backboard with metal clips

Print can be cut to size to fit the frame if necessary

Dark card can be used to create a border around an image

Spiral-bound album with color prints arranged beneath plastic overlay

Framing prints

Prints can be enlarged, then mounted in frames for display. Of the many easy framing and mounting kits available, those shown here use clips to hold the glass and backboard together. Others have wood or aluminum frames.

Framed prints

PICTURE-TAKING ERRORS

Modern camera film is made to very high standards. It is unusual for there to be anything wrong with quality or consistency when it leaves the factory. Even own-brand and promotional packs of film should present few problems – they have more than likely been produced by a leading film manufacturer. Remember that film should always be kept in a cool place, out of direct sunlight, in low humidity, and away from all sources of chemical fumes, such as household cleaners and bleaches. Many photographers store their film in a refrigerator. Always use and process film by the date indicated on the carton.

COLOR AND EXPOSURE PROBLEMS

Some pictures display odd color faults, such as an orange or blue color-cast. Such faults usually have nothing to do with film quality; color-casts are caused by exposing film designed for specific lighting conditions incorrectly. On color print film, casts can be corrected or minimized by the printer. With color slide film, however, there is no printing stage, so always use the correct film for the light source, or use a correcting filter over the lens. A green color-cast can result from using old or badly stored film. Most modern cameras have an automatic exposure control that will generally produce good, well-exposed images in average conditions (where the subject is frontally lit and the entire frame has evenly distributed light and dark tones). Autoexposure problems are most likely to occur if the subject is lit from behind or if it is much lighter or darker than its surroundings. If you consistently experience exposure problems, have your camera tested and serviced.

CAMERA CARE AND USE

Faults such as tilted horizons, lens obstructions, and framing problems that often result in a subject being chopped in half, are the typical errors of inexperienced photographers or those working with a camera that is new to them. The only cure is patience and attention to detail. Before exposing each frame, take extra care that the image you see in the viewfinder is the way you want it and that there is nothing obscuring the lens. Your fingers or the camera strap can get in the way, especially if you are using a compact camera. Establish a simple routine for camera care, checking that the lens is not dusty or smudged, and that the inside of the camera is free of hair, dust, and grit. This will guarantee a high percentage of successful, sharply focused, blemish-free photographs.

COLOR-CASTS

Overall orange color-cast
This usually occurs when film made for use in daylight or flash is exposed indoors by domestic tungsten lighting. Be sure to use the correct film for the lighting conditions or use a correction filter over the camera lens or light source. An orange cast can also occur if flash is bounced off an orange-colored surface before reaching the subject. Use neutral surfaces for bouncing light.

Orange color-cast

Overall blue color-cast (i)
This problem is rare and usually the result of exposing tungsten-balanced film by daylight or by flashlight. Again, use the right film for the lighting conditions, or use an appropriate correction filter. A blue cast can also occur if flash is bounced off a blue-colored surface before reaching the subject. Use neutral surfaces for bouncing light.

Blue color-cast

Overall blue color-cast (ii)
A strong blue cast can be caused by a very smoky atmosphere in the room where a shot is taken or excessive amounts of ultra-violet light, which are particularly associated with coastal areas and mountain landscapes. Attach a clear UV filter to the lens to minimize this problem. A polarizing filter can sometimes have a stronger effect than a UV filter, but it will result in increased exposure times.

Blue color-cast

Overall green color-cast
In outdoor shots, this usually means that the film is old or has been badly stored. Always check the use-by date on film cartons. A green cast on photographs taken indoors may mean that daylight-balanced film has been exposed by fluorescent lighting. Overcome this problem by finding out precisely what type of fluorescent lighting is being used, then use the appropriate correction filter, if available.

Green color-cast

COMPOSITIONAL ERRORS

Obstruction

If you are using an SLR camera, always check the viewfinder before taking a photograph to see if there is anything obscuring the lens. If you are using a compact camera, be sure that your fingers and camera strap are well away from the lens, because they will not appear on the direct vision viewfinder.

Lens obstruction

Parallax error

This occurs when parts of a subject are accidentally omitted. This usually happens when the parallax correction marks in the viewfinder of a compact camera are not taken into account, or the shot is taken too close to the subject. Frame your subject within the marks and do not come in closer than the nearest recommended focusing distance. Also examine your negatives carefully to check that this problem is not due to a printing error.

Subject partly obscured

Image distortion

Distortions can be caused by using the wrong type of lens to photograph a particular scene – for example, when a wide-angle lens is used too close to a subject or when a converging vertical distortion results from tilting the camera up to include the top of a tall building. To avoid distortion, be sure always to select the correct lens and camera position.

Distorted image

Tilted image

To avoid this problem, look carefully through the viewfinder before taking a picture to make sure that the horizon is parallel to the top or bottom of the frame.

Subject tilted in frame

FLASH FAULTS

Flash-lit subject overexposed

This occurs when the flash is used too close to the subject, if the wrong aperture is used, or if the flash has been set with the wrong film speed. Follow your flash instructions regarding the correct working distance and aperture required for your unit, and make sure that you set the correct film ISO number on nonautomatic flash units.

Subject overexposed

Flash fall-off

This describes underexposure of all or part of a flash-lit subject. Check that the subject is within the recommended working distance for your flash unit (assuming that you are shooting indoors with enough reflective surfaces to bounce the light back). Outdoors, flash fall-off is rapid, so move closer to the subject or select a wider aperture. If you are using a manual flash, set it to the correct film ISO number.

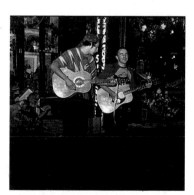

Subject underexposed

Unsynchronized flash

This results in all or part of the image being black, and is most often associated with SLR cameras; it is caused by the flash firing when the shutter has only partially cleared the film plane. On manual cameras, check that you have set the flash-synchronization speed (usually 1/125 or 1/60 second) or the lightning flash symbol on the shutter speed dial correctly.

Image partially blacked-out

Vignetting

This shows as dark edges and corners on an image and can be caused if the spread of light from a flash is inadequate for the angle of view of your lens. Fitting a diffuser over the flash or bouncing a flash off reflective surfaces helps. Vignetting on nonflash images can be caused by using the wrong lens hood on a wide-angle lens, using more than one filter on a lens at the same time, or if a polarizing filter is fixed to a lens.

Vignetted image

CONTRAST AND EXPOSURE

Camera shake
This results in multiple images of the subject and general blurring. Adopting a steady, relaxed shooting posture is the best way to avoid it. If the shutter speed being used is very slow and likely to result in camera shake, support the camera on a tripod or level surface, such as a wall or the roof of a car. Using a fast film often allows a sufficiently fast shutter speed to be selected, which will avoid the problem altogether.

Blurred image

Multiple exposure
More than one image recorded on the same film frame indicates that the film has not been correctly loaded and is therefore not advancing properly. Be sure to follow the loading instructions in your camera manual carefully. If your camera has a rewind crank, check that it turns in the opposite direction from the direction the film is wound (this means that the film is loaded properly).

Double exposure

Subject movement
Part of the subject is blurred but all stationary parts of the scene are sharp. This occurs when the shutter speed being used is too slow to arrest the rapid movement of part of the subject. If possible, use a faster shutter speed, or find a more head-on camera viewpoint so that subject movement is effectively minimized.

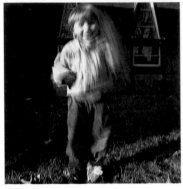
Moving subject blurred

Excessive contrast
The shadowy areas of the print are too dark or highlight areas too bright. Unfortunately, the recording ability of film cannot resolve detail in both very bright highlights and deep shadows. Decide which is more important for the composition of the image and set the exposure accordingly. Alternatively, wait until contrast is less extreme, or, for close-ups, artificially lessen contrast by using a flash or a reflector.

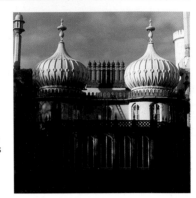
Excessive contrast

Flat contrast
This is when there is very little difference between the brightest and darkest areas of the image or subject, which is a problem if the photographer is relying on shape to make the image interesting. This problems occurs often in twilight shots. To light an appealing foreground or subject in such conditions, use a fill-in flash to create artificial contrast.

Image with flat contrast

Pale image or colors
Assuming that it is not a lighting problem, washed-out colors or a distinct lack of image contrast are often caused by a dirty lens or lens filter. Make sure all front lens elements, filters, and, on an SLR, the back lens element, are clean and free of scratches.

Image with washed-out colors

Overexposure
This is when too much light reaches the film, causing light shadow areas and bleached-out highlights. The fault lies in selecting the wrong shutter speed/aperture combination for the film speed. If overexposure happens consistently on an autoexposure camera, there may be a problem that needs professional repair.

Image overexposed

Underexposure
Like overexposure, this is when the wrong shutter speed/aperture combination has been selected for the film speed, resulting in too little light reaching the film, which causes heavy shadow areas and dull highlights. If underexposure happens consistently on an autoexposure camera, there may be a problem that needs professional repair.

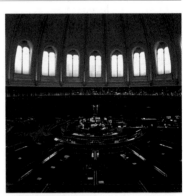
Image underexposed

MISCELLANEOUS FAULTS

Unexposed film
Processed film that is perfectly clear has never been exposed. This happens as a result of the film not advancing. Follow the loading instructions in your camera manual carefully and always remember to wind the end of an exposed film back inside the cassette.

Unexposed film frame

Image out of focus
If the final image is partially blurred, the aperture selected may have resulted in insufficient depth of field. Autofocus cameras may focus incorrectly through glass or if the subject is not center-frame. If the subject is off-center, use the focus lock (if your camera has one) and consult your camera manual regarding potential autofocus problems. If the shutter speed is below 1/30, slight camera shake can also cause this problem.

Image out of focus

Blemishes on print
These usually take the form of spots, lines, and scratches on the film caused by dust, dirt, hair, or grit inside the camera. Check the inside of the camera whenever you remove a film. Blemishes or out-of-focus spots are also often due to raindrops on the lens when the photograph was taken.

Out-of-focus spot on image

Red eye
A subject's eyes glowing red usually happens when the built-in flash on compact cameras and SLRs is very closely aligned with the lens. If you cannot bounce the flashlight from a nearby wall or ceiling before it reaches the subject, use a film that is faster and correct for the available light minus the flash.

Subject's eyes glowing red

Film fogging
This happens when non-image-forming light reaches the film, usually when you open the back of a camera before rewinding the film. Remember always to rewind the film before removing it. An ill-fitting or loose camera back can also allow enough light in to cause fogging.

Film fogged by light

Flare
Never point the camera directly at a bright light source unless the lens is adequately shaded, otherwise bright patches of light (flare) will obscure parts of the film and produce a washed-out image. Flare can also be caused by fine scratches on the mat-black interior of the camera.

Flare surrounding light source

Grainy image
Using the wrong film speed results in an overly grainy image. This usually occurs if extremely fast film is used. It is most apparent when an image is greatly enlarged – a smaller print minimizes it. To avoid excessive graininess, use a slower, finer-grain film with an increased exposure time, or add extra lighting. Grain shows up more in the neutral and light-toned areas of an image.

Overly grainy image

Half-framed image
This happens when you try to squeeze an extra frame of film at the end of a roll. Although film comes in standard lengths, you can occasionally take an extra frame. If the picture is important, however, it is worth taking the shot again when you have reloaded, in case the processing laboratory has to cut into the frame to detach the film from the core or attach a clip to the end while the film is drying.

Half-framed image

PRINTING ERRORS

At a large processing laboratory, films requiring the same type of chemical processing (E-6 for most color slides and C-41 for color negatives) are processed in long strips and passed through a series of chemical baths, which are constantly monitored to ensure that they are at the correct temperature. Depending on the volume of film being processed, the chemical solutions are constantly renewed to give consistent results; likewise at the printing stage. Each film image is printed by an enlarger that automatically analyzes its density and color content and sets the required color filtration and exposure length. A conveyor-belt system transports the individual sheets of exposed printing paper through another series of chemical baths and hot-air dryers, delivering hundreds of finished prints every hour.

HOME DARKROOM PROBLEMS

Naturally, the degree of automation in a film laboratory is not possible or desirable in the home darkroom, where you can work creatively on individual images as you process them. Inherent in home processing, however, is the likelihood of error. The most common problems to be avoided are related to darkroom cleanliness; dust, hair, or grit on the surface of a negative or positive will result in a blemished and flawed print, even if filtration and exposure are perfect. More serious is the contamination of one processing solution with another. Even one drop of bleach or fixing agent spilled in a developer solution will mean a waste of expensive paper and chemicals.

CHEMICAL PROCESSES

The temperature of solutions and the timing of the separate chemical stages of print processing are other major sources of potentially avoidable problems for the home darkroom user. Some chemical solutions, particularly those used in color printing, have only to be fractionally off the exact working temperatures stated in their accompanying instructions to seriously affect the color balance of the print. It is also worth remembering that only a fixed number of chemical solutions can be used to process prints. Avoid having to throw away ruined printing paper and wasting your creative efforts by keeping accurate records of the number of prints passing through these solutions before their chemical action is exhausted.

BLACK AND WHITE PRINTS

Blurred prints
If a negative is sharp but the resulting print blurred, first check that the enlarger is focused correctly. As an aid, use a focus magnifier to view an enlarged part of the projected image on the baseboard prior to exposure. Also use a printing frame to ensure that the printing paper cannot move during exposure.

Blurred image

Inaccurate highlight detail
This can happen even though a negative has been correctly exposed. If details in the highlight areas of a negative do not appear in the corresponding dark areas on the processed print, you may need to print on a softer grade of paper, because hard grades yield fewer intermediate tones.

Lack of highlight detail

Soft print with "muddy" tones
Black and white prints can sometimes turn out too soft and muddy looking, even though the negative is satisfactory. To achieve increased contrast – when there are areas of solid black and bright white present – try using a harder grade of paper, which eliminates more intermediate tones to create a crisper, more contrasty image. Also make sure the developer you use is not contaminated.

"Muddy" tones

Spots and lines on a print
These are generally caused by dust, hair, or similar debris on the negative and are very noticeable on a print. The only way to prevent such blemishes is to keep your darkroom scrupulously clean. Inspect both sides of a negative each time you load one into the enlarger. When cleaning negatives, take particular care with the emulsion side, which scratches easily.

Spots and lines

COLOR PRINTS FROM NEGATIVES

Brownish streaks on print

The most likely cause of brownish streaks appearing on a print is that light hit the paper before exposure and fogged it. Be sure that your darkroom is completely sealed against white light, especially around doors and windows. If you have a safelight, check that it is the correct type for color printing, that the filter cover is secure, and that the bulb is the right wattage.

Brown streaks

Dark image lacking in contrast

Usually caused by exhausted bleach solution. Keep a note of the number and size of all prints passing though the solution. Discard and replace it before exhaustion point is reached. Read the instructions accompanying the chemicals to determine how often they should be renewed.

Lack of contrast

Heavy shadows and color-cast

These are probably due to the temperature of the developer solution being incorrect. The correct working temperature of the solution can be found in the instructions accompanying it. Use a thermometer to gauge the exact temperature of a solution before pouring it into a print drum. A thermostatically controlled processing unit for solutions and print drums makes these critical controls easier to maintain.

Heavy shadow areas

Pale, reversed image

If a processed print shows a pale image, reversed left to right, the paper was probably placed under the enlarger with the emulsion side face down, so that the paper was exposed through the back. (Note that prints like this can also have a blotchy, cyan color-cast.) Practice with a spare, waste piece of paper until you are confident you can tell the emulsion side by touch in complete darkness.

Image reversed

COLOR PRINTS FROM SLIDES

Purple color-cast

If the print has a purple color-cast, the paper was slightly fogged by white light before exposure, which destroyed most of the top yellow dye layer. Seal the darkroom completely against white light, and if you are using a safelight, make sure it is the correct type for color printing, that the filter cover is securely in place, and that the bulb is of the recommended wattage.

Light purple color-cast

Magenta color-cast

This problem is most likely to occur if you are new to darkroom procedures and either neglect to set the enlarger filtration before printing or accidentally change the setting. Familiarize yourself thoroughly with your equipment and check that everything is in order before exposing the paper.

Bright magenta color-cast

Blotchy, uneven image

This is usually due to the printing paper being loaded into the processing drum with the emulsion side the wrong way up, so that uneven amounts of each chemical solution reach the emulsion. The same happens if the paper is correctly oriented but not enough solution is used. Be very careful at every stage.

Unevenly processed image

White or colored scratches

These indicate that the delicate surface of the printing paper has been damaged. Scratches often come up white, but can also be blue, yellow, magenta, or cyan, depending on the depth of the scratch. Always handle the paper gently, especially when still wet, because this is the time when the emulsion is most easily affected.

Scratches on print

GLOSSARY

A

Accessory shoe See *Hot shoe*.

AE See *Autoexposure*.

Aerial perspective Illusion of depth and distance in a photograph due to the light-scattering effect of atmospheric haze. In distant views, in particular, colors tend to appear bluer and tones lighter than usual.

AF See *Autofocus*.

Air brushing Method of retouching a negative or print by spraying with dye or pigment.

Ambient light See *Available light*.

Angle of incidence Angle created between an incident light ray striking a surface and an imaginary "normal" line set at right-angles to that surface.

Angle of reflection Angle created between an incident light ray being reflected from a surface and an imaginary "normal" line set at right-angles to that surface.

Angle of view Most widely separated parts of a scene that a lens is capable of resolving into an acceptable image on a piece of film. The angle of view varies according to the focal length of the lens and the camera format.

Antihalation layer Coating of dye on the back of films that absorbs light passing directly through the emulsion. Without this layer, light would be reflected back from the film base, through the emulsion, so creating ill-defined haloes around sources of bright light in a scene. See also *Halation*.

Aperture Circular opening within a lens that determines the amount of light that is allowed to pass through to reach the film. On all but the simplest of cameras, the size of the aperture can be varied by a diaphragm, which is set to different-sized openings, known as "stops," calibrated in f-numbers.

Aperture priority Type of semi-automatic exposure system whereby the photographer sets the aperture and the camera selects the corresponding shutter speed to ensure correct exposure of the scene.

ASA Abbreviation for American Standards Association, the film speed rating system in general use before the ISO standard was internationally adopted.

Autoexposure Camera system designed to set both the size of the aperture and the shutter speed to ensure correct exposure of a scene. Film speed is also taken into account.

Autofocus Automatic system that uses a motor, either in a lens or the camera itself, to stop the movement of the lens when the image is correctly focused. Some advanced autofocus systems transmit a beam of infra-red light or ultrasound and time the delay before it is received back from the subject in order to estimate subject distance.

Autowinder Automatic mechanism that advances the film one frame each time the shutter is released. See also *Motor drive* and *Motorized film transport*.

Available light Light that is normally available in a scene, not including artificial light such as flash. Domestic tungsten lighting also counts as available light if it is present. Also known as ambient or existing light.

Averaged light reading Type of exposure system that measures the brightness of many different areas of a scene to produce an average exposure value for the scene as a whole. The priority of each area is weighted according to the sensitivity patterns of its light-measuring cells.

B

B (Bulb) setting Shutter setting found on many cameras that holds the shutter open for as long as the release is depressed. Used for manually timed exposures that are longer than the longest automatic timed setting available. The name comes from the early days of photography when the shutter was fired using an air bulb and tube. See also *T (Time) setting*.

Back projection Projection system that throws a film image onto the back of a translucent screen. This technique is often used to create a backdrop for a person or object placed in front of the screen.

Backlight compensation control Manual exposure control found on many modern cameras that opens the aperture by a predetermined amount to compensate for when the main subject is lit from behind. Most exposure-measuring systems tend to underexpose a backlit subject because the side of the subject facing the lens is in shadow.

Backlighting Lighting that illuminates the subject from the rear. This type of lighting may cause exposure problems unless compensated for. See also *Backlight compensation control*.

Ball-and-socket head Simple type of camera-mounting system found on some tripods. It consists of a ball that can be rotated in a cup-shaped fixture, allowing sideways and up-and-down camera movements. A clamp keeps the ball steady in one position before the exposure is made. See also *Tripod*.

Barn doors Set of four hinged metal flaps on a frame that fits around a lighting head. Moving the flaps in or out of the light beam controls the spread of light.

Barrel distortion Design fault, usually associated with wide-angle lenses, that causes vertical lines near the edges of the frame to bulge outward. Good-quality lenses are built to avoid this fault – so barrel distortion should not be a problem unless lenses wider than about 24mm are used on 35mm-format cameras.

Baseboard camera See *View camera*.

Bellows See *Extension bellows*.

Between-the-lens shutter Shutter system on most fixed-lens cameras that is built within the lens itself. See also *Focal-plane shutter*.

Blur Unsharp image area caused by camera or subject movement, inaccurate focusing, or the use of an aperture that gives a shallow depth of field.

Bounced flash Light from a flash that is first directed at a surface, such as a wall, ceiling, or reflector, before it reaches the subject. This creates a broader, softer area of lighting than is possible using direct flash.

Bracketing Taking a series of photographs of the same scene with each frame at a different exposure setting. Bracketing is useful when you want to select slightly darker or lighter prints than the exposure system would normally produce, or when it is difficult to judge the best exposure.

Burning-in Photographic printing term used to indicate those parts of an image which would benefit from extra exposure. Parts of the image not requiring burning-in have to be shaded from the enlarger light during this process.

C

Cable release Mechanical or electrical device used to trigger the shutter. A cable release is usually used when a camera is mounted on a tripod, because it is particularly important that the camera is not jarred at the moment of exposure.

CAD See *Computer-aided design.*

Camera obscura Origin of the present-day camera, consisting of a darkened room with a small hole in one wall. The hole allowed an image of outside objects to be thrown onto a screen on the opposite wall.

Cassette Metal or plastic film holder for 35mm cameras. A spool inside the cassette releases film when the film advance mechanism is turned, and collects the exposed film again when it is rewound.

Catadioptric lens See *Mirror lens.*

CC filter Abbreviation for color compensating filter. Any of a range of pale-colored filters used to compensate for or introduce a color-cast. Different-strength filters are available in magenta, cyan, yellow, red, blue, and green.

CCD See *Charge-coupled device.*

Center-weighted light reading Type of exposure-measuring system that assumes the subject is usually placed in the center of the frame and so weights the exposure in favor of that area. See also *Averaged light reading.*

Charge-coupled device Device found in electronic-image video cameras. Light passing through the lens falls on a grid of light-sensitive cells making up the surface of the charge-coupled device (CCD). Depending on the intensity of the light striking each cell, the CCD transmits an electrical signal of varying strength, which creates a pattern that can be stored on electromagnetic tape or on a computer-readable floppy disk.

Chromatic aberration Lens fault that causes the different wavelengths of light to focus on slightly different planes. This should only be a problem with some cheap camera lenses where chromatic aberration appears as a series of different-colored fringes around the subject.

Circles of confusion Disks of light on an image that are formed by the lens from points of light coming from the subject. The smaller these disks appear, the sharper the resulting image. When they are sufficiently large to be seen as disks, as opposed to points, the image is out of focus.

Clip test Small length of film clipped from the beginning of an exposed roll. This is processed in advance so that processing times can be adjusted if necessary for the rest of the film.

Closing down See *Stopping down.*

Color-cast Unnatural color affecting the whole image. Color-casts often occur when daylight-balanced film is exposed in tungsten light, or vice versa. Casts can also occur when flash is bounced from a colored wall or ceiling, or when daylight is reflected from a colored building or filtered through green foliage. The human brain compensates for color-casts, so that a white handkerchief always looks white even if viewed under red-colored lighting. Film, however, records colors as they actually are, making no compensation at all.

Color compensating filter See *CC filter.*

Color correction filter Pale-colored filter used to warm up or cool down slightly the overall color content of a scene.

Color temperature scale Calibrated in degrees Kelvin (K), this rates different light sources according to their color content. Daylight and flash are rated at 5400K, studio tungsten lamps are rated at between 3200 and 3400K, and most domestic tungsten lights at about 2800K.

Compact camera Small, usually highly automated 35mm camera with a permanent fixed lens and a direct vision viewfinder.

Complementary colors In a photographic context, this term refers to the colors yellow, magenta, and cyan, which are complementary to the primary colors blue, green, and red. Colors are complementary to one another if, when mixed in the correct proportions, they form white or gray.

Computer-aided design (CAD) Design executed using a computer. Computer design programs are capable of rendering text in the correct typeface and size and of manipulating scanned images of photographs or artworks, altering their size, colors, contrast, and so on.

Contact sheet A print with the images from the same roll of film exactly the same size as the negatives. Contacts are produced by placing the negatives in contact with a sheet of photographic printing paper, pressing them down under a piece of glass, and exposing them to light.

Continuous tone Term used in black and white photography to describe a negative or print that has gradations of tones from black to white, which correspond to the different tones of the original subject.

Contrast Difference between the darkest and lightest parts of an image. The degree of contrast is dependent on factors such as the inherent contrast of the subject itself, the contrast-recording ability of the film used to record the original image, the angle and direction of lighting, the type of enlarger used to create the print, and the paper used to print the image.

Contrast filters Filters used in black and white photography to alter the film's response to the colors of a scene, rendering them as either lighter or darker shades of gray.

Contre jour Another term for backlighting. See *Backlighting.*

Converging verticals An effect usually associated with a wide-angle lens that occurs when the film plane and the subject are not parallel. This results in the vertical sides of a tall building appearing to converge when the camera is tilted back to include the top. An effect similar to converging verticals occurs when parallel lines, such as the sides of a road, appear to converge as they become more distant from the camera.

Converter lens Lens that fits into the lens mount of a camera body and changes the focal length of a fixed focal length lens. For example, a x2 converter doubles the focal length of any lens it is attached to, while a x3 triples it. Often there is some loss of image quality when a converter is used, and there can also be a loss of lens speed.

Coupled rangefinder Focusing system in which the rangefinder and focusing control are linked. The photographer sees a direct view of the subject in the viewfinder, the central portion of which is overlaid with a secondary image. The focus control is moved until both images exactly correspond.

Cropping Removing unwanted parts of the image. Cropping in the camera means selecting the correct camera distance and focal length to include only the desired part of the image; cropping in the darkroom means enlarging only part of the negative. Prints can be cropped simply by cutting off unwanted areas.

D

Daylight-balanced film Film designed to reproduce correct subject colors when exposed in daylight or by the light of electronic flash or blue flash cubes. See also *Tungsten-balanced film.*

Dedicated flash Type of flashgun designed to be used with a specific camera or range of cameras. Once attached to the camera, the flashgun effectively becomes an extension of that camera's circuitry, controlling shutter speed, receiving film speed information, and using the exposure meter.

Delayed action timer Manual camera control that delays the firing of the shutter after the release is depressed. Most often used to take a self portrait or to trigger the shutter smoothly if a cable release is not used.

Depth of field Zone of acceptably sharp focus extending both in front of and behind the point of true focus. Depth of field varies depending on the aperture selected, the focal length of the lens (or zoom setting), and the focal distance. Depth of field is increased if a smaller aperture is set, if a lens with a shorter focal length is selected, and if the lens is focused at its maximum focal distance.

Depth of field scale Pairs of f-numbers engraved on a lens barrel that indicate the effective depth of field surrounding a subject when that lens is focused on the subject and the desired aperture has been selected.

Depth of focus Distance that the film plane can be moved without requiring the camera to be refocused.

Development Chemical process of converting exposed silver halide film emulsion to a visible image. The dilution of the developing agent, the temperature of the resulting solution, and the degree of agitation of the solution during the development stage all affect the outcome of the process.

Diaphragm Adjustable aperture of a lens. The size of the aperture affects the amount of light that reaches the film.

Diaphragm shutter Between-the-lens camera shutter that also performs the function of the iris diaphragm.

Diffuser Any material that is used to scatter and soften light.

DIN Abbreviation for Deutsche Industrie Norm (German standards organization), one of the film speed rating systems that was formerly in use before the ISO standard was internationally adopted.

Direct vision viewfinder Sighting device found on compact and other non-reflex cameras that allows the user a direct view of the subject.

Dodging Photographic printing term used to describe using a small device to block those parts of an image that would benefit from less exposure under the enlarger. Parts of an image that require dodging have to be shaded from the enlarger light while the rest of the paper receives normal exposure.

Downrating Exposing film as if it were less sensitive to light than its nominal ISO rating indicates. Allowances for downrated film have to be made during development.

DX film-speed recognition Automatic film-speed recognition system found on most modern cameras that uses a series of sensors placed inside the film chamber to read a coded pattern printed on the side of the film cassette. Each speed of film has its own unique code, but if the camera encounters a non-DX-coded film it automatically defaults to ISO 100.

E

Electronic flash Type of flash that discharges an electric current through a gas-filled tube to produce a short burst of bright light. Power is usually provided by batteries, although studio flashes require plug-in power.

Emulsion Light-sensitive coating on photographic film and printing paper consisting of silver halides suspended in gelatin.

Enlargement Any size of print that is larger than the transparency or negative from which it is produced.

Enlarger Darkroom device that projects the image of a negative or transparency onto a piece of photographic printing paper.

Enprint Smallest standard-sized enlargement from a 35mm negative that is made by most commercial, automatic printing machines.

Existing light See *Available light.*

Expiration date Date printed on the box of all films that indicates the month and year by which the film should be used and processed. This date is usually conservative but film emulsion may deteriorate more rapidly if not properly stored. Factors that reduce the shelf-life of film include heat, excessive humidity, and proximity to fumes from substances such as household cleaners.

Exposure Amount of light received by a photographic emulsion such as film. Overall exposure is the product of the intensity of the light received by the film and is controlled by aperture size. The length of time that light is allowed to act on the film is controlled by the shutter speed.

Exposure latitude Amount by which a film may be over- or underexposed and still produce an acceptable result when given standard processing. Fast films in general have a wider exposure latitude than slow films.

Exposure lock Feature found on many automatic SLR cameras and some compacts that allows the photographer to take a light reading from one part of a scene, lock that reading into the camera, and then to recompose the picture and shoot. A useful feature when the subject is backlit or when the main subject is either much lighter or darker than the surrounding scene.

Exposure meter Device, either built into the camera or available as a hand-held accessory, which measures the amount of light reflected from or falling on the subject and, taking the film speed into account, recommends a shutter speed and aperture to achieve correct exposure. Also known as a light meter.

Extension bellows Close-up attachment for SLR cameras and view cameras that fits between the camera body and the lens. The bellows unit is made of flexible material and mounted on rails. Any degree of subject enlargement is possible within the design limits of the unit. Automatic metering may be possible.

Extension tubes Similar in principle to an extension bellows, extension tubes are made of metal in different lengths and can be used singly or in combination to give fixed degrees of subject enlargement. Automatic metering may be possible.

F

False attachment Compositional line-of-sight effect in which the subject appears to blend into an object that is visible in the background. If used intentionally, false attachment can indicate a connection between otherwise disparate objects, or it can also be used for humorous effect.

Fast film See *Film speed.*

Fast lens See *Lens speed.*

Fill-in light Supplementary lighting from a flash or reflector that is used most often to lighten shadowy areas of the subject and reduce overall contrast. Also used to add highlights if the subject is flatly lit.

Film A thin plastic base coated with a light-sensitive emulsion that produces an image of the subject when exposed in a camera.

Film back Preloadable film holder designed for use with a medium-format camera. It is possible to change from black and white to color, or from color negative to color transparency film at any time, even halfway through a film, simply by removing the film back from the camera and attaching another, loaded with the appropriate film. A thin, dark plate protects the film from accidental exposure.

Film plane Plane on which the film lies in a camera. The camera lens is designed to bring images into focus precisely at the film plane to ensure correctly exposed pictures.

Film speed The more sensitive a film is to light, the "faster" it is. The speed of a film is indicated by its ISO number. Each doubling of the ISO number represents a doubling of light sensitivity (for example from ISO 100 to 200 or from ISO 400 to 800). Slow films are in the range ISO 50–100; medium-speed films ISO 200–400; and fast films ISO 800–3200.

Filter Glass, plastic, or gelatin disks or squares that fit over a camera lens or, less commonly, the light source, in order to change the appearance of the finished image.

Filter factor Most filters subtract some of the light passing through them. Through-the-lens (TTL) exposure-metering cameras automatically compensate for any extra exposure required, but for non-TTL and manual cameras, the mount of the filter may be engraved with a filter factor that indicates the additional exposure that has to be given.

Finder See *Viewfinder*.

Fisheye lens Extreme wide-angle lens that produces highly distorted, circular images, sometimes with an angle of view in excess of 200°. Depth of field at every aperture is so extensive that focusing is unnecessary.

Fixed-aperture lens Lens with a fixed aperture, which is found only on very simple cameras. Exposure compensation (if available) is achieved by changing shutter speed.

Fixed-focal-length lens Lens with a fixed focal length, also known as a prime lens. See also *Zoom lens*.

Fixed-focus lens Lens that is set to one subject distance from the camera and cannot be selectively focused closer than or beyond the subject. Used only on the simplest of cameras, the lens is usually set at the hyperfocal point, which, when coupled with a small maximum aperture, renders most subjects relatively sharp. See also *Hyperfocal point*.

Flare Non-image-forming light caused by light scattering as it passes through the glass surfaces of a lens, or light reflected from inside the camera body itself. Air-to-glass surfaces inside the lens are coated with a special solution to reduce light-scattering flare, and the insides of the camera are painted mat-black to absorb any non-image-forming light.

Flash Portable light source, usually electronic, that produces an intense beam of short-duration light when an electrical current is discharged through a gas-filled glass tube.

Flash fall-off Progressive underexposure of those parts of a subject that are beyond the working distance of the flash.

Flash fill-in See *Fill-in light*.

Flash meter Type of hand-held exposure meter designed to register the very brief burst of light produced by a flash. Some exposure meters can be used in both continuous light and flashlight.

Flash synchronization speed Shutter speed that ensures the shutter has completely cleared the film plane when the flash is fired.

Flash umbrella Umbrella-shaped reflector that casts a broad area of soft, diffused light onto the subject when flashlight is bounced off its inside surfaces.

Flashgun Any type of add-on flash unit.

Flats Large pieces of plywood or fiberboard used for building sets in a studio. Flats, if painted an appropriate color, can also be used as reflectors to ensure an even spread of light.

Floodlight Studio light designed to produce a broad beam of light.

f-number Series of numbers engraved on the barrel of a lens representing the different sizes of aperture available. Moving the aperture ring up one stop (for example from f4 to f5.6) makes the aperture smaller and halves the amount of light passing through the lens. Moving the aperture ring down one stop (for example from f11 to f8) makes the aperture larger and doubles the amount of light passing through the lens. The scale of f-numbers is calculated by dividing the focal length of the lens by the effective diameter of the aperture, so a 110mm lens and an effective aperture diameter of 10mm would equal f11. f-numbers are commonly referred to as f-stops.

Focal length Lenses are most often described by their focal length, measured in millimeters (mm), which is calculated by measuring the distance between the rear nodal point of the lens when the lens is focused on infinity, and the focal plane. See also *Nodal points*.

Focal plane Plane at which light from the lens is brought into focus. In order to ensure sharp images, the focal plane and the film plane must precisely coincide.

Focal-plane shutter Type of shutter consisting of fabric or metal blinds situated just in front of the focal plane. Focal-plane shutters are normally found only in cameras with interchangeable lenses. Otherwise, a between-the-lens shutter would have to be built into every lens. This type of shutter also shields the film from light when the lens is removed from the camera body.

Focal point Point of light on the optical axis where all rays of light emanating from a given subject converge and come into sharp focus.

Focus lock Feature found on many automatic SLR cameras and some compact cameras that allows the photographer to focus the lens on one part of a scene, lock that setting into the camera, and then recompose the picture and shoot. A useful feature when the subject is off-center, since most autofocus systems focus on anything that is positioned center-frame.

Focusing Adjustment of the lens-to-film distance in order to achieve a sharp image of the subject. Many modern cameras are equipped with an automatic focusing device.

Focusing screen Glass or plastic screen mounted inside the camera that allows the image to be viewed and focused accurately.

Format Size or shape of a film original, printing paper, or camera viewing area.

Front projection Way of projecting a background scene from the front of a set onto a special reflective screen located behind the main subject.

f-stop See *f-number*.

G

Gelatin Translucent medium used to hold light-sensitive silver halide grains in suspension before being coated onto a plastic film or paper base as an emulsion.

Grain Exposed and developed black silver halide grains making up a photographic image.

Graininess Term describing the visual appearance of irregular clumps of exposed and developed silver halide grains on films and printing papers. Graininess is most apparent in light-toned areas of an image.

Granularity Qualitative measurement of the degree of clumping together of silver halide grains within a photographic emulsion.

Guide number Measure of the maximum output of an electronic bulb or flashgun that varies according to the film speed used. Lens apertures can be calculated by dividing the guide number by the distance between the subject and the flash. Suppose the number is 160, then at 10ft (3m) the lens would be set at f16, at 20ft (8m) f8, and so on.

H

Halation Haloes of light surrounding bright sources of illumination in a photograph. Caused by light passing through the emulsion and reflecting from the film base to form a slightly out-of-register secondary image. Due to an anti-halation layer in modern films, halation usually occurs only in long nighttime exposures of scenes that include bright lights such as street lamps.

Half-frame camera Camera format that uses only half the area of a standard 35mm negative. This allows 72 pictures to be taken on a 36-frame film.

Half-tone Mechanical printing process that reproduces the photographic image in ink as a pattern of tiny dots that simulate the effect of the continuous-tone original.

High-key image One that is composed predominantly of light tones or colors. See also *Low-key image*.

Highlights Brightest parts of a subject or print.

Hot shoe Metal plate usually found on the top of the camera, which is designed to receive a flashgun. Electrical contacts on the base of the hot shoe correspond to contacts on the bottom of the flash, so completing a circuit when the shutter is fired.

Hot spot Very bright spot caused by light reflected off any shiny objects in a scene, such as glass picture frames, mirrors, or areas of greasy bare skin.

Hyperfocal point The nearest point of sharp focus to a camera when a lens is focused on infinity. At the hyperfocal point, depth of field extends from infinity to a point halfway between it and the camera.

I

Image plane Plane commonly at right angles to the optical axis at which a sharp image of the subject is formed.

Incident light Light falling on a subject as opposed to that being reflected by it.

Incident light reading Measurement taken with an exposure meter of the amount of light falling on a subject, rather than that reflected from a subject.

Infra-red focusing index Marks on the focusing ring that indicate the adjustment that needs to be made when using infra-red film, since infra-red light comes into focus at a slightly different point from visible light.

Infra-red light Wavelengths of light, invisible to the human eye, which occur beyond the red end of the visible color spectrum.

Intensification Method by which the density of a photographic image can be strengthened. Most applicable to negative material. Works better on negatives that have been under-developed rather than underexposed.

Internal focusing Internal adjustments of the glass elements of a lens to account for different subject distances. In most lenses, the lens barrel either extends or contracts when focused on subjects at different distances from the camera.

Inverse square law Law that states that a doubling of the distance between a subject and a compact light source, such as a flash, results in a quartering of the light illuminating the subject.

ISO Abbreviation for International Standards Organization, the internationally agreed film speed rating system that replaced ASA and DIN

J

Joule Unit of light output from electronic flash, equivalent to one watt-second or 40 lumen-seconds.

K

Kelvin (K) Unit of measurement used to describe the color temperature of light sources. See *Color temperature*.

Key light See *Main light*.

L

Large-format camera See *View camera*.

Latent image Invisible image on film or photographic printing paper formed by the action of light from the subject and made visible by the development process.

Lens Glass or plastic optical instrument that can refract light. A modern photographic lens consists of different-shaped glass elements arranged in groups to form a compound lens. In a compound lens, some elements are convex in shape, causing rays of light to converge, and some concave, causing rays to diverge. The effect of the combination of these elements is to cause all the wavelengths of light to converge at a common point – the focal point.

Lens hood Attachment made of metal or rubber that screws into the filter mount on the front of a lens and prevents unwanted light from reaching the surface of the lens and so affecting the image.

Lens speed Refers to the maximum aperture of a lens. Lenses with wide maximum apertures admit most light, and so can be used in dimmer lighting conditions or to compensate for faster shutter speeds; these are known as fast lenses. Slow lenses have relatively small maximum apertures.

Light box Box containing fluorescent tubes with an opaque glass or plastic top used for viewing transparencies.

Light meter See *Exposure meter*.

Light source General term for any light source used in photography, e.g. sunlight, flash, or tungsten light.

Lighting head General term for the light-emitting part of a flash unit.

Linear perspective Sense of depth and distance in a two-dimensional photograph caused by the apparent convergence of parallel lines receding from the camera.

Lith film Highly sensitive form of line film that produces very high contrast images when used with a special lith developer.

Long-focus lens Lens with a focal length longer than the diagonal of the film format with which it is used.

Low-key image One that is composed predominantly of dark tones or colors. See also *High key*.

M

Macro lens Lens with an extended focusing range that is designed to give the best resolution of subject detail very close up.

Macro mode Setting on some zoom lenses that gives the lens an extreme close-up facility.

Macrophotography Close-up photography without the use of a microscope, in which the film images are larger than the original subject.

Main light Principal lighting unit responsible for the overall illumination of a subject or scene.

Medium-format camera Camera with a picture format larger than 35mm but smaller than a view camera. One of the many camera types using 6cm roll film, including 6 x 4.5cm, 6 x 6cm, 6 x 7cm, and 6 x 9cm format cameras.

Microphotography Production of extremely small photographs using ultra-fine grain film in a special camera. The image must be enlarged for viewing through a microfilm reader.

Miniature camera General term for any 35mm-format or smaller camera.

Mirror lens Telephoto lens with mirrors replacing some of the glass elements found in a traditional lens. The effect of the mirrors is to reflect light rays up and down the length of the lens to produce a long focal length in a relatively short lens barrel. The aperture of such lenses is usually fixed at around f8. Also known as a catadioptric lens.

Modeling lamp Low-wattage, continuous-output lamp mounted in the lighting head of a flash unit. Allows the photographer to preview the effects of light and shade, especially the fall of the shadows that will be produced when the flash fires.

Monochromatic Describes a photographic image that is solely or predominantly composed of a single color or shades of a single color.

Montage Composite picture made from a number of photographs.

Motor drive Automatic film advance system, either built into the camera or available as an add-on accessory. The system advances film on continuously after each exposure while the shutter-release button is depressed. Rate of exposure varies depending on the motor drive model and shutter speed, but up to six frames a second is possible.

Motorized film transport Automatic feature found on many modern cameras, which uses a motor inside the camera to advance the film at the beginning of a roll, advance the film after each exposure, and rewind the film after the last shot is taken.

Multiple exposure Technique of making more than one exposure appear on the same frame of film. Sometimes done for special effect but can also occur due to a fault with the film advance system.

Negative Developed film image in which colors or tones of the original subject are reversed. An intermediate stage in the production of a print.

Neutral density filter Gray-colored lens filter that reduces the amount of light reaching the film without affecting color balance.

Nodal points The front nodal point in a compound lens system is the point where the rays of light entering the lens appear to converge. The rear nodal point is the point where the rays appear to have originated, after passing through the lens.

Normal lens See *Standard lens*.

Off the film (OTF) Describes a light-reading system that gauges exposure by measuring the amount of light being reflected by the film.

Open flash Button on some flashguns that allows the flash to be fired manually without exposing the film. Very important feature on any flash unit if exposure using a flash meter is required.

Opening up Increasing the size of the aperture to allow more light to reach the film.

Orthochromatic Describes a photographic emulsion that is sensitive to all wavelengths of the visible spectrum, with the exception of deep orange and red.

Overexposure Occurs if a film receives too much light, either by exposing it to too bright a light or by allowing the light to act on it for too long. It results in light prints or slides and a reduction in subject contrast.

Pan-and-tilt head Versatile type of camera-mounting system found on some tripods. The tripod head can be swiveled from side to side or tilted up and down, and the camera turned either horizontally or vertically and locked securely in any position. See also *Tripod*.

Panchromatic Describes a photographic emulsion that is sensitive (but not necessarily evenly so) to all color wavelengths of the visible spectrum.

Panning Action of turning the camera while the shutter is open to keep pace with a moving subject. The subject should appear reasonably sharp while all stationary parts of the scene are blurred.

Panorama In a photographic context, this is a broad, continuous scene taken either with a panoramic camera or produced by taking a series of photographs of different segments of a scene and joining the individual pictures together to create a panoramic view.

Panoramic camera Camera with a scanning lens that swivels about its rear nodal point to produce a long photographic image on a curved plate or length of film.

Parallax error Framing error almost always associated with direct vision viewfinders, which results in a slight difference in viewpoint between the image as seen in the viewfinder and that recorded on the film.

Pentaprism Five-sided prism usually found on the top of 35mm SLR cameras. Its inside surfaces are silvered so that the image produced by the reflex mirror appears in the viewfinder the right way up and correctly oriented left to right.

Perspective Visual representation of depth and distance in a two-dimensional photograph.

Perspective control lens See *Shift lens*.

Photoflood See *Floodlight*.

Photogram Picture made by placing opaque and/or translucent objects in contact with photographic printing paper or suspended above it, exposing the paper to light, and then developing normally.

Photomicrography Production of larger-than-life images of small subjects by attaching the camera to a microscope.

Pinhole camera Simple camera consisting of a light-tight box with a piece of film at one end and a tiny pinhole in the other (instead of a lens) through which light is transmitted.

Plane Imaginary straight line on which image points may lie or which passes through a set of points perpendicular to the optical axis.

Plate camera Camera originally designed to take glass plates, but often adapted to accept sheet film.

Polarizing filter Colorless gray filter consisting of two disks made of stressed plastic. When the disks are correctly oriented in their filter mount they serve to reduce reflections from glass or the surface of water.

Portrait lens Lens with a focal length of about 90mm (for a 35mm camera).

Positive See *Slide*.

Posterization Darkroom printing technique that converts a continuous-tone image into a series of distinct, flat tones, similar to those used in some poster printing processes.

Power pack Heavy-duty voltage storage unit used to provide power for studio flash lighting heads. Power packs recharge almost instantaneously and can deliver a virtually limitless number of flashes.

Preview button See *Stop-down button*.

Primary colors In a photographic context, the term usually refers to the colors blue, green, and red. In terms of painters' pigments, the primary colors are blue, yellow, and red.

Prime lens See *Fixed focal length lens*.

Printing-in See *Burning-in*.

Prism filter Special effects filter that produces a series of repeated secondary images surrounding the main image.

R

Rangefinder Focusing system that measures the distance from camera to subject, usually by comparing two views of the subject. When they coincide, the subject is in focus. See also *Coupled rangefinder*.

Rebate Non-image area on a film in which the frame numbers and, on some films, the sprocket holes are located.

Reciprocity failure Loss of sensitivity of a photographic emulsion when given either a very brief or a very long exposure. Color material may also experience uncorrectable shifts in color balance.

Red-eye Fault caused by light reflected from a subject's eyes when exposed by flash. Normally only a problem with small, compact cameras with built-in flash, since the lens axis is parallel and very close to the direction of the light from the flash. If possible, move the flash unit to one side or bounce the light before it reaches the subject.

Reflected light reading Gauges exposure by measuring the amount of light reflected back from the subject toward the camera. All TTL (through-the-lens) exposure-measuring systems take a reflected light reading. See also *Through-the-lens metering.*

Reflector Any material that reflects light. Common colors for a reflector are white or gray, since these do not introduce unwanted color-casts.

Reflex camera Camera design that uses a mirror between the lens and focusing screen to correct the upside-down image produced by the lens.

Retouching Removing blemishes and/or changing the tonal values of negatives, slides, or prints.

Ring flash Circular flash lighting unit that fits around the outside of the front of the lens. Most often used in close-up photography to produce localized, shadow-free illumination.

Roll-film camera See *Medium-format camera.*

S

Safelight Low-output darkroom light filtered an appropriate color (orange is best) so as not to affect unexposed printing paper. Black and white printing paper is not affected by safelighting, but some color papers can be.

Saturation Degree of purity of a color. The less a color is affected by other colors, the more saturated it is said to be.

Sheet film Large-format film made in sheets cut to a specific size rather than in roll form.

Shift lens Type of lens in which some elements can be shifted slightly vertically or horizontally off-center to overcome the type of problem encountered when a camera is tilted to include, typically, the tops of tall structures. Also known as a perspective control lens.

Shutter Mechanical device that controls the moment of exposure and the length of time light is allowed to act on the film to produce an image. See also *Between-the-lens shutter* and *Focal-plane shutter.*

Shutter priority Type of semi-automatic exposure system whereby the photographer sets the shutter and the camera selects the corresponding lens aperture to ensure correct exposure of the scene.

Silhouette Photograph in which the subject is rendered as a solid black shape against a much lighter background.

Silica gel Crystals that readily absorb moisture in the atmosphere. Often packed with new photographic equipment in order to prevent humidity damage.

Single lens reflex (SLR) Type of camera design that uses an angled mirror behind the lens, and, in 35mm SLRs, a series of silvered surfaces inside a top-mounted pentaprism, to show exactly the same scene in the viewfinder as encompassed by the lens.

Skylight filter Pale red filter that can be used with color film to introduce a slight, natural-looking color-cast. Useful with cold-looking scenes and to counteract the tendency of some films to produce a blue cast in shadow areas.

Slave unit Fires additional flashes when the principal flash lighting unit connected to a camera fires.

Slide Positive film image designed to be viewed by projection. Also commonly known as a transparency or a positive.

Slide sandwiching Placing two slides in the same mount and projecting them together.

Slow film See *Film speed.*

Slow lens See *Lens speed.*

SLR See *Single lens reflex.*

Snoot Type of flash head used to direct a narrow beam of light over a small area.

Soft-focus lens Lens designed to produce a slightly soft image, with not all in-focus elements critically sharp. A portrait lens may also be a soft-focus lens.

Solarization Complete or partial reversal of an image, caused by massive overexposure to white light.

Spot meter Type of exposure meter with an extremely narrow angle of view. A spot meter is used to take a light reading from a specific part of a subject.

Spotlight Unit that produces a strong beam of light, which can easily be trained on a subject.

Spotting Removing blemishes or small unwanted areas of detail on a print using a paintbrush and dyes, watercolors, or graphite.

Standard/normal lens Lens with a focal length approximately equal to the diagonal of the film format with which it is used. With 35mm format film the standard lens is 50–55mm, and 80mm with medium format. A standard lens reproduces about as much of a scene as you would see with the naked eye.

Starburst filter Special effects filter that produces starlike patterns around the sources of light in a photograph.

Stop Another name for aperture. See *Aperture.*

Stop bath Chemical solution (usually weak acid) that halts the action of film or paper developer and neutralizes any developer residues, so preventing contamination of other processing chemicals.

Stop-down button Manual control that closes down the aperture to that selected for exposure. The photographer can then judge depth of field on the focusing screen. Also known as a preview button.

Stopping down Closing down the aperture to restrict the amount of light reaching the film.

Strobe light Low-output flash light that is capable of delivering many thousands of flashes per second.

Studio flash Large flash units, often connected to heavy-duty power packs and mounted on adjustable stands, and designed to illuminate large areas of a photographic studio or for use on location.

T

T (Time) setting Shutter setting found on some cameras that locks the shutter open when the release is depressed and closes it only when the release is depressed a second time. This setting has been largely replaced by the B setting on modern cameras. See also *B setting.*

Technical camera See *View camera.*

Telephoto lens Compact long-focus lens. The term is often incorrectly applied to all long-focus lenses irrespective of their construction.

Test strip Strip of printing paper or film that is given a range of trial exposures.

Through-the-lens metering Describes a type of light-measuring system used commonly in reflex cameras to measure the light that is reflected from a subject and then passes through the lens. Commonly abbreviated to TTL.

TLR See *Twin lens reflex.*

Tonal range Range of shades of gray, between the extremes of black and white, which can be distinguished in a photograph.

Tone An area on a print or negative that has a uniform density and that can be distinguished from other lighter or darker parts.

Transmitted light Light that is passed through a transparent or translucent material.

Transparency See *Slide.*

Tripod Camera-steadying device consisting of three legs and some form of mounting system to hold the camera. Tripod legs are extendable so that the camera height can be adjusted, and most also have an extendable central column (on top of which the camera is mounted) for finer height adjustments. The two most commonly available camera-mounting heads are ball-and-socket and pan-and-tilt types.

TTL See *Through-the-lens metering.*

Tungsten-balanced film Film designed to reproduce correct subject colors when exposed in tungsten light. If exposed in daylight without the appropriate correction filter over the lens, subject colors will appear unnaturally blue. See also *Daylight-balanced film.*

Tungsten-filament light Artificial light source produced by passing electricity through a tungsten filament inside a sealed glass bulb.

Tungsten-halogen light Compact and improved type of tungsten light with a consistent color temperature due to the fact that the bulb is non-blackening.

Twin lens reflex (TLR) Type of medium-format camera that uses two lenses of identical focal length mounted one under the other on a lens panel. The top lens is used for viewing and focusing and the bottom lens for taking the picture. A limited number of interchangeable lenses is available for this camera format, but these are expensive since both have to be changed each time.

Ultra-violet (UV) filter Colorless filter designed to remove excessive ultra-violet from the light passing through the lens. A UV filter may be left on the lens all the time to protect the lens from dirt, knocks, and scratches. UV filters do not affect exposure.

Ultra-violet light Part of the electro-magnetic spectrum beyond visible blue. In distant scenes, such as mountainous areas, ultra-violet radiation increases the effects of aerial perspective by creating a blue haze. Ultra-violet effects can be minimized by using an ultra-violet lens filter.

Underexposure Occurs if a film receives too little light, causing dark prints or slides and a reduction in subject contrast.

Uprating Exposing film as if it is more sensitive to light than its nominal ISO rating indicates. Allowances for uprated film have to be made during development.

UV filter See *Ultra-violet filter.*

Vanishing point Point at which parallel lines appear to converge in the distance. Used by artists to give realistic perspective in a two-dimensional representation.

View camera Large-format camera, using individual pieces of 5 x 4in (12.7 x 10cm) film or larger, with a lens panel mounted on a flexible bellows and a ground-glass screen at the image plane for viewing and focusing. This type of large and cumbersome camera is normally mounted on a sturdy tripod. Press cameras have a baseboard to support the bellows and are more portable. Also known as a technical camera.

Viewfinder Viewing system that allows a camera to be aimed and, usually, focused accurately. The viewfinder often contains exposure-related information around the edges of the screen.

Viewpoint In photography, the position from which the picture is taken in relation to the subject. Very small changes in camera viewpoint can result in considerable differences in finished prints or slides.

Vignette Gradual fading of a photographic image to white or black. This darkroom technique is achieved either by holding light away from the edges to create a white vignette (see *Dodging*) or by giving a large amount of extra exposure to the edges to create a black vignette (see *Burning-in*).

Visible spectrum That part of the electro-magnetic spectrum between infra-red and ultra-violet that is visible to the naked eye.

Wide-angle lens Lens with a focal length shorter than the diagonal of the film format with which it is used. Commonly used wide-angle lenses for 35mm cameras include 35mm, 28mm, and 24mm focal lengths. Lenses wider than this will normally show some signs of barrel distortion.

X-ray fogging Overall gray veil produced when unprocessed photographic emulsions are exposed to excessive X-ray radiation. This can occur as a result of baggage screening at airports, but modern systems use X-ray dosages that should be safe for most emulsions. Repeated screenings of films, especially fast films, may have a cumulative effect.

X-sync socket External socket found on some cameras that accepts a cable connecting the shutter to an electronic flashgun used off-camera. It ensures that the firing of the flash is synchronized with the opening of the shutter.

Z

Zoom lens Type of lens designed so that groups of internal elements can be shifted in relation to each other to produce a range of different focal lengths. One-touch zooms have a single control for focusing and zooming, while two-touch zooms have two separate controls and are slower to use. Fully automatic cameras may have a power zoom switch that continues to zoom the lens until the switch is released. Changes of framing can be monitored in the viewfinder. See also *Fixed-focal-length lens.*

INDEX

A

B

C

ACKNOWLEDGMENTS

Author's acknowledgments:

Producing this book was essentially a team effort. Special thanks go to Jane Ewart,
Steve Gorton, Alison Melvin, and Robyn Tomlinson. I would also like to thank
Miranda Talbot, Auberon Hedgecoe, Jenny Mackintosh, Mrs Surridge, Mrs Last,
and, of course, the many models who appear in the book.

Dorling Kindersley would like to thank the following:
Jemima Dunne for all her work on the initial stages of the project; Roddy Craig, editor for the last three
months of the project; Claire Edwards and Nathalie Godwin for design help; Lorna Damms, Julee Binder,
and Camela Decaire for editorial help; Leigh Priest for the index; Pippa Ward for administrative help;
Iain Pusey for computer image manipulations; Carol Hart for make-up; Slag for supplying the hats on
pp.74–5; Richard Lewington for supplying the butterflies on pp.188–9; Hazel Taylor and Doreen Mitchell
for supplying the pets on pp.210–11, and Ben Pulsford for building the sets on p.236, pp.238–9, and
p.241. Thanks also to the following for modeling: Anna Kunst, Ella Milroy, Tim Ridley, Hilary Nash and
Nuala Morris (Take 2 models), Lucy Fawcett, Kate Douglas, Lucy Keeler, Ivan Inversion, Kevin O'Kane,
Arthur Pita, Georgia Cooper, Jo Cligget, Sandra and Rosie Kuys, Oliver Swan-Jackson, Emily Gorton,
Alice Surridge, Jennifer Smith, Freddy Harrold, Daniel Evans, Shaun Rebbeck, and
Croydon Kings American football team (coach Brian Smallwood).

All photographs by John Hedgecoe with the exception of the following by Steve Gorton:
photo set-ups; cameras and equipment (pp.2–3, pp.18–19, pp.20–21, pp.22–3, p.25, pp.26–7, pp.28–9,
p.30, p.33, p.174, p.187, pp.242–3); darkroom (p.236, p.241); home studio (pp.238–9); and
photographs of John Hedgecoe (p.1, p.3, pp.6–7, p.13, p.35, p.67, p.215, p.237).

Illustrations:
Janos Marffy: p.14, p.15, p.16, p.17, p.240
Dave Pugh: p.24, p.46, p.47, p.69, p.119, p.133, p.163, p.183, p.205

Information and assistance was kindly provided by:

C.Z. Scientific Instruments Limited
Canon (UK) Limited
The Flash Centre
Johnson's Photopia
Leeds Photovisual Limited
Linhof & Studio Professional Sales
Nikon (UK) Limited
Olympus Optical Company (UK) Limited
Pentax UK Limited
Polaroid (UK) Limited
The Pro Centre
Teamwork

Special thanks to Joe's Basement, London W1, for technical
assistance, notably Kerrin Roberts and Godfrey Pope (color),
and Ian MacMaster and Simon Lloyd (black and white).
Thanks also to Danny at DGP Photographic, London W1.

Photographic location credits:

Holkham Hall, Norfolk (Seat of the Earls of Leicester):
p.25 (kitchen), p.61 middle right, p.125 (kitchen), p.172, p.174, p.176
Black Sheep Mill House, Ingworth, Norfolk: p.192
Felbrigg Hall, Norfolk (National Trust property): p.198
Blickling Hall, Norfolk (National Trust property): p.27 & 167
(views of garden pavilion), p.194, p.195 top, p.200 bottom, p.201
The Mill House, Corpusti, Norfolk: p.199, p.200 top, p.217 top left
Porchester Centre Baths, London: p.220 (bottom three photos)
The Lloyds Building, London: pp.164–5